Hungry for Wisconsin

Pastries await you at Craverie Chocolatier Cafe at the Shops at Woodlake in Kohler.

Hungry for Wisconsin
A Tasty Guide for Travelers

Mary Bergin

ITCHY CAT PRESS

Designed and produced by Flying Fish Graphics
Printed in Korea

Library of Congress Cataloging-in-Publication Data

Bergin, Mary, 1955-
  Hungry for Wisconsin : a tasty guide for travelers / by Mary Bergin. -- 1st ed.
    p. cm.
  Includes index.
  ISBN 978-0-9815161-0-3 (alk. paper)
  1. Restaurants--Wisconsin--Guidebooks. 2. Cookery--Wisconsin. 3. Wisconsin--Guidebooks.
  4. Wisconsin--Description and travel. I. Title.
  TX907.3.W6B47 2008
  641.59775--dc22   2008022788

Itchy Cat Press
Blue Mounds
Wisconsin 53517 USA
608.924.1443
www.itchycatpress.com
ffg@mhtc.net

On the front cover, clockwise, from top left: Montmorency cherries from Door County; Cream City beer from Lakefront Brewery, Milwaukee; SarVecchio cheese from Sartori Foods, Plymouth; and chocolates from Gail Ambrosius, Madison.
At center: Harbor View Café, Pepin.

Dedicated, with gratitude, to:

Herb Hiller of Florida, who reassured me that it's fine and legitimate to stay close to home when travel writing.

The Reverend Kelly Crocker of Madison's First Unitarian Society, for her "Spirituality of Food" class, which taught how growing, cooking and eating can enhance our perspectives, connections and soul.

Brother Fred, who laughs easily and has long demonstrated a high tolerance for his sister's odd weekend itineraries.

The dozens of friends and colleagues whose good humor and generosity of spirit enriched this research. Your expertise, resources and companionship are valued.

Dave Zweifel's *Capital Times*, which opened its photo and text archives for this project. Long may our progressive outlooks prosper. No boss will ever be better than Dave.

CONTENTS

Milwaukee & Area

Northeast

NOTE:

Call before you begin driving; much can change on short notice in the highly competitive food business.

INTRODUCTION

The people and businesses in *Hungry for Wisconsin* may seem to have little in common. Some flip burgers. Others turn entrées into edible art.

We share glimpses of dirt-in-nails farm life and coat-and-tie ambiance. We find joy in buying Belly Flops (misshapen jelly beans) near Kenosha and Garden Ganache (elegant blends of heavy cream and chocolate) in Kohler.

One-of-a-kind efforts—like the cranberry science class at Pittsville High School, or the to-die-for cookies made for Midwest Airlines—earn national attention, but it's a slew of craft brews, artisan cheeses and secret-recipe sausages that define our core character.

We know who we are, and we are proud of it: horseradish to sauerkraut, "funeral wieners" in Whitelaw to roller-skating carhops in Oshkosh and La Crosse. Many business owners do their work proudly and quietly, cooking for their neighbors.

Chefs whose work could earn diamonds on the U.S. coasts settle for under-the-radar, peaceful living in Plover, Downsville, Suamico, Monticello and numerous other small towns. But why would it be a surprise that restaurateurs who truly believe the "buy local" mantra live in or near rural areas?

What everybody in this book has in common is integrity of product. When we have our way with food, we are making statements about authenticity: our values, quirks, obsessions, ethnic pride.

It is no coincidence that Wisconsin routinely dominates national and world cheese championships. Or that Milwaukee hosts on its lakefront some of the nation's largest ethnic festivals.

This isn't a comprehensive guide to food in Wisconsin, or a "best of" bible. I have tried to not duplicate places that got attention in my first book, *Sidetracked in Wisconsin: A Guide for Thoughtful Travelers*. Occasionally, I can't help myself.

The concept of *Hungry for Wisconsin* was planted during Wisconsin Public Radio's *Conversations with Larry Meillor*, when a caller asked me for suggestions about fine dining in remote locations. We had ideas, but it was a woefully low representation of what exists statewide.

When I was features editor at *The Capital Times* in Madison a few years ago, it was my priority to print a daily food feature. "You all have one thing in common," I observed. "You have to eat, regardless of your gender, education, fetishes, career aspirations, criminal record, political beliefs or the type of car you drive."

Most people enjoy eating, but it's also easy to get into a culinary rut. *Hungry for Wisconsin* is full of ideas about what to savor while learning about the state's food heritage and diversity—sometimes in unlikely locations.

When you travel, you eat. Food can be good theater as well as sustenance. We watch chefs at work, bike between barns, chat with farmers at markets, whoop it up over rutabagas and mushrooms, turn fruit picking into a family outing. These choices are a terrific beginning. Have a great meal, wherever you go!

The author at the Stable Grill of Quivey's Grove, Madison.

ABOUT THE AUTHOR

Mary Bergin grew up on a farm that had no garden, cooks often but not well, supports local farmers but knows she could do more. She is a lifelong journalist whose interest in food writing has been more about people, passions and trends than kitchen techniques and restaurant critiques.

The Sheboygan County native has lived in Madison since the 1980s and since 2002 has written a syndicated travel column that appears weekly in daily newspapers throughout Wisconsin. She appreciates a good steak sandwich while driving but also knows how to linger for hours over a five-course meal with matching wines.

Hundreds of homemade pie slices are sold during the Cumberland Rutabaga Festival.

TELL ME ABOUT:
Wild Rice Heritage

Native Americans have long referred to it as *manoomin*, food that grows on water, and some circles consider it to be the nation's oldest agricultural crop.

Indigenous wild rice has a place at special occasions, from funerals to celebrations. The harvest is a sacred act that involves giving up as well as gathering.

"My dad says you want some of the rice to fall into the river, so the rice will reseed itself and keep the rice bed thick and full of rice," says a story in *Mazina'igan*, published by the Great Lakes Indian Fish and Wildlife Commission. "You also want the waterfowl to have their share. We can't take it all and must think about future ricers, and the animals and birds who also rely on manoomin for food."

Brian Wiggins and Lisa Ash promote and preserve truly wild rice for the next generations.

Truly wild rice—that which grows freely in cool, northern rivers, shallow lakes and other wetlands—commands top dollar because its harvest is done by hand. The rice quality is fiber rich, flavorful and noticeably nutty.

Native Americans, the Ojibwe in particular, for generations have turned their pilgrimage to the ripened rice beds into a ritual that involves the entire family. The harvest does not begin until elder rice chiefs decide it is time.

The fall journey into the jungle-like rice patches is a two-person job. One uses a wooden pole to navigate a canoe through rice beds. Canoe paddles and motorized boats are shunned because they can damage the delicate grains. The other harvester uses two ricing sticks, one to bend rice reeds into the canoe, the other to gently tap seeds away from the plants. When rice is ready for harvest, these seeds fall easily into the canoe bottom. Upon returning home, the rice is dried and tossed until the hulls fall off, then cleaned and packaged.

This is about more than upholding a tradition, says **Brian Wiggins** of Trego, an Ojibwe who grew up on northern Wisconsin's **Bad River Reservation**.

"It is a way of life, a part of what we want to bring back" to younger generations, he says about wild ricing. His tribe feels the same about other aspects of Native American culture, such as language and traditions.

Tribal schools are involved in getting youth reconnected to their heritage, Brian says, but fewer people than when he was a boy (in the 1950s) participate in the autumn rice harvest. Brian says nothing has changed in the harvesting ritual, although modern canoes are used instead of the handmade birchbark vessels of his ancestors' era. He considers commercially grown wild rice, nicknamed "paddy rice," to be inferior in flavor and requiring more time to cook.

It's hard to know how much wild rice is gathered in Wisconsin. The Department of Natural Resources has the authority to regulate the harvest, purchase and sale of wild rice, but rules do not apply to Native American tribes that have retained harvest rights.

The DNR considers it illegal to collect wild rice with any mechanical device. A drop in lake levels and building developments along shorelines threaten the crop's health.

Brian Wiggins and **Lisa Ash** are operators of **Bear Clan Wild Rice**, which sells a part of the annual yield to businesses and individuals. Brian says fall 2007 was the first time that no rice harvest occurred, because of the lack of rain and subsequent low water levels.

Bear Clan Wild Rice
715-466-5368

•

SIDE DISH: Wild Rice Dessert Topping

1 cup cooked wild rice
½ cup brown sugar or maple sugar
½ cup raisins or dried cranberries
½ cup chopped pecans

Combine all ingredients. Cover and refrigerate. Spoon mixture over vanilla ice cream, pudding or custard.

Brian and Lisa distribute this recipe and others at events about Native American culture and traditions.

BARRON: Safari Cuisine

It is shortly before 1:30 p.m. when we reach downtown Barron, population 3,200, and the door to **Safari Cuisine** is locked. The restaurant, which specializes in East African and Mediterranean food, is supposed to be open from noonish until 10 p.m. So we give a call, and owner **Noor Arte** apologetically meets us at the entrance.

"Come in," he says, smiling. "It is OK." And then he heads back to the kitchen, where he is single-handedly cooking up a storm.

The dining room is painted a pretty sky blue; filling one wall are murals of palm trees and beach scenes. You wouldn't call it fancy—plastic tablecloths, no center-pieces—but the surroundings are clean and practical.

In the same room is a little ethnic market: cans of fava beans and mango pulp, bags of red lentils and adzuki beans, jars of ghee (a type of clarified butter) and an unpredictable mix of other products.

Soon the doors open for everyone, and the place fills, mainly with a dozen or two Muslim men who have just finished midday prayer at a mosque down the street. Our table is one of only two with women. It is a sticky midsummer day, so our limbs are exposed—which would be taboo in traditional Muslim communities. Here, we feel outnumbered but also politely tolerated.

We eat a dish labeled "KK" on the menu: chopped and curried goat meat, with basmati rice, salad and *jabati*, a flat East African bread. Meat stews and *sambusa* (similar to an eggroll) would have been other logical options, had we the time or a big appetite. Meal prices are under $10. White cornmeal (*ugali*) mixed with cabbage and spinach, then served with braised meats, is called *soor*. *Mkate wa mayayi*—a sandwich of ground beef, eggs and onion—also is listed, but an online search at home brings up nothing with that name.

A man from Marinette tells us that he drives this far (about 300 miles) routinely, to get to a mosque. Noor, who opened Safari Cuisine in January 2007, says everyone is welcome—women and men, Christians and Muslims. The

It's palm trees on the wall and halal-certified meat in the entrées at Safari Cuisine.

Somalia native is one of about 500 who in the late 1990s moved to this part of Wisconsin; many took jobs at the local poultry processing plant.

"Many entry-level jobs are now available on an annual basis, some in agriculture and some in food processing," reports West CAP, a nonprofit community action association. "There are more of these jobs than the local labor supply can fill."

The ethnic composition has changed dramatically, also involving Laotian and Mexican populations, and the growth of diversity poses an ongoing challenge and opportunity for Barron. "To me, everything I see is fine," Noor insists. "Everybody is equal."

Safari Cuisine and Grocery
531 E. La Salle Avenue, Barron
715-637-0555

•

TIDBITS

Meat served at **Safari Cuisine** comes from the **Browse & Grass Farmer Association**, whose lambs and goats graze freely on natural pastures. They do not receive antibiotics or hormone injections.

The association's products are sold under the Shepherd Song label, a reference to **Shepherd Song Farm**, operated by **Larry** and **Judy Moses Jacoby**, Downing. The products are halal-certified, to meet the religious requirements of Muslim customers. *Halal* refers to the manner in which the animals are raised and slaughtered. It means being respectful to all creatures, and, when it is time for slaughter, the process proceeds in a specific and merciful manner.

"For those of us raising pastured animals, the lack of humane slaughter facilities to properly complete the process for our special animals is very apparent," the Jacobys say online, through another enterprise, Spirit of Humane, the developer of slaughtering systems that meet the farmers' needs. This explains why they began selling their equipment.

www.browseandgrass.org 715-861-4823
www.shepherdsongfarm.com 715-265-7637
www.spiritofhumane.com 715-861-4823

Wild Rice Restaurant turns dinner into art.

BAYFIELD: Wild Rice Restaurant

Wild Rice Restaurant is a whiff of whimsy and immersion in fine dining amid acres of woods and Lake Superior shoreline.

The restaurant opened in 2001 and is named after owner **Mary Rice**, a watercolorist, philanthropist and one of the area's biggest wizards of creativity. Bayfield's more casual flamingo-filled Maggie's and the Egg Toss Cafe have been among Mary's other bright and image-boosting ideas for this part of northern Wisconsin.

At Wild Rice, a glass-to-ceiling "wine cube" shows off dozens of types of wine. It is dramatic décor as well as a functional architectural feature. One wall of glass in a small-group dining room allows customers to watch the chefs at work, and their dishes are delicate exercises of artistry.

Open seasonally, and a good stop when attending Warren Nelson's spirited Lake Superior Big Top Chautauqua tent shows (**www.bigtop.org**, **888-244-8368**) at the base of Mt. Ashwabay Ski Hill.

Wild Rice Restaurant
84860 Old San Road, Bayfield
www.wildricerestaurant.com 715-779-9881
•

BLOOMER: Czech Out the Bakery

Bread is Mike Hable's specialty at Bohemian Ovens.

Since 1997, a wood-fired, brick oven has helped bakers **Mike** and **Sally Hable** produce authentic European breads at **Bohemian Ovens**. Mike and his brother **Bill** saved a few bucks by making their own oven, 2,128 bricks that are held together with a metal frame. The device weighs almost 15,000 pounds and can bake 40 loaves of bread at one time.

Mike is a former dairy farmer who is especially proud of his Power One recipe—a tasty bread whose flours are mixed with oatmeal, tomato juice, flaxseed, almonds, walnuts and cranberries.

The sourdough rye is a Czech specialty.

The bakery (with friendly, nothing-fancy restaurant) also produces from-scratch pastries and soups. Saturdays are "make your own pizza" nights.

It's an especially good day when you catch a lunch special with Bohemian Chicken or Sveckova Beef dumplings. Mike says everybody in town seems to have a dumpling recipe that is a point of pride.

He's a guy with a dry sense of humor, selling T-shirts that say "I knead it daily" and "Czech out my buns."

Bohemian Ovens
905 Martin Street, Bloomer
www.madpages.com/bohemian
715-568-3676
•

CUMBERLAND: Rooting for Rutabaga

Our timing is dreadfully off for this escapade, or so we assume. The month is August, the destination is a town of 2,300 and the event is a Sunday parade.

We get to the **Cumberland Rutabaga Festival** about one-half hour after the procession begins, probably ruining a once-in-a-lifetime experience by shopping too long in Duluth. We're braced to catch only the tail end of the spectacle and hope to at least get a parting shot of the Rutabaga Queen—kind of like Santa waving goodbye at a holiday parade.

Wrong. The 'baga royalty breezed through at the beginning, so our heart sinks further. We watch, wait and wait . . . until it's evident that this is small-town pageantry at its finest. The parade is no quick hit; it lasts more than two hours (it used to take three and a half).

Every little community festival for a 100 miles—Osseo to Hudson—seems to contribute a set of queens for a day. They wear tiaras and matching gowns and have perfected the Wave. It is no wimpy flutter, but an ardent and synchronized gesture, strong in its precision, disciplined in its execution.

There is room for all of these floats, many school bands, even a shiny waste disposal truck. Everybody seems to belong, and everybody has a role. That includes the spectators, who reinforce the sense of community and pride.

Parades, at any time of year, validate that something is worth celebrating. It has been that way in Cumberland for more than 75 years, although you'll have a hard time tracking down a rutabaga on most days—including much of the festival weekend.

We were about to give up on the root vegetable, which used to be harvested in large quantities near Cumberland and given away during the festival. "It's a little early for the harvest this year," one local decides. "You should have checked the farmers' market yesterday," another admonishes.

Then we spotted a Rutabaga Fries sign, outside of the **Spot Bar** on Second Avenue, and quickly placed an order. While waiting, we found a lone raw rutabaga to examine and hold. Big as a softball. Kind of like a turnip on hormones.

The 'baga fries came crinkle-cut and coated with a light batter, ranch dressing on the side for dipping. What's it taste like? Cabbage, our friend Marjean suggested. "Eggplant strips, but not as mooshy," also was scrawled in our notes. Soon we were sharing a bench on the sidewalk and feeling like experts, as others asked what we were eating.

Cumberland Rutabaga Festival
Weekend preceding Labor Day
www.cumberland-wisconsin.com
715-822-3378
•

Viking Brewing Company salutes its heritage.

DALLAS: Something's Brewing

Together, now: 23 bottles of beer on the wall, 23 bottles of beer . . .

The last time we checked with **Ann Lee**, that's how many types of beer her family was producing at their microbrewery, which since 1995 has operated out of a building that was a Ford dealership in the early 1900s. After that, the structure was a creamery, egg processing plant, welding shop.

Five of the **Viking Brewing Company** labels—Blonde, Vienna Woods, CopperHead, Whole Stein and Big Swede—are produced year-round. They are sold in four-packs, typically at liquor stores in Minnesota and Wisconsin. CopperHead, a ruby Martzen-style lager, is the most popular.

"The younger crowd has never known of a beer market without microbrewed products in it," Ann notes. "So now, it's about what's new, and we introduce at least one new beer every month." Example: Hot Chocolate, a chocolate stout made with Fair Trade cocoa, milk, sugar and "a dash of cayenne pepper for warmth." It shows up in December.

Son **Darren** has come up with a well-received root beer that is lighter and less syrupy than typical root beer. A hint of wintergreen and pepper are a part of what makes the beverage a pleasant standout.

Packaging products in groups of four instead of six "dresses them up," says Ann, who believes people are more apt to try four-packs and classify them as high-end products. Fans include chef Nathan Berg at Native Bay Restaurant on Lake Wissota, who has created four-course dinners to match the Viking beer line. It's also not unusual to see these beers accompany lutefisk dinners, because of the brewery name. Husband **Randy Lee** is Norwegian. Ann is Swedish.

A goal is to become more environmentally friendly, perhaps through the addition of a bio-diesel boiler. Viking already uses refitted bulk tanks, from farms, to process and hold the beer.

"We liked the area and wanted something we could do together," Ann says, about settling in the Barron County town of 350. The family (which also includes daughter **Jennifer**) started out bottling their products by hand: Wash, label, fill. Wash, label, fill. Now a bottling machine hikes production to 120 cases at a time, and Ann says the next phase of technology "will pull in 10 times as much, so we'll have to hire employees."

The Lees had been accustomed to making beer in five-gallon batches. Their research about style of beer and who brewed it is extensive. Some formulas have been based upon beechwood smoked malts in Baumberg, Germany.

"There's no point to brewing what everybody else is doing," Ann explains. Today she does most of the brewing and bottling while Randy works as a computer programmer.

There are not many other reasons to visit Wisconsin's version of Dallas, Ann acknowledges, unless you count pretty Pine Crest Golf and its tree-lined fairways. So when the mayor encouraged her to liven things up, Ann seized the opportunity.

"The town is yours," she's been told, so in 2004 free, outdoor movie nights began in summer. Free cans of spinach went to the first 20 people who showed up on "Popeye" nights.

On the first Saturday of October, the town kicks it up for Oktoberfest, an event that didn't exist before the Lees' involvement. A Viking-themed encampment, steel combat (as in sword-and-shield demos), gun show, polka dancing and—you betcha—beer drinking fill the weekend.

Viking Brewing is open for tours most Saturdays and by appointment.

Viking Brewing Co.
234 W. Dallas Street, Dallas
www.vikingbrewing.com
715-837-1824
•

Fresh baked breads and seasonal menus spell success for The Creamery Restaurant & Inn.

DOWNSVILLE: Mellow Hospitality

It's not often that we lead people to a community of 180 residents as an overnight destination, but the **Creamery Restaurant & Inn** makes Downsville an exception.

"Mellow hospitality" is a part of the promise.

The classy, revamped dairy creamery is near the 14.5-mile Red Cedar State bike/hike/ski trail, which connects to the 24-mile Chippewa River State Trail. So that gives you something to do besides eat, which is a good thing, since Creamery cooking means killer quality, with creative flair. Any place with sockeye salmon on the menu gets my attention.

Trout (served smoked on crostini—as a nibbler, or with roasted tomatoes and cheese—as a sandwich) comes from the nearby **Bullfrog Trout Farm**. **Promise Farm Buffalo**, also in the neighborhood, provides fresh bison.

Creamery cuisine contains a southern European influence. Two cheeses, provolone and goat, cover the Garlic Ramekin—a popular appetizer of stewed leeks, artichokes and mushrooms in cream and white wine.

"The menus, like the surrounding countryside, change seasonally," founding proprietor **Richard Thomas** explains online. The operation generally is closed in March and a part of April.

Dinner for two will run about $100 and be worth it. Lighter, casual fare is served in the lounge. The popular bakery, known for its breads and dog biscuits, shares quarters with a gift shop that sells local artwork, imported crafts and unusual toys (including puppets).

The bakery releases a monthly schedule of breads to be baked, and the choices change six days a week. Think honey brioche, soft pretzels, chocolate/cherry sourdough, sweet potato/spiced pecan, raisin rye. Want one out of order? Just file a request for four or more loaves, one week before pickup.

Overnight accommodations, bright and modern in 12 rooms, are $130-160 per night. Eight are in the Woodland Terrace addition, which has a living room large enough to handle a bridal shower or be the activity center for a family that wants to call the entire building "home" for a reunion. Another large room is designed for business meetings.

Richard actually had his eye on the Downsville general store as a cafe site in 1978, but his architect father convinced him the long-abandoned creamery had more charm and potential. The Creamery's restaurant opened in 1985.

A university marketing study predicted its rural location spelled failure, but instead it helped it succeed. It is a sanctuary where people come to forget about the high-tech world for a while.

The Creamery Restaurant & Inn
E4620 Hwy. C, Downsville
www.creameryrestaurant-inn.com
715-664-8355
•

Luscious breads, cakes, other desserts and dog biscuits fill the bakery cases.

EAU CLAIRE: Dinner and a Show

If you were in college from 1969 to the early 1970s, you may know of this place as the Barr, a beer and live music joint where ages 18-20 could imbibe. **Larry Barr** built the business in the town of Union, one-half mile outside of Eau Claire, to avoid head-butting with rules that prohibited such conduct among the young within city limits.

Buses would haul college students from UW-Eau Claire to the Barr until liquor laws changed and the destination tamed down, morphing into the Country Supper Club. When the name Fanny Hill was added, it was a reference to the erotic eighteenth-century novel.

By 1978, the property was staging live theater. A decade later, the first seven rooms for overnight stays were built. Today each of 11 rooms is uniquely decorated in quaint Victorian style. Hilltop gardens overlook a stunning panoramic view of the Chippewa River and its lush terrain.

Inside are hundreds of teddy bears, from small to huge, in display cases; one nurses a fake cocktail at a table in the bar. Running above and around customers are toy train tracks, loops for a trolley and other antique miniatures. At least two decorated Christmas trees are up year-round. The bar has a built-in fish tank.

All are fun, unusual touches. Before Halloween, 3,000 pumpkins are delivered to Fanny Hill, and local groups get paid to carve them. Lights inside the pumpkins produce a dramatic decorating effect.

The theater, where customers eat during performances, seats about 165 in five tiers. On off days, it's a conference or meeting area. Elsewhere is dinner seating for the nontheater crowd, and casual dining occurs on the deck.

Paid actors present light fare—comedies and musicals—throughout the year. Locals say the restaurant has the area's best brunch and best view.

At the bar: Rudy's Choice is whiskey and amaretto, lemon-lime soda and a tad of cherry juice.

Entrée examples: Pretzel-crusted chicken. Pecan-crusted walleye. Portabella mushrooms layered with spinach, asiago, pesto and sun-dried tomatoes.

In demand is the house dressing, a honey poppyseed. "We get people hooked on it," jokes **Lois Hodgins**, who heads group sales. No, you can't have the recipe.

The signature dessert is a chocolate mousse and Bailey's Irish Cream cheesecake combo, but our eye also lingers on Lemon Bliss, which is lemon mousse inside a pastry shell, with a dollop of lemon curd.

Fanny Hill Dinner Theatre
3919 Crescent Avenue, Eau Claire
www.fannyhill.com
800-292-8026
•

TIDBITS

Fanny Hill has a **Lois Club**, for people named Lois. They get together for matinees and other events. The first gathering attracted 74 people with the name.

Lois Lane cocktails come in two versions: mild-mannered and super. People wear "I'm Lois" or "Lois Wannabe" buttons.

Who is in charge of reservations? Lois Hodgins, who argues, "What could be better than a room full of Loises?"

•

A fine destination for a casual lunch is **Northwoods Brewpub**, 3560 Oakwood Mall Drive, Eau Claire, where it is easy to drool over two menus: beer and pie. It's an odd combination, but appropriate in this setting, because **Jerry Bechard** owns the brewpub and the highly revered **Norske Nook** restaurants (in Osseo, Hayward and Rice Lake).

So thick and luscious pies sit in a glass case that is within view of the beer vats. Dine on the patio, with a sweet pond view, or cozy up to the fireplace, inside the lodge.

Some of the pies, and the beers, have won national awards. Our guy Dick was so smitten with Floppin' Crappie, an ale, that he bought a T-shirt with the beer name on it.

www.northwoodsbrewpub.com 715-552-0510

•

In downtown Eau Claire, the farmers' market bustles with up to 70 vendors under the skylight arches at Phoenix Park's open-air pavilion on Wednesdays, Thursdays and Saturdays.

The seasonal outdoor market ends in late October.

www.ecdowntownfarmersmarket.com 715-834-5697

Sandra Isaacs Bell serves authentic Jamaican fare within view of the Mississippi River.

HAGER CITY: Barbeque at the Harbor

When the Food Network visited during Father's Day weekend, it was to film a "Barbecue Bites" segment at **Harbor Restaurant and Bar** in Hager City, which is just a bridge away from Red Wing, Minnesota.

Bathroom signs say Inboards and Outboards instead of Women and Men. Chainsaw art is plentiful. Mississippi River boaters might have an easier time finding the place than motorists, and Minnesotans likely know the laid-back Jamaican food joint better than the average Wisconsin resident.

Owner **Brad Smith's** jerk sauce is a secret blend of spices and other ingredients. Meats are marinated in it before hitting the grill, and this is what lured the Food Network to Hager City. But the aura of authenticity doesn't end there. Jamaican residents join the Harbor Restaurant staff from April to October or November. Reggae and blues performers provide live music outdoors when the weather is good.

To find the Harbor Restaurant by car, follow Highway 63 and take the last exit before crossing the river into Minnesota. Find Island Road, head toward the water and you're there.

Harbor Restaurant & Bar
N673 825th Street, Hager City

•

Décor and menu are one-of-a-kind at Turk's Inn.

HAYWARD: A Turkish Surprise

One of Wisconsin's quiet culinary icons is **Marge Gogian**, a gracious woman who has long been accustomed to greeting and feeding a crowd as the years end and begin. Marge owns the one-of-a-kind **Turk's Inn**, two miles north of Hayward. The colorful restaurant, whose hours depend upon time of year, has been in business since 1934. It is an elegant surprise amid the ruggedness of Wisconsin's Northwoods.

Rich hues of red, Persian textiles, unusual artifacts and reminders of family or celebrity customers make the restaurant an attraction as well as a fine ethnic dining experience in an unexpected location. A Byzantine-style bar fills the Harem Lounge. In and near the Kismet Dining Room are wonderful nooks for intimate dining.

The Kennedys—John, Robert and Ted—all have been here, as have the late U.S. Supreme Court Justice Harry Blackmun, the Spiegels of catalog shopping fame and U.S. and state politicians of conservative and liberal persuasions.

Marge's parents, **George** and **Isabelle Gogian**, selected farmland next to the Namekagon River for this business venture and planted 50,000 pine trees on the property. They were both Armenian, but born in Turkey, and were brought together through an arranged marriage that lasted 53 years.

On the menu are steaks and seafood, but the unusual draws are the shish kabobs, pilaf, borek (cheese-filled phyllo pies), Turkish coffee and baklava. A signature dessert is the crème de menthe parfait.

"No one could work for them because they were so fussy," Marge says of her parents, smiling. Much of the work continues from scratch. One example: the restaurant ages and cuts its own meat.

Regarding baklava, the flaky ethnic dessert: "We make our own syrup that includes rosewater and lemon juice. It's not as sweet as the Greek version." Creamy bar specialties include George's Polar Bear (Galliano, crème de cacao, ice cream) and Harem's Delight (Cointreau, crème d'amande, ice cream).

Marge was a fashion stylist and dress designer in New York City before returning to Wisconsin to help with the restaurant after her father had a debilitating heart attack.

"I wanted a career and to travel, to not be tied down," she confides, but as an only child she considered it her responsibility to continue the family business.

Turk's Inn
11320 N. U.S. 63, Hayward
715-634-2597

•

SIDE DISH: Cracked Wheat (Bulgar) Pilaf

1 cup cracked wheat
1¾ cups chicken or beef broth
¼ pound butter (1 stick)
½ cup chow mein noodles, broken up
½ teaspoon salt
¼ teaspoon pepper

Stir cracked wheat and broth over medium flame until broth is absorbed. Add butter, chow mein noodles and seasonings. Let simmer for 5 minutes over a lower flame. Do not stir while cooking. Serve.

*Variation*s: Add sautéed chopped onion. Use ½ cup of both wild rice and cracked wheat. For pink pilaf, omit noodles and use one cup of broth and one cup of tomato juice.

The **Turk's Inn** suggests serving the pilaf with steak, wild game or poultry. Have leftovers? Use it for breakfast: reheat in a skillet with butter, drop eggs on top and let simmer until eggs are cooked soft.

Kevin Cain sells berries and fun to berry pickers.

HIXTON: Berries of Blue

Wisconsin is not known for its blueberry production, which means you're in for a sweet surprise when discovering a patch.

For a handful of weeks in midsummer, cars clog the pathways of Cain's Orchard, which also grows grapes and at least two dozen varieties of apples.

Up to 3,000 people travel from as far as Chicago to pick blueberries on Saturdays, some arriving hours before the orchard opens with the ringing of a bell at 7 a.m. It turns into a charming family outing in a pretty and secluded setting, just a couple of miles off of I-94.

"They just run," owner **Kevin Cain** says, to describe customer reaction to the bell ringing. Showing up with kids is encouraged, but dogs are not. Early birds get free coffee. Up to ten tons of berries are harvested per picking day, which tends to be weekly.

"Sure, we're selling blueberries," Kevin says, "but we're also selling entertainment."

It takes up to a dozen people to orchestrate car parking. People in wheelchairs are welcome; employees find a place that is flat and level for them to do their picking.

Ice cream buckets are filled with up to nine kinds of highbush berries, and they grow on 20 acres. Some berries may be the size of quarters. Although herbicides aren't used, the crop is not organic because of fertilizer applications. Fencing, to keep deer away, surrounds it all.

The business is largely about picking your own product, and it began after Kevin and his wife, **Diane**, bought a weathered, 160-acre farm in the 1970s, shortly after they married. "We were too dumb to know better," Kevin jokes. Little by little, they transformed it, cosmetically and with regard to crop content.

"Apples didn't have the production that I wanted on the lower ground, so we planted blueberries," Kevin says, giving Diane credit for the transition. He grew up on a dairy farm near La Crosse; she is a registered nurse.

Hills surround and shelter three sides of their property. "No wind gets in," Kevin says. "It's a microclimate" that is a good match for the berries.

A small gift shop stocks jams, salad dressings, syrups and other items that come from Upper Midwest harvests. "If Wal-Mart sells it, we don't," is how Kevin puts it. "And we try to limit the blatant commercialism because that's just not our style."

The specific dates and times for any fruit picking will depend upon the growing conditions of the year.

The lineup of six cash registers is evidence of how busy this place gets. A bucket of freshly picked berries is under $10. It is not possible to avoid the labor and simply show up to buy berries.

Blue Ray, Berkeley and Elliot are types of highbush blueberries that can survive in a northern climate. They vary in looks, taste and ripening. The bushes are pruned, in rotation, every six or seven years.

The Cains list both their orchard and residence phone numbers on their website. So do they get a lot of oddball calls?

"If we didn't like people," Kevin says, sidestepping the question, "we wouldn't do this." He describes his customers as "easy to deal with," with sunny dispositions, "not 'concrete' people but active people who probably like to hike and bike."

Cain's Orchard
W13885 Cain Road, Hixton
www.cainsorchard.com
715-963-2052
•

Native Bay presents fine dining in an outwardly casual setting.

LAKE WISSOTA: Native Son at Native Bay

Chippewa County's Lake Wissota got a sliver of Hollywood exposure in 1997, when mentioned during the movie *Titanic*, but the 6,300-acre lake didn't exist until six years after the ship sank in 1912.

We love "gotcha" moments, don't we? Perhaps the blessing is that the blooper didn't cause too many interlopers to discover, overrun and ruin this lovely, manmade lake.

As it is, Lake Wissota State Park isn't far enough north to be a trendy Northwoods locale for summer vacations. That's a shame, or a relief, depending upon your point of view. This peaceful and wildlife-filled area is one of many good reasons to visit the Chippewa Valley. You also won't be disappointed when in search of food.

Native Bay Restaurant and Lounge presents the finest of dining in the most unlikely of places. The property faces Lake Wissota and looks like an ordinary watering hole—umbrella tables outside, with a plastic banner or two, to identify the spot.

Inside, chef **Nathan Berg** gathers ingredients from Wisconsin farmers and works magic. "A northern Wisconsin style of menu—lots of cranberries, wild rice, maple syrup, freshwater fish" and other locally produced items are at front and center.

"Incredibly fresh food makes for better food," asserts Nathan, and buying local products keeps the local economy strong. He also likes getting to know the farmers whose food he's buying.

Nathan mentions **Bob** and **Martha Hamblin's Romar Greenhouse**, Augusta, where he purchases heirloom produce. This is one of about 40 local vendors that he'll contact, which makes life more complex than "going online and typing in an order to get all that I need delivered the next day from one or two providers."

His job also has involved busting myths about expectations. It is not a private club, there is no need to wear a suit, and a meal need not break the bank.

Our dinner choice, for $32, was locally raised buffalo, a juicy and lean rib eye, served with au gratin potatoes, made with a swiss gruyère.

Although one part of the business is fine dining, the lounge's casual fare also patronizes local food producers. So the burgers are organic, grass-fed beef. The cheese curds are white cheddar from **Castlerock Organic Farms**, Osseo, with a sourdough bread wrapping and dipping sauce of smoked heirloom tomato vinaigrette. Also impressive is the lengthy menu of microbrews.

Boats sputter and coast up to the pier, then dock for an hour or two, just as they did before Nathan, a Chippewa Falls native, was born. The business was a typical lakeside supper club, called Waters Edge.

Nathan was drawn to restaurant work as a teen, when he worked as a dishwasher. Like a lot of young adults, he veered away from home to widen his work experience and view of the world. A goal was to own his own restaurant, and when Waters Edge went up for sale in 2005, Nathan, then 29, seized the opportunity.

He conducts cooking classes and hopes to soon figure out a way to present multiple courses of fine dining on the pontoon boats that can be rented at Native Bay.

Native Bay Restaurant and Lounge
9504 Hwy. S South, Chippewa Falls
www.nativebayrestaurant.com
715-726-0434

•

Legacy Chocolates are based on percentages: 41 to 99% cocoa.

MENOMONIE: Leaving a Legacy

When Valentine's Day approaches, consider adjusting your notion of how fine chocolates should look, and how heartfelt sentiments should be expressed.

Eliminate the heart-shaped box, the crinkly brown paper candy cups and the business of squishing the bottom of a confection to identify the filling before taking the first bite.

The exquisite choices in Menomonie are not about cream or coconut center, toffee or caramel texture. Both the chocolatier and the customer must deal with percentages: 41 to 99. The higher the number, the bigger the kick of cocoa; it comes from a specific type of bean in South America.

And the display? Each wonderfully dense truffle sits in its own little covered plastic container, the same kind used for a helping of mayo, tartar sauce or salad dressing in a cafeteria line or takeout bag. That keeps the candy fresh and cuts the possibility that one aroma will mingle or interfere with another.

So forget about lovely glass platters that present these candies as small pyramids of edible gems. What these products—from **Legacy Chocolates**—lack in presentation is made up in purity of chocolate taste that is not sugared down. The flavors for sale— champagne to espresso—change daily.

How good is the quality? Good enough to win "Best Chocolate" honors three years in a row in a poll of Twin Cities readers (through the alternative weekly newspaper *City Pages*). Why would Minnesota residents choose **Mike** and **Cathy Roberts's** Wisconsin company for this prize? The second outlet for Legacy Chocolates is in St. Paul.

What you give others in this world is much less about pretense and extravagance than spirit and kind intentions. Keep the opportunity for significant connections in mind when you prepare for the next Valentine's Day. Make your words and actions more memorable than the material goods.

Legacy Chocolates
632 S. Broadway Street, Menomonie
2042 Marshall Avenue, St. Paul, Minnesota
www.legacychocolates.com
715-231-2580

•

TIDBITS

Wisconsin has no shortage of exquisite candy makers. Here is a sample:

The Chocolate Caper, 105 S. Main Street, Oregon. Claude Marendaz and his recipes are from Switzerland. The two-layered Swiss pralines are his specialty.
www.chocolatecaper.com 608-835-9294

•

Wilmar Chocolates, 1222 N. Superior Street, Appleton. Boxed assortments include the Award Collection of candies that have earned the Wisconsin State Fair Seal of Excellence.
www.wilmarchocolates.com 920-733-6182

•

Seroogy's, 144 N. Wisconsin Street, DePere. In business since 1899, it is best-known for flavored meltaways (mint, peanut butter, almond, chocolate, chocolate crisp).
www.seroogys.com 800-776-0377

•

Beerntsen's Confectionary, 108 N. Eighth Street, Manitowoc. The third-generation family business produces chocolates in unusual, fun molds and also has a store in Cedarburg.
www.beerntsens.com 920-684-9616

•

Oaks Chocolates, 1206 Oregon Street, Oshkosh. In business since 1890; products include the popular Melty Bar candy bars.
www.oakscandy.com 920-231-3660

•

Kehr's Candies, Milwaukee Public Market, 400 N. Water Street, and factory store at 3533 W. Lisbon Avenue. Making candy since 1930, and the old-fashioned feel of the factory store is worth a visit, but orders also are shipped.
414-223-4305

•

Candinas Chocolatier, 2435 Old PB, Verona, and 11 W. Main Street, Madison.
Swiss-trained confectioner **Markus Candinas's** artisan chocolates earn raves from *Consumer Reports*, *USA Today* and the *Financial Times* of London.
www.candinas.com 800-845-1554

The blackboard menu at Harbor View Cafe changes twice a day.

PEPIN: Sit, Stay, Eat

Breezing into the **Harbor View Cafe**, looking for a meal to go, I hear a gentle but direct and swift admonishment.

"This is a come-in-and-sit-down place," says **Judy Krohn**, head cook, but we do find something to suit my desire to stay on schedule. A cup of chilled ginger-carrot soup—perfect for sipping on a steamy summer day—and a porketta sandwich on a slightly chewy, toasted bun make excellent driving companions. The shaved and succulent pork carries a hint of garlic, enough to notice but not define you later in the day. Add a side of aioli and—what, pickled onions? The meal has panache.

A loaf of the house specialty, crusty French bread, also goes home for the ride. Slices accompany diners' soups and salads. Cafe owners **Chuck Morrow** and **Ruth Stoyke** take pride in the from-scratch cooking that revolves around ingredients—pheasant to cheese—that sometimes come from just down the road.

The menu is written on a big chalkboard above the bar and changes twice daily. Expect to wait for a table on summer weekends, but that's a fine time to settle into one of the Adirondack chairs outside the cafe, facing Lake Pepin's pretty harbor.

Ruth, from northern Minnesota, started out as a cafe customer, then a server. "I'm still a server," the co-owner says, with a laugh.

Fresh seafood, flown into Minneapolis daily, makes the biggest mark on the menu—but don't expect a traditional Wisconsin fish fry. "We don't deep-fry anything here," Ruth says. "We sauté and grill."

Halibut in black butter caper sauce is a specialty. "We have fish every night—four or five choices," says Ruth. "It's not just for Fridays."

Don't expect to dine at the cafe, open seasonally, between 2:30 and 5 p.m. The kitchen closes between lunch and dinner.

Minnesotans, through magazine and newspaper polls, have selected the Harbor View Cafe as the area's best day-trip restaurant.

Harbor View Cafe
314 First Street, Pepin
www.harborviewpepin.com
715-442-3893
•

TIDBITS

Thanks to glacial movement long ago, the widest "naturally occurring" part of the Mississippi River is Lake Pepin (2 miles wide, 20 miles long, 10,500 years old, says the National Park Service), although Lake Onalaska near La Crosse is 4 miles wide because of the work of Lock and Dam No. 7.
•
Six miles north of Pepin is the riverfront bluff community of Stockholm, population 97, and the place hops during summer. More than 100 artists sell their work during the Stockholm Art Festival, on the third Saturday in July.

Art galleries, Amish furniture, a dog biscuit bakery and kitchen boutique are among the specialty shops.

Order Swedish pancakes with lingonberries or salmon cakes with poached eggs at the **Bogus Creek Cafe & Bakery**, N2049 Spring Street. To go: a loaf of cranberry walnut bread or a fruit-filled kolachi. Open seasonally.
www.stockholmwisconsin.com 715-442-2266

While farmers harvest cranberries, teens turn into tour guides.

PITTSVILLE: Quick-study Tour Guides

Until the new millennium, Pittsville was merely known as the geographic center of Wisconsin. Now the town of 850 also is heralded as home to the nation's only cranberry science class for high schoolers.

The lessons can be as much about dealing with the public as they are about bogs and berries. By the time the crop is ready to harvest in October, the students are splitting up the narration of two-hour tours that explain the industry from beginning to end—first-year beds to final freezing.

Wisconsin leads the U.S. in cranberry production, and Pittsville High School is in the heart of it. About 20 students per fall semester take the specialty agriculture class, taught by Bill Urban.

"A cranberry grower approached the school [in the mid 1990s] to say he'd pay an extra 50 cents an hour to students who took the class, then worked for him," says Bill, who also is the school's Future Farmers of America advisor.

The idea didn't take off, but the seed had been—hah!—planted.

Cranberry science, a relatively stale topic for teens, became cool to study after Bill struck up a deal with local tourism and cranberry industry leaders. They devised a plan to grow tourism as students learned and berries ripened.

Students uncomfortable with public speaking could help prepare a lunch that includes a variety of cranberry products. The meal is included in the tour price. Money raised from tour fees ($20 per person) would go into a scholarship fund.

"People want to see the red color" when visiting cranberry bogs, Bill acknowledges, so that frames the timetable for giving the tours. Field trips for fourth graders, while studying Wisconsin history and culture, are among the customers.

Close to 400 people go on the Pittsville tours per year, and they have come from as far away as Japan. Tour segments are split into at least seven parts, so many students have the chance to be tour speakers. The revenue means that Pittsville can award $500 college scholarships instead of $100, and that 10 to 12 teens can go to the national FFA convention instead of one or two.

When the cranberry harvest ends, so do the tours, although the class lasts until mid-January. "We go on to learn about other Wisconsin products," Bill says.

"This has put Pittsville on the map" and shown off the state "as the cranberry bread basket of the country," he says.

Splash of Red Cranberry Highway Tours
Pittsville High School
www.pittsville.k12.wi.us/cranberry
715-884-6412
•

TIDBITS

Tours begin when the cranberries are ready to harvest, and that sometimes does not coincide with the **Warrens Cranberry Festival**, the world's largest, held during the last weekend in September.

The festival presents a one-hour cranberry marsh tour. The event's farm market contains more than 100 vendors. Cranberry products are the predominant theme, but much more is sold. Pickled mushrooms, Amish-made noodles, maple syrup, beef jerky and buffalo sausage are some of the other likely products.

www.cranfest.com 608-378-4200

No boarding pass is required for these airline cookies.

RIVER FALLS:
The Best Secret

The cookie that helped make an airline exceptional comes from a modest, family-owned business in northwest Wisconsin which has been in operation about 65 years.

Private-label work typically is top-secret information, but Midwest Airlines has let the world know who has been making its chocolate chip cookie dough since 1986. That's because a new product—packages of the frozen dough, marketed under the airline name—is being sold at a chain of specialty food markets in Milwaukee.

The manufacturer is **Best Maid Cookie Company** of River Falls, which produces 45 kinds of cookies in a dozen sizes and forms. You won't find any mention of the company's work with the airlines at the Best Maid website.

Most products are sold to food service systems in schools and hospitals, which means the Best Maid label isn't on the average person's radar. So "modest" means a lack of horn tooting for a company whose 100 employees make 650,000 pounds of cookies/dough per week.

"Kids would probably get [a Best Maid cookie] before the parents do," says **Deb Dartsch**, cookie company co-owner with **Ron Thielen**. "The University of Wisconsin has used our cookies forever," she adds.

Fly Midwest Airlines, and attendants bake dough from Best Maid on board, filling the cabin with a delightful fragrance before passengers are handed two warm cookies at a time. It's the most memorable part of a flight with Midwest, and a part of the reason that the company routinely earns best airline honors from Zagat, *Travel+Leisure* and *Conde Nast*.

Gas up at a PDQ, and it may be possible to buy a similar Best Maid cookie, weighing in at three ounces, but it's sold prewrapped and at room temperature.

The amount of chocolate used and the way the cookies are baked make the airline's product distinct from those sold under the Best Maid label, Deb says. "They're a little different, but they're still good," she says of her company's house brand.

Deb considers Midwest Airlines "a wonderful organization and a nice fit" for her company because both are Wisconsin based. Her dad, **C. Arthur Erickson**, started Best Maid in 1943, using no preservatives and vowing to include fine chocolate in 25 percent of his recipes.

"Our cookies had been on board other airlines" before the work with Midwest began, Deb says, but these products didn't stand out because the cookies weren't baked as planes flew.

Best Maid operates two outlets where product overruns and imperfect cookies are sold.

Best Maid Cookie Company
1147 Benson Street, River Falls
www.bestmaid.com
715-426-2090
3940 Minnehaha Avenue, Minneapolis
612-722-5035

•

TIDBITS

When Midwest Airlines Genuine Chocolate Chip Cookie Dough— 32 individual, ready-to-bake, 1-ounce cookies—made its debut, six Sendik's Markets in the Milwaukee area (Grafton, Elm Grove, Franklin, Mequon, Wauwatosa and Whitefish Bay) got the nod to sell the product exclusively.

Next up, says James Reichart of Midwest Airlines: consideration of dough sales in other parts of Wisconsin, and possibly Kansas City.

•

The cookies are baked only on-board Midwest Airlines flights that depart after 10 a.m.

•

Midwest Airlines sells cookie merchandise—3-inch refrigerator magnets, cookie-shaped zipper pulls, T-shirts, sweatshirts and mock turtlenecks—at **www.midwestairlinesstore.com**. Cookie lovers blog at **www.savethecookie.com**, a name that refers to stepped-up efforts to prevent a change in airline ownership.

Area residents have their artwork for sale at Racheli's.

WASHBURN: Doing Double Duty

When **Ugo** and **Marcia Racheli** moved to northern Wisconsin from the Twin Cities, it was to retire, but their pace of life has been anything but leisurely. **Racheli's**, the deli, opened in 2004. The couple's homey, sit-down restaurant opened less than two years later. The cuisine is rooted in recipes from Ugo's native Italy, but with significant accommodations.

For sale are five types of lasagna: two meat-based (beef, pork sausage) and three vegetarian (one with eggplant, another with gluten-free polenta instead of noodles, the third a more traditional veggie mix).

About ten kinds of soup are prepared and sold, in rotation. Other products—such as pizzas, baked crackers, pasta entrées—sometimes are adapted to meet dietary restrictions.

"I've been concerned for a number of years about industrial food production," Ugo says. "It's not good for the health of the people."

He weekly delivers his restaurant's foods, which have no preservatives or additives, to grocery stores and other businesses as far away as Hayward and Superior. That's more than 200 miles per triangular swoop, and Ugo does double-duty along the way.

"We are scouting suppliers and buying products along the same routes," he says.

He seeks small-scale producers of quality cheeses, breads, meats and other items. Distribution of Racheli's prepared foods seems to work especially well in small-town IGA markets; "they give us some space and let us advertise," Ugo observes.

Sons **Joseph** and **Larry** work with their parents in Washburn, and the deli/restaurant contains a small gift shop that sells sleek wood-carved items—from bowls to cutting boards. Some of these beautiful pieces are handcrafted by Larry.

The Washburn deli/restaurant used to be a dairy farm and milk bottling plant. It continues to have an agricultural ambiance.

"We want to help extend the growing season and improve the agricultural land-scape around us," Ugo says. He is a fan of FEAST (Food security, Education, Access, Sustainable agriculture and Traditions), a group for foodies in Ashland and Bayfield counties.

"We are following our conscience," he says. "Wisconsin has always been a place of small businesses and small farmers—a place for individuality."

Racheli's Deli & Restaurant
77130 Hwy. 13, Washburn
715-373-5008

•

Larry's handcrafted wood items are functional and handsome.

ELSEWHERE IN THE NORTHWEST

The biggest bash in Birchwood, which calls itself the state's bluegill capital, is the summertime **Bluegill Festival**. Buying a festival button earns you a discount at the weekend fish feed, where platters are heaped with fish, cole slaw, fries and a dinner roll.

The year 2008 was the forty-fifth such festival. It's not all that unusual for a bald eagle to fish the same lakes that you do, especially when choosing a waterway that is accessible only by canoe. Besides bluegill, the chains of lakes—Spider, Birch, Chetac, Red Cedar and others—are home to northern pike, walleye, bass and crappies.

www.birchwoodchamber.com   www.birchwoodwi.com
800-236-2252

•

Before leaving the Chippewa Valley, head to the **Jacob Leinenkugel Brewing Company**, 124 Elm Street, Chippewa Falls, for a free tour, beer sample and shopping for Leinie merchandise at the Leinie Lodge, which also has cozy furniture for hanging out. The warm-weather tap is Summer Shandy, beer with honey and lemonade, served April through August. Don't be offended if you hear talk about grabbing a Big Butt. That's the doppelbock, a cool-weather option.

Biggest event for the Leinie family (which includes you, if you choose) is the annual family reunion, on the day before Father's Day. Expect music, free food and beer samples.

www.leinie.com 888-534-6437

•

Nobody in the world grows or processes more horseradish than **Silver Spring Foods** of Eau Claire, a family business that began in 1929. Its expanding line of products—mustards as well as horseradish, condiments as well as seafood sauces—includes national award winners.

Silver Spring processes about 3,500 tons of horseradish each year, from 7,000 acres in Buffalo, Pepin and Chippewa counties to 2,000 acres in Clearbrook, Minnesota. Horseradish also is bought from farmers in Collinsville, Illinois, and Tule Lake, California.

"It's a secret blend," says **Ed Schaefer**, company president. Like grapes for wine, horseradish quality and character are shaped by soil and climate. The Eau Claire horseradish is "a little sweeter" and has a wild root lineage. The California contribution is "more fibrous," and Illinois horseradish arrives muddier, because of its proximity to the Mississippi River.

NORTHWEST ROAD TRIP:
Abundance in the Heart of Wisconsin

Wisconsin Dairy State Cheese Company has more than 100 varieties of cheese.

Central Wisconsin is the nation's hub of cranberry production, but that doesn't mean the snack and meal choices are one-dimensional.

Enjoy the sight of cranberry blossoms in early summer, berry-red bogs in autumn and sandhill cranes nearly all year, while exploring a grand scale of culinary delights.

1. **Breakfast** at the **Little Pink Restaurant**, 910 Dura Beauty Lane, Wisconsin Rapids, will awaken your senses while being kind to your pocketbook. The cozy diner is deep pink, inside and out, making it hard to miss (or snooze). Don't expect to hog a table for four; it is customary and necessary to take a seat anywhere during peak meal times.

If you have a hankerin' (and you should) for a loaf of **Helen's** bread, or her cinnamon rolls, order in advance. **715-421-1210**

2. **The squeakiest cheese curds** around come from **Wisconsin Dairy State Cheese Company**, Hwys. 34 and C, Rudolph. Watch cheesemakers at work, from behind a glassed-in observation deck. Antique butter/cheese dishes fill display cabinets. For sale are more than a dozen flavors of ice cream, and more than 100 types of Wisconsin cheese. **715-435-3144**

3. **Organic foods and Fair Trade coffees** show up in an unlikely place, on the outskirts of the tiny town of Rudolph. Visit **Back to the Country Store**, 7220 Third Avenue, and its friendly staff, who can help address many types of diet restrictions. **www.backtothecountrystore.com 715-435-3492**

4. **For lunch**, it's a lemon phosphate and burger at **Herschleb's**, 640 Sixteenth Street North, Wisconsin Rapids, which has been in business since 1939. The old-time

soda fountain setting is what makes this a nostalgic stop; the owners sell ice cream by the gallon and the cone.

Silky ice cream is made on the premises, and the cookies also can be tremendous. Blueberries, cranberries and white chocolate fill the All American Cookie. **715-423-1760**

The direction for dinner depends on your mood.

5. **Piegatta (folded pocket pizzas)** and traditional pizzas come from the wood-fired oven at **Cafe Mulino**, inside the Hotel Mead, 451 E. Grand Avenue, Wisconsin Rapids. **www.hotelmead.com 715-422-7055**

6. **Gourmet preparation** of steak and fish is routine at **Baker Street Grill**, 1716 Baker Street, Wisconsin Rapids, so don't assume that the sports bar motif means just burgers and fries. **715-421-5858**.

7. **Drive about 20 miles southeast**. The **Hide-A-Way**, 1682 Apache Lane, Rome, presents classy-casual dining (their white linens, your jeans) with pretty Lake Petenwell views and a nautical decor. Consider the Greek specialties: flakey spanako-pita, spiced rack of lamb and saganaki (the traditional cheese appetizer that is set aflame at tableside). Ommpahh! **715-325-6550**

8. **And when it's time to sleep** it all off, nestle into private quarters at the **Stone Cottage**, 2480 Highway D, Wisconsin Rapids, a former foreman's quarters on a still-operating cranberry estate. **www.cranberrylink.com 715-887-2095**

Outstanding in a cranberry bog

Your outlet for shedding pounds gained is the 50-mile Cranberry Highway. Instead of getting behind the wheel, bike it or the 29-mile Cranberry Trail.

www.visitwisrapids.com
800-554-4484

Judy Hageman teaches budding gardeners.

TELL ME ABOUT: Farm/Fork Relationships

By the time most people begin planting spinach, **Snug Haven Farm** is reaping the last of its harvest.

The first of the farm's cherry tomatoes begin ripening less than two weeks later, way ahead of the typical Midwest garden.

The timing is strategic, the bounty impressive and the quality superb. What Belleville farmers **Bill Warner** and **Judy Hageman** harvest ends up on the plates of upscale Chicago restaurants, and that makes them different from the average vegetable grower.

"Sweet and quite lovely," says Brian Enyart of Frontera Grill and Topolobampo in Chicago, when asked to describe the spinach, which is sautéed with roasted garlic in olive oil, or steamed, pureed with tomatillos and used as a sauce for grilled fish.

These two Rick Bayless restaurants garner raves, from the *New York Times* to *Conde Nast Traveler*.

"They are incredible," says Sarah Stegner, formerly head chef at the Chicago Ritz-Carlton, a Four Seasons hotel. That's her response to both Snug Haven spinach and tomatoes.

Snug Haven sauce tomatoes are like a roma, and less watery than average. They are frozen whole, and the farm can keep 18,000 pounds in storage; Chicago restaurants get them from late October to mid-June.

"The consistency, for our sauces, is absolutely perfect, every time," Brian says.

There is mutual support and loyalty between supplier and customer, and this example is not unique. Snug Haven operates independently, but there are about two dozen Wisconsin family farms in **Home Grown Wisconsin**, a cooperative founded in 1996 that has fostered communication—and business—between farmers and chefs. Today more than forty Chicago restaurants, including the acclaimed Tru, Blackbird and Charlie Trotter's, are regular customers.

The business deals were not cemented overnight. They have been built on trust that had to be earned by both sides.

Chef Rick Bayless, a PBS food show host as well as restaurateur, was a participant in the original conversations. "It was one of the most bizarre experiences in my life," he says, of his first meeting with the new co-op. "I felt like I was their biggest nightmare, not the answer to their dreams."

Would the restaurants order enough to make it worth the farmers' time? Would they take all that was ordered? Every week? Could the farmer count on being paid?

Similarly, the farmers had to prove they were dependable, that they could produce a high-quality product consistently and that communication would be quick if something out of their hands—like frost damage—affected production.

Rick says he invited the co-op to visit his restaurant and introduced them to the complex flavors that their vegetables could help produce. "We offered them a taste of what we do," he recalls. "We had to promise to buy $1,000 in produce per week." His first order was for $2,500 worth. "Now we spend $500,000 on 30 farms per year. A dozen are our major suppliers, and we've seen some farms go from minuscule to great."

Many of the chefs appreciate intimacy between themselves and the farms. They like to visit their suppliers, see the picturesque rural settings, hear the farmers' stories, feel a sense of place and connection between farmer and food.

"The number of restaurants that embrace the organic presence is exploding, and Rick (Bayless) is leading the charge," says Jim Slama, co-founder of *Conscious Choice* magazine.

The Frontera Farmer Foundation, established in 2003, provides short-term loans for farm projects. Loan money comes from donations, plus a $100-per-plate dinner and silent auction.

Snug Haven was able to add freezer equipment because of Frontera's help. The restaurant prebought enough tomatoes to finance the purchase.

Judy and Bill have tried to anticipate their customers' needs. The spinach, for example, is hand cut, leaf by leaf. When it gets to the restaurant, it's clean and has no stems. It is grown in hoop houses, where temperature, water levels and, ultimately, quality can be controlled. They take up less than one acre.

"We wanted to get a jump on the season," says Judy, to explain the logic of off-season growth cycles. "That's how you do well" in sales.

"In summer, it tastes too much like spinach," Bill says, of their product. Grown as it is, "there's no bitter aftertaste. It's sweeter."

The Chicago chefs, and others, have encouraged the farmers to trust their instincts.

"What do you want to grow? What grows well? What product excites you? We are chefs who can prepare whatever you give us," if it is of high quality, Rick Bayless says.

Snug Haven, a longtime Dane County Farmers' Market vendor, also sells cut flowers, arugula (a salad green), radishes and early potatoes. Bill and Judy were interim managers of the market in 2001; Judy also is a former manager of Home Grown Wisconsin.

Home Grown Wisconsin
www.homegrownwisconsin.com
608-347-3054

•

TIDBITS

The relationship that Snug Haven Farm has with upscale Chicago restaurants is a simple example of value-added agriculture.

The farmers do more than grow a product for generic sales. They have refined quality to match a specific customer's standards and needs. They have established a market niche.

Farmers historically have been straightforward commodity producers who benefit the most when they keep expenses low and demand exceeds supply. In the value-added approach, "they differentiate a product enough to be able to command a higher price for it."

The explanation comes from Arlen Leholm, dean and director of the University of Wisconsin Cooperative Extension.

Bill McKnight and Tanya Laiter produce the Rolling Pin Bake Shop's tempting treats.

FITCHBURG: Russian Riches

Bake it, and they will come.

When **Tanya Laiter** and **Bill McKnight** opened the **Rolling Pin Bake Shop** in 2003, it was with no advertising, fanfare or business connections.

"Where are the customers?" Tanya asked, doubting herself.

"Wait," Bill reassured. "We'll create our own traffic."

And that is what has happened. Word spread; now the business that was built on a dream and secondhand furnishings thrives. It has expanded twice, to include seating for three dozen breakfast/lunch diners, and caters full meals for a crowd.

Display cases are filled with all the decadence that various combinations of chocolate, butter, sugars, whipped cream, fruit and nuts can produce. One case rotates seductively, and it is for refrigerated goods: tiny and large cream puffs, eclairs, mousse-filled cakes, fruit tarts, cheesecakes. Another holds huge and petite cookies, scones, pastries, muffins, cinnamon buns.

The relatively small space is big on diversity, particularly ethnic temptations. There typically is Russian white bread, teacakes and rugalah (a filled, Jewish pastry); Challah bread; lady locks (a cream-filled puff pastry); and heart-shaped linzer cookies.

If you see a cake and just want to buy a slice, ask. If your dream dessert isn't on the shelves, or comes in the wrong size, the bakers truly want to know.

A six-inch cake—envision raspberry-lemon-poppyseed—feeds more than you'd expect, because of the delicious richness of ingredients.

Tanya, a native of Russia, has made more than 300 types of pastries and cakes. She sometimes relies on her mother-in-law's cookbook from 1959, which is ten years older than the baker.

She and Bill are friends who worked in a North Carolina bakery before moving to Wisconsin. Tanya's husband, Mikhael Lyubchenko, is a physicist. It is his work that brought them all to the Midwest.

The business partners began to collect usable bakery equipment—a stainless steel table to baking pans—in North Carolina. Battered furnishings that would cost $5,000 new were bought for $200. Then they scraped, scrubbed, painted and decorated with their own artwork.

Much of Tanya's artistry is more fleeting, evident in the cookies and cakes that she elaborately decorates. She does it freehand, with no tracing of pictures, and quickly—like the Noah's ark scene that took less than an hour. Or the "looks-alive" rainbow trout, the intricate Yellow Brick Road, the comical SpongeBob SquarePants.

"I make the doughs and the batters, so Tanya has more time for decorating," Bill says. She has a master's degree in fine art and taught art to children and adults until 1993, when she moved to the United States. Her first job was in a grocery store, as a bagger; she did not speak English.

Rolling Pin Bake Shop
2935 S. Fish Hatchery Road
608-270-9611

•

TIDBITS

What's for lunch? Don't expect too much that is ordinary, or a menu that stays the same at the **Rolling Pin**.

Salad possibilities: Chicken Gorgonzola and Grilled Pear, Roast Beef with Lemon-Basil Mayo and Roasted Red Onions, Portobello and Granny Smith Apple.

Selections with ethnic roots: Beet Borscht, Russian Peasant Soup, Italian Wedding Soup.

And for breakfast? Egg choices may include Potato and Leek Flat Omelet, and Popeye's Omelet (feta with, yes, spinach).

*Chuck Deadman, with sons Chuck Jr. and Dave,
hoist super premium cones of Chocolate Shoppe Ice Cream.*

MADISON: Supreme Ice Cream

It's almost 7 p.m. on a sweltering weeknight, and the **Deadman** brothers—**Dave** and **Chuck Jr.**—are still at work, sweetening up the masses before a downtown Madison concert begins.

The summer is their time to run long and hard. Sixteen-hour workdays are not unusual.

Their product—**Chocolate Shoppe Ice Cream**—comes in 110 flavors, although no location sells more than 50 kinds at once. It all is made at one Madison ice cream plant, then ends up in coffeehouses to sandwich shops in seven states.

This enterprise, a hands-on family business, has been around since 1962 and has survived all sorts of tests. Some have come from nationally known brands: Dairy Queen, Maggie Moo's, Ben & Jerry's, Culver's, Cold Stone Creamery. It employs about 50 at its Madison factory and retail outlets, and it is not unusual for employees to seem like family. They include Bev Kriel, who is in her seventies and works at the State Street shop; she has been with the company since 1972.

Three factory-owned stores in Madison are training grounds for wholesalers who sell Chocolate Shoppe products. New wholesale customers get two days of training on all aspects of serving and storing the treats, cleaning and maintaining store equipment, training and managing staff.

"Scoop training" is a 12-step process that includes how to hold the scoop, put ice cream in a cone, handle a cone, and avoid breaking it. Learning to make a malt or shake takes twice as many steps.

"We're not in many grocery stores, and that has been a deliberate decision," says Dave. "We want to sell to ice cream shops. It makes the brand more visible."

It's also a way to have more control over quality because "we take it off our trucks and put it right into the freezer, so there is very little shocking [thawing and refreezing] of the product."

The family is proud that most of its deliveries can be made, roundtrip, in one day.

"We constantly get calls from other places that are farther away, saying 'we want to pick up your product,' but we want to support all our customers well and stay closer to Madison," Dave says. The ice cream stays special, he believes, because it's of high quality and not easily accessible everywhere.

At the east Madison ice cream plant, up to seven flavors per day are funneled into three-gallon cartons and frozen. Ice cream production for other companies is a part of this business, too, and those work contracts are kept confidential.

The primary Chocolate Shoppe product—super premium ice cream—is not for dieters. It is all-natural, high in butterfat, smooth in texture and dense: a carton weighs 19.5 to 20 pounds, compared to the commercial industry average of 14 pounds.

The product line has grown more complex since the business began as a one-machine operation in the back room of a retail store on Monona Drive. That's when the average ice cream cone cost a nickel.

Today the product line also includes sherbet, Italian ice, nonfat yogurt, no-sugar flavors and nondairy (soy) versions.

Chocolate Shoppe Ice Cream has withstood nationwide competition as well as local. The Vanilla Bean (whose vanilla flavoring, from Madagascar, costs $250 per gallon) won a blue ribbon for vanilla ice creams at the National Ice Cream and Yogurt Retailers Association contest. Its Zanzibar Chocolate was one of three ribbon winners in the "new flavor" category.

Are there more flavors to come? Of course, the Deadman brothers say. That part is easy. Finding the right name is more difficult.

Chocolate Shoppe Ice Cream
various locations throughout Wisconsin
www.chocolateshoppeicecream.com
608-221-8640
•

Wisconsin's State Capitol is the perfect backdrop for a farmers' market.

MADISON: To Market, to Market

Where we live, farmers' markets are plentiful and in multiple locations, almost daily in summer and at least weekly in winter. This is our good fortune.

The Dane County Farmers' Market is a giant nationally; up to 300 vendors surround the State Capitol on Saturdays, spring to late fall. *Eating Well* magazine is one of the most recent to proclaim this market as the best in the nation.

Only agricultural items made or grown in Wisconsin can be sold. There is a three-year waiting list for vendors who want to participate. It is about ostrich and emu meat as well as homemade cottage cheese and dog treats, asparagus to trout, potted plants to pea vines.

This all makes the Capitol Square the hottest place to be on a Saturday morning in Madison, and thousands will toddle counterclockwise to absorb the array of street musicians, political causes and vendors that garnish the food. Spectators move at a leisurely pace, and serious shoppers tend to either arrive early or gravitate to the smaller markets, which have fewer vendors, but more elbow room.

It seems like just about every little Wisconsin town has a summer farmers' market; the U.S. Department of Agriculture is aware of more than 100 in our state. Nationwide, 82 percent of these markets create enough income to cover their expenses, and 19,000 farmers sell their products only this way.

Now big-box chain stores have made it clear that they intend to sell more naturally grown and organic food. These powerhouses in global purchasing/pricing threaten our local, charming, vital markets and will be a new test for consumers.

Must lowest price always be our bottom line? Is there value in seeing and interacting with the people whose food reaches your table? Do you appreciate the freshness and flavor of berries or tomatoes picked shortly before being sold?

If step one is to support the local farmers and their products, step two is to favor the independent restaurants whose menus rely upon locally grown ingredients. It is these chefs who make sure that endangered foods and food products do not vanish because of high-yield and highly engineered corporate farm practices. More than three dozen Madison area restaurants work together as one in marketing, education and outreach.

Check out the list, and keep these businesses in mind, whenever you're on the road or not in the mood to cook.

Dane County Farmers' Market on the Square
www.dcfm.org
608-455-1999

•

Madison Originals
www.madisonoriginals.org
608-228-0684

•

TIDBITS

Madison foodies rally downtown for all kinds of reasons. Among our favorites:

Local chefs are coaxed into making sweet and savory donations for Pie Palooza, in mid-June. The pies are sold by the slice, with salad and a beverage.

Choices might range from bastilla (a Moroccan chicken and vegetable phyllo dough pie) to chocolate ancho pecan tart. Traditional favorites—like pumpkin, apple and rhubarb cus-tard pies—also are likely.

Rhubarb custard, anyone?

The event location varies. Proceeds support the REAP (Research, Education, Action and Policy) Food Group, a nonprofit that wants people to eat locally produced and sustainable foods.

REAP Food Group annually hosts the mid-September Food for Thought Festival, a gathering of foodies who lecture, cook and exhibit their products, political positions and food philosophies.

The free event gets bigger every year and usually brings in at least one heavyweight speaker (like Mollie Katzen, *Moosewood Cookbook* author).

www.reapfoodgroup.org 608-294-1114

•

The annual Taste of Madison, around the Capitol Square, showcases the specialties of locally owned restaurants, although chains also participate.

Event organizer Keith Peterson describes the Madison area as being "absolutely flooded with fantastic local cuisine" and "we would really like to showcase all the flavors that are distinct to Dane County and beyond."

Middleton's Capital Brewery in 2005 became the event's exclusive beer sponsor. A goal is to draw in more businesses from New Glarus, Mt. Horeb and other outlying communities. The event attracts about 150,000 people.

•

Herd of cows? Of course you have, and a bunch of breathing bovine take over a part of the Capitol Square on the first Saturday morning in June.

That's when the celebration of June Dairy Month kicks in, during Cows on the Concourse, at Main Street and Martin Luther King Boulevard.

For kids, it's a great way to learn about dairy products, see where milk comes from and compare cow breeds. All ages benefit from fresh dairy treats, sold for a nominal price.

www.danecounty.dairy.com

Kimiko Miyazaki won the 2003 Food for Thought Recipe Contest.

•

A Farmers' Market Alliance for south central Wisconsin has been formed, to help expand and improve seasonal market operations.

"Small markets often are managed by a farmer who also is trying to sell" his products, says Miriam Grunes of the REAP Food Group.

Wisconsin has five farm atlases, each covering a different part of the state. These are free publications.

Each atlas is updated annually and lists dozens of farms, markets and

A basket of bounty from a farmer's garden.

other businesses that sell local products directly to consumers.

Central Wisconsin Farm Fresh Atlas
www.farmfreshatlas.org 715-343-6214

•

Farm Fresh Atlas of Eastern Wisconsin
www.farmfresheastwi.org 920-898-1814

•

Farm Fresh Atlas of Western Wisconsin
www.wifarmfresh.org 715-726-7950

•

Southeast Wisconsin Farm Fresh Atlas
www.slowfoodwise.org 262-857-1945

•

Southern Wisconsin Farm Fresh Atlas
www.reapfoodgroup.org 608-294-1114

Chris Weng prepares sushi at Edo Japanese Restaurant.

MADISON: Ethnic Eats

In Minneapolis, 17 blocks of Nicollet Avenue are nicknamed "Eat Street" because about 55 restaurants and markets sell food from around the world.

In Madison, 20 blocks of South Park Street have the potential to be branded the same way. Of the 30 places to buy food, about two dozen are independently owned businesses, and they represent at least a dozen types of ethnic cuisine.

Many are family-run, some owners speak little English, and only one is active in the South Metropolitan Business Association. Therein lies the authenticity and charm, the obstacles and challenges.

"We claim Park Street as Madison's international street," says **Lindsey Lee**, of Park Street Partners, a group at work to enhance the area. He also owns **Cargo Coffee**, 1309 S. Park Street, which used to be a Jiffy Lube.

Newer culinary businesses include **Inka Heritage**, 602 S. Park Street, a Peruvian restaurant. **Maritza Paz** moved here from Miami, where she had a cable TV cooking show and specialized in Peruvian seafood recipes; after helping to open this restaurant, she became chef at **El Corral**, 3302 Packers Avenue.

In 2007, **Jerry Canon** opened **Azzalino's Bar & Grill**, 416 S. Park Street, a soup/sandwich/salad spot, with daily specials (spaghetti, prime rib, goulash, lasagna, cod/catfish) on weekdays.

"I looked at how Park Street was changing and saw an opportunity," says Jerry, who also is a financial planner. What he used to consider "a harsher area" of Madison holds new opportunities for business growth because of hospital and residential renovations.

"These are down-home, everyday people and restaurants," says Rob Waterman, of the South Metropolitan Business Association. "They're less about the show"—as in outdoor dining and flashy buildings and decor. "It's no frills but great food."

The association has about 100 members, most of whom run small businesses, but Lindsey is the only member who sells food and beverages on South Park Street.

Others are welcome to join but "these are typically mom-and-pop operations, people who feel they can't leave the confines of their business," Rob rationalizes.

"Your world is the four walls in which your business operates," echoes Lindsey, regarding the work of being your own boss.

He also owns **Ground Zero**, 744 Williamson Street, "so I see two different perspectives" regarding multiculturalism in Madison.

"We are seeking diversity on Willy Street," he says. "Park Street *is* diversity," a reflection of its business mix as well as its residents.

South Park's business operators "first and foremost are serving their own ethnic community," those in outlying communities as well as the neighborhood.

South Metropolitan Business Association
www.madison.com/communities/smba
•
Park Street Partners
www.madison.com/communities/parkstpartners
•

TIDBITS

Special diets are accommodated at **Taj Indian Restaurant**, 1256 S. Park Street, where the menu includes a modestly priced lunch buffet, and the curry entices diners before they even open the door. "We are very friendly here," co-owner **Satnam Singh** says, and customer Bal Kishan agrees. "They have good karma," he says. "I was a customer, and they made me a family friend."

•

The head sushi chef at **Edo Japanese Restaurant**, 532 S. Park Street, is from New York City, where he worked at sushi restaurants. Sushi entree choices include hand-rolled combinations. The Edo Love Boat is 30 pieces of sushi and sashimi (raw, sliced seafood), enough for two to four people.

•

Italian sausage from longtime family recipes comes in mild, hot and double-hot versions at **Fraboni's Italian Specialties**, 822 Regent Street. Turkey sausage, brats and a cheese/parsley/wine sausage are other options. Seasoned porketta roasts are made with a four-generation family recipe.

•

A popular dish at **Inka Heritage**, 602 S. Park Street, is the Lomo Inka Heritage: grilled tenderloin, rice and beans, plus a fried egg and plantains. The Ronda Criolla, a hot appetizer platter, is a good way to sample several Peruvian foods.

Menudo (a traditional Mexican soup, with tripe) and pozole rojo (a soup with hominy corn, pork and chili) are popular meals at **Taqueria Guadalajara**, 1033 S. Park Street. The former American Lunch has nine diner seats, a couple of tables for two and outdoor seating at the rear of the restaurant. "Excellent and authentic," concluded an eastsider, having a late lunch of budget-priced tacos.

•

Customers are encouraged to linger over a cup of tea at the **Oriental Shop**, 1029 S. Park Street, whose Japanese merchandise—groceries to videos—is accompanied by pretty decor: bonsai trees, ethnic dolls, Zen-like artwork. Shopkeeper **Tamaki Haase Wu** is glad to share recipes.

•

A sign outside of **Yue-Wah**, 2328 S. Park Street, describes it as an Oriental grocery store, but dozens of other cultures—Mexican, Middle Eastern, African—are represented. Owner **Ken Ma** is a native of Vietnam.

•

More than a dozen types of Danish kringle have been made daily at **Lane's Bakery**, 448 S. Park Street, for 30 years. The third-generation family business, on this street since 1957, also makes cakes topped with heavy whipping cream. "People will go out of their way if you have a quality product," says co-owner **Chuck Lane**, "just like a fine dining restaurant."

Ken Monteleone stocks the world's best artisan cheeses at Fromagination.

MADISON: The Cheese Wiz

Let's be direct: you're not a know-it-all about cheese just because you live in Wisconsin.

That's no reason to get sheepish. **Ken Monteleone**, owner of **Fromagination**, 12 S. Carroll Street, and staff are able to help. The food specialty store, whose inventory base is the world's best artisan cheeses, is about both education and epicurean delights.

Many places sell cheese, but the high level of reverence and priority for the artisan product makes this business unusual in Wisconsin.

"We're not looking for things that are ordinary," Ken says of his wares, which also include cheese accessories (fondue sets, display cases) and accompaniments (wine, beer, unusual crackers) and other types of artisan food.

"Everything we're selling, and doing, has a story behind it." That includes the reclaimed building materials from floor to ceiling, the lighting fixtures made of recycled materials (and for sale), the proud history of pastas to chocolates that have been made by the same small companies for many decades.

What might the average Cheesehead not know about cheese?

- The best wrapping for cheese storage is a waxy paper, not plastic.

- Blue and stinky cheeses also should have a foil wrapping.

- To fully experience the taste of a hard or semi-hard cheese, remove it from refrigeration two hours before eating.

- If you are the first to get your hands on a wedge of brie, don't cut off the "nose" (narrow end of the wedge). Cut a small slice in a way that allows the narrowed end to stay intact.

- When serving more than one kind of cheese, have a cutting knife for each, so flavors don't blend.

- Avoid freezing cheese.

- It's OK to store similar cheeses together, but they shouldn't touch.

For other advice, check out the "Cheese Care & Etiquette" handout at Fromagination. Relevant books and videos (like the Wisconsin-produced "Living on the Wedge") are for sale.

Cheese class titles have included "How to Taste Cheese," "Wine and Cheese Pairings," "Winter Ales with Aged Cheese" and "Risotto Techniques."

"I didn't want to just open another cheese store," Ken says. "It's not that hard to do little things to make a difference."

For example, Ken lends vintage blankets for impromptu picnics on the Capitol Square lawn, just across the street.

Fromagination
12 S. Carroll Street, Madison
www.fromagination.com
608-255-2430
•

MADISON:
It's Kosher at Greenbush Bakery

Marv Miller wears a Packers cap in phonetic Hebrew and holds a tray of fresh fritters.

Marv Miller's Greenbush Bakery has had a certified kosher dairy kitchen since 1998.

Because of the bakery's location, in a tavern-heavy neighborhood, his double-chocolate doughnuts and blueberry fritters are a hit with college students as well as the Jewish community.

It is not happenstance that business hours are until midnight on weekdays, 3 a.m. on weekends, and that the exhaust fan produces a waft of fresh doughnuts as bar time nears.

Marv, who has been an insurance salesman as well as a flight mechanic for the Navy and an Oscar Mayer equipment mechanic, says the aroma is a great marketing device. Another is selling, at University of Wisconsin Hospital, four-packs of filled krullers called the Rabbi's Delight.

Greenbush Bakery
1305 Regent Street, Madison
608-257-1151

•

Live music heats up the Harmony Bar & Grill.

MADISON: Neighborhood Harmony

The first time **Keith Daniels** saw this place, in 1989, it looked like a sty. Dark, dingy, run-down.

His buddy, Byron Marshall, assumed that they'd keep searching. This was prospective business site no. 35, but this is where their hunt ended.

Keith had quickly rejected all the other locations but saw potential in this neighborhood, in this bar and grill, even in the building's neglected 1910 tin ceiling. Rent from two second-story apartments would cover the mortgage. Excellent food and a congenial atmosphere would build customer loyalty.

That was the plan, and the east-side **Harmony Bar & Grill** is a good neighbor as well as a successful business.

Instead of a fish fry ("the kitchen's too small for that"), there are handcrafted pizzas. In addition to sponsoring 24-30 softball teams—plus pool, soccer, volleyball and bowling teams—the bar would host fundraisers, typically monthly.

We could talk about the blues, bluegrass and rock that swell the house on weekends, the creative menu that redefines the term "bar food," the lack of ferns and pretense. Keith has no lofty aspirations for the Harmony, but he is proud of his neighborhood and believes in doing what he can to keep it healthy.

"He's amazing," says Becky Steinhoff, of the Atwood Community Center. Two annual Harmony fundraisers—Jimmy Buffett Night in April and the Harmony Golf Scramble in June—have raised more than $13,000 per year.

"He's just always there," Becky says, "not just for us, but for other community events, too."

The barkeep is matter-of-fact about his involvement. "We do tons of benefits," he says, without elaboration. Becky says there are other contributions, from sponsorship of a music stage during Atwood Summerfest to cash donations.

That doesn't mean he's an easy mark. Keith leans left and supports causes that he believes in, but he expects patronage in return. So don't ask him to sponsor a bowling team, then drink elsewhere after league play.

"The clientele has remained pretty much the same—it's aged as I have," Keith says. Grad students to aging baby boomers come here for libations and a game of cards or pool, a bowl of soup or plate of quesadillas.

Undergrads are less likely to make their way to the Harmony, since it's two miles from campus. Business "went up considerably" after Madison's ban on smoking in bars, and "if they would revert it, I'd stay nonsmoking."

He works almost every day, but not much behind the bar anymore. The place feels like home to Keith, who as a kid ran errands, swept the bar floor, sorted beer bottles and played a lot of pinball at another Harmony Bar & Grill—the family business in Burlington.

Then he saw the world while in the Navy from 1973 to 1977—"we went to Egypt, Europe . . . wherever the ship went"—and during a 1980s backpacking trip that took him to Athens and Wales, Sydney and Hong Kong, Bombay and Bali.

He's always liked bar work because "I like people and this allowed me to be out while getting paid for it, without spending my own money" or drinking to excess.

Keith considers the Atwood area to be a strong and well-kept neighborhood, one with a strong sense of community.

"In this business, a lot of owners aren't nearby anymore," he notes. "The bars are just investments for their money."

Harmony Bar & Grill
2201 Atwood Avenue, Madison
608-249-4333

•

Keith Daniels is proud of his neighborhood's independent streak.

TIDBITS

Phil Ladwig, the kitchen manager of **Harmony Bar & Grill** since 1994, keeps the bar's menu lively. His 17 pizza choices include the Puttanesca (garlic, kalamata olives, capers and anchovies), the Margherita (mozzarella, plum tomatoes and fresh basil), the Abruzzi (pesto, spinach and sausage or mushrooms) and more predictable combos.

An award-winning Walnut Burger, created by Daniels's ex-wife, Jo Raggozino, remains on the menu. So do the hot (as in temperature, not seasoning) potato chips, served with bleu cheese dip.

MADISON: Savor the Harvest

The shagbark hickory nut is an endangered food, and Tami Lax is out to save it.

October is the time of year when **Tami Lax** collects shagbark hickory nuts, just as she did as a girl with her parents and grandparents south of Green Bay.

Crack open enough of them, and your hands will smell a bit like maple syrup.

Sometimes the nutmeats are just toasted and eaten, or served with cheese. They are a part of Tami's holiday turkey stuffing. They also become candy clusters when she drenches them in chocolate.

Tami savors the flavor of the shagbark nut, plus the memories of family and rituals that the taste triggers. She also recognizes how important the shagbark tree and nut were to American Indians, then American colonists, as a long-lasting source of heat and hand-tool material, as well as food and oil.

"I come from a family of foragers and farmers," says Tami, owner of **Harvest Restaurant**, 21 N. Pinckney Street, "and I realize the next generation may not have the passion or the knowledge about how foods like these can and have enriched people's lives."

The shagbark hickory nut is on the endangered food list that is being compiled by Slow Food USA, an organization that works to protect and preserve culinary history, uniqueness and character. Tami put the nut there, first by nominating it to the list, then by being on the eight-member panel that evaluates the nominations.

The shagbark tree is extremely slow to grow, almost impossible to transplant because of its long taproot and thus not farmed or harvested commercially. It also has been a tempting tree to remove; one cord of the hardwood emits as much energy as one ton of coal.

"The stewards of these nuts are, generally speaking, our elders," Tami wrote in her shagbark nomination to Slow Foods USA. "Our parents and grandparents still cherish them for their scarcity and unique flavor."

The nut gathering and processing is labor-intensive work that few seem to appreciate. Jennifer De Bolt of Madison is an exception; she sells wild fruits and nuts to local restaurants.

"It's a labor of love," she says. "One pound of these nuts takes me about four hours to process."

Jennifer seeks shagbark nuts within a 45-mile radius of Madison, often on public hunting grounds. It takes about 220 nuts to get one pound of nutmeat, if the nuts are of average size.

"It's kind of a gamble," she acknowledges. A tree that produced four bushels of nuts for her last year, for example, may yield nothing this year. Nutmeat size is another variable.

Tami calls the shagbark hickory nut a regionally unique food, one whose quality and flavor are superior to many commercially sold nuts.

She contends the nut's future is "threatened by our shrinking rural areas, overuse of the timber and a new generation that isn't always interested or well informed about early American food sources."

Southern Wisconsin is on the northern edge of the shagbark growing range in the United States. The tree can live more than 300 years. Although the total number of hickory trees in the state has increased, fewer are 100 years or older.

Special meals at Harvest often celebrate regionally significant foods, and the restaurant also has hosted Slow Food meals that specifically focus on the organization's endangered food list.

For more about Slow Food USA's Ark of Taste—foods and products considered endangered—go to www.slowfoodusa.org/ark. What else is on the list? American artisanal cider, hand-crafted root beer, poi, wild catfish and much more.

Harvest Restaurant
21 N. Pinckney Street, Madison
www.harvest-restaurant.com
608-255-6075

•

Tory and Traci Miller value fresh and local ingredients.

MADISON: Rural Reverence

It is not unusual for **Tory Miller** to cook on Thanksgiving, but in 2006 he had an unusual crowd to feed. That is when the executive chef of **L'Etoile** restaurant fed 100 at the James Beard House in New York City's Greenwich Village.

Being invited to cook at the James Beard House is one of the highest honors that an executive chef can earn. Few from Wisconsin have gotten the nod. They include L'Etoile founder Odessa Piper, who cooked Thanksgiving dinner there in 1994.

For Tory, the roasting of sweet potatoes and Cinderella pumpkins began around 8 a.m. Then came the sauces, including one with tart and tiny red currants. It was dished up with rainbow trout, a sweet potato puree, toasted hickory nut butter and braised red cabbage — the third of five courses. The cabbage recipe came from the chef's grandmother.

"I was adamant about bringing Wisconsin foods with us," says Tory. So more than 50 products from three dozen farms and other vendors were packed into a van and driven east. That included cream and milk from **Blue Marble Dairy,**

Barneveld, and organic eggs from **New Century Farm,** Shullsburg.

It would have been easier, and less expensive, to simply order meal ingredients from the Beard House purveyors. But "simple" is not what Tory or his meals is about.

"When I created this menu, I first thought about who we'd serve," the chef explains. "I want them to know that we have more than just cheese that we wear on our head, and a bunch of beers, in Wisconsin."

The L'Etoile staff served turkeys from Matt Smith's **Blue Valley Gardens,** Blue Mounds. The birds are a heritage breed, raised over roughly 36 weeks, not the hormone-pumped turkeys that mass-market producers slaughter after one-third or one-fourth of the time.

The turkeys were filled with a sage stuffing that contained George's Kielbasa, from **Willow Creek Farm,** Logansville. "It's my Polish grandfather's recipe—they'd make it on Friday nights" at his butcher shop, farmer Sue Renger says, of the sausage.

Names of Wisconsin product providers routinely fill the menus at L'Etoile. "If we don't nurture the farmers and land," Tory believes, "we will lose them."

He nods toward the Capitol Square, from a second-story restaurant window. "It is such a blessing to have them right outside," he says, alluding to the outdoor Dane County Farmers' Market. "To not use these farmers would be sinful."

Tory and his sister, Traci, have been co-owners of L'Etoile since May 2005. They were raised on a Racine farm, where older brother Trever still lives.

"He has great gardens and plans to start antique apple orchards—something for the next generation," Tory says.

The James Beard Foundation has long been aware of L'Etoile because of founder Odessa's reputation. *Gourmet* magazine lists L'Etoile as one of the nation's 50 best restaurants.

●

L'Etoile
25 N. Pinckney Street, Madison
www.letoile-restaurant.com
608-251-0500

●

TIDBITS

Tory and Traci Miller also operate the more casual **Cafe Soleil**, on the street level of the same building that houses L'Etoile. Known for its fine pastries and soups, this laid-back eatery also has stepped up its eco-friendly practices, introducing compostable coffee cups and all-fluorescent lighting, in addition to scrutinizing the smallest elements of the menu. Truly local and sustainable.

•

L'Etoile staff conducts cooking classes, typically monthly. Dinner classes include a three-course meal, with wine and recipes.

•

Tory and pastry chef **Eva Ringstrom** work with middle school students twice a month during the school year, to help them better understand how fresh produce is grown and ways to prepare it at home.

•

What does L'Etoile mean? It is French for "the star."

The Cafe Soleil setting is casual, but the eat-local mission matches big sister L'Etoile.

Nilda Molina Miller creates arresting chocolates and candy.

MADISON: Tantalizing Toffee

Silly burglar. Why choose an ex-cop's business for your break-in?

Nilda Molina Miller says the late January incident was more annoying than financially destructive. It's not like the former Madison police officer would be lax enough to actually leave money sitting around, but her intruder didn't know that until casing the place.

It left a mess when the busy-ness of Valentine's Day was just around the corner. Then the owner of **Nilda Chocolates** prepared for an Olbrich Botanical Gardens fundraiser that enabled 350 participants to sample locally made chocolates and wines.

It was a way for Nilda to meet some of her Madison competitors (our thought, not hers). Although her storefront opened in summer of 2006, sizing up the competition has not been a priority.

"I don't have the time to go around to see the other places, or try their products," she says, referring to herself as a one-woman show. "I like the idea of creating my own flavors and chocolates" without being subconsciously influenced by other artisan chocolatiers.

Press a bit more, and you'll learn that Nilda doesn't really consider the others as competition because "we each have our specialty," and Madison has enough chocolate

Nilda's toffees are tempting treats.

lovers to provide good business for all.

"There are only a handful of chocolatiers who make their candy on site" locally, she notes.

Nilda sells assorted truffles but her specialty is toffee, ten kinds of it— buttery, small-batch toffee that is made in individual molds instead of a huge pan that is topped with chocolate, then broken into jagged edges of random shapes and sizes.

Toffee is "one of the top candies I'd enjoy as a kid," she says. And as her signature product, "it's what makes me stand out."

She began with two varieties, the base recipe and one with almonds added to it. "Some flavors take longer than others to make, because there are more ingredients" that need to be distributed by hand. An example is Cranberry Passion: the dried berries go into each mold, and the hot toffee needs to be poured and spread evenly, before it hardens.

"More of a modern toffee" is how she defines it, because the neat, round chocolate discs look more upscale.

So that's how Nilda stands out, but she is not looking to be the boss of a business that requires her to play administrator more than chocolatier.

"I want to keep the business model intimate," she says. "Maybe a couple of part-time, seasonal employees. That's it."

Owning a business can be "all-consuming" but "you really don't know that until you step into it," she notes. Her candy can be ordered online, but it's otherwise an "exclusive product" that isn't sold throughout Madison. You can buy it at her business or at **Java Cat Coffee and Espresso**, 3918 Monona Drive.

Nilda Chocolates
2611 E. Johnson Street, Madison
608-819-0414
www.nildachocolates.com
•

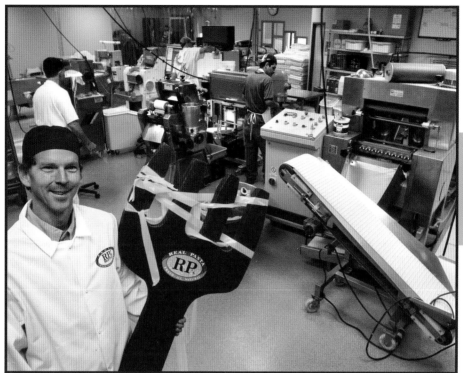

Peter Robertson's love of pasta has been lifelong.

MADISON: Using the Noodle

For **Peter Robertson**, a love of pasta took hold when he was about six years old, during a trip to Italy with his family. Years later, he spent weeks in that country, as a stage carpenter for the Martha Graham and Merce Cunningham dance companies.

"When we stopped touring, I began making my own fresh pasta," Peter recalls. First it was just a holiday gift for friends. Then the owner of an Italian restaurant began to place orders.

By 1996, the pasta maker had opened his own shop, **RP's Pasta Company**. He and employees make 20 flavors and 15 cuts of pasta, plus tortellini and ravioli, for grocery stores and restaurants.

There also is walk-in customer business. About 7,000 pounds of fresh pasta—which is not dried, but packaged and kept refrigerated or frozen until it's time for meal preparation—is made per week.

"The concept of fresh pasta still is very foreign to some people," Peter says. His products are all natural, with no preservatives.

Six machines, including an extruder—which cranks out pasta in a specific shape and size—simplify the work, "but only the hand can tell when the dough is ready, smooth enough" to be turned into pasta, he contends.

The business began with two pasta flavors: egg and spinach. Now all kinds of combinations come and go or stay—cilantro garlic, garlic parsley, toasted sesame. Farmers' Market customers have recommended some of these; others were the ideas of chefs.

"The possibilities are endless," Peter says.

What hasn't withstood taste tests? Beer pasta and Cheddar pasta—proof, he says, that Wisconsin loyalties are not unconditional.

The perfect pasta, Peter contends, need not be complicated by multiple ingredients: "All you have to do is put butter on it, or olive oil and Parmesan."

The company's newest product line is Ecco La Pasta flours for making homemade pasta, gnocchi and pizza crusts. KitchenAid includes Ecco La Pasta products with the Pasta Culinary Kit sold for its Stand Mixer. The pasta flour also has received favorable attention in the *New York Times*.

"It's the same as doing it from scratch, without the complications," Peter rationalizes. "Making pasta at home—that's the real fresh pasta experience."

RP's Pasta Company
1133 E. Wilson Street, Madison
www.rpspasta.com
608-257-7216

•

TIDBITS

The menu is small, the choices are classic, and the passion is obvious. This is what the **Fork & Spoon Cafe** at **RP's Pasta Company** is all about. The low-cost luncheon spot is under the guidance of **Peter Robertson's** team of chefs.

"When I originally envisioned RP's, this was it"—pasta production, a storefront and a restaurant, acknowledges the pasta meister.

On the menu are a half-dozen types of pasta—spaghetti with marinara to linguini with basil pesto sauce—a house salad and an antipasto plate.

Peter's goal is to present a good and affordable restaurant that serves a simple menu with locally grown and fresh ingredients.

www.forkandspooncafe.com 608-257-7216

Huma Siddiqui cooks with the spices and recipes of her native Pakistan.

MADISON: Queen of the Samosa

Although much of **Huma Siddiqui's** life has changed since her upper-class upbringing in Pakistan, much of the food has stayed the same.

That has been a comfort, particularly during times when "change" meant "upheaval" and uncertainty about the future. When her environment changed drastically, kitchen aromas stayed familiar. Traditional food rituals also have helped reinforce core values.

When Huma decided to end her marriage, she brought her children, then ages 9 and 13, to Mount Horeb. This is where a brother lived, and this is where her life began again.

"I grew up in a protective environment," she says of her childhood. "I had to learn to take care of myself."

Being a good parent and learning to be self-sufficient were the priorities. CPA is one title that she has earned. Another is "Samosa Queen," because food is her passion and anchor.

Not just any food, but the spices and recipes of her native land.

Samosas are deep-fried pastries that contain potato chunks and various spices. Huma routinely makes the appetizer—up to 150 at a time—for potlucks and treats.

"We create a lot of stereotypes about people, but the gaps lessened, and food was a big part of it," she says.

A Muslim but "not a mosque-goer," as a newcomer she celebrated the end of Ramadan by inviting 15 people to her home. A few years later, there were 105. Ramadan, the holiest month for Muslims, is a time of fasting as well as celebration.

Then she began conducting Pakistani cooking classes, which she still does at several locations, in addition to a televised cooking show. After students told her the recipe spices were hard to find, she began White Jasmine, an online tea and spice business.

She also has written a well-received cookbook, *Jasmine in Her Hair: Culture and Cuisine from Pakistan*, in which she shares tidbits about her life as well as long-time family recipes and insight about Pakistani culture.

"Nothing is impossible in my opinion and experience," she writes. "It entirely depends on the person—whether they decide to be the victim of circumstances or step up, take control and prove themselves."

In her classes, recipes remain authentic but shortcuts are introduced, because Huma knows few people desire or have the time to spend all day cooking.

"Pakistani cuisine recognizes the importance and characteristics of spices," she notes. They are meant to enhance the flavor of a recipe, not overpower the other ingredients.

Commonly used spices are garlic, ginger, chili powder, turmeric, coriander, cumin and garam masala (a combination of cloves, green and black cardamoms, cinnamon and cumin).

"You can still change things to match your own mood or taste by adding less or more of each spice," Huma says.

The cuisine sometimes is mistaken for Indian cooking, but the spicing and cooking techniques differ. Indian recipes shy away from meat; Pakistanis don't use pork or wine. Both cuisines define curry as a type of sauce, not a specific spice.

White Jasmine
www.whitejasmine.com
608-437-1250

•

ELSEWHERE IN MADISON

Who makes the best hot dogs in Madison? If you like 'em Chicago style, one place to head is to a **Home Depot** food cart.

That is the opinion of **Mitch Kite** and **Kevin Sherfinski**, software quality assurance engineers who are so enamored with Chicago-style hot dogs that they have designed a website—**www.hotdogchicagostyle.com**—to explain their passion and guide hot dog lovers to the area's best.

What makes it a Chicago dog? The guys provide this assessment: It is a Vienna beef hot dog topped with chopped onions, diced/wedged tomatoes, a dill pickle spear, pickled hot peppers ("sport peppers"), pickle relish, mustard and celery salt, served on a poppy seed bun.

"A good hot dog can be a thing of beauty and a stupendous culinary experience," they contend online. Their website has hot dog history, trivia and do-it-yourself dog dressing tips.

•

Cameron Ramsay compares a loaf of bread dough to a three-month-old baby. "It's a living thing, a life form—that's what it's all about," he says.

The subject is sourdough, and his passion for making it. Like a baby, the dough needs attention: time to eat, rest, perspire . . . give off a little gas. All the kneading and rising can be both a science lesson and a spiritual process, Cam contends. That helps explain how his six-hour and $250 bread-making class is about more than sharing recipes.

The owner of **Madison Sourdough Company**, 6640 Mineral Point Road, used to be a trader on the Chicago Mercantile Exchange. He would work with wood and bake bread to relax. Then he worked himself into a network with French artisan bakers, and one hobby became a business.

Is his class an expensive indulgence? Cam dismisses the notion: the $250 fee will "weed out people who don't really care" about bread-making, and it is "cheap for what students will be getting." That includes his advice, long after the class ends.

Who has the time to make bread? Cam winces. Of course there is time, he says. The hands-on work takes merely 20 to 25 minutes, albeit over 6 to 24 hours.

Madison Sourdough sells exquisite French and Viennese pastries, as well as breads. There used to be a limit of two pastries per person. To get more, you needed to place an order. **www.madisonsourdough.com 608-833-8009**

•

We've eaten and made plenty of meatballs while on this planet, but none has tasted as good as the ones from **Artamos**.

Artamos, which is Greek for "butcher," is an organic meat market at 714 S. Whitney Way. Co-owners **Jason Kreutzer** and **Eric Roenning** have degrees in biology and wildlife management, with an emphasis on grassland ecosystems.

That's a mouthful, and so is the array of sandwich choices here. Turkey is sold five ways (from black forest to peppermill), liverwurst can be fresh or smoked, and hoagie rolls range from asiago to wheat. Like mustard? There are six kinds to dress up a sandwich, plus a wide assortment of cheese.

Available side dishes include tomato basil mozzarella, penne rigate salad and bleu cheese chicken. We also could have ordered a hot meat with gravy over mashed potatoes.

This business is pretty much all natural, all the time. That includes organic poultry, steaks, chops, roasts and other meat cuts.

www.artamos.com 608-442-5929

•

Sometimes we get busy, forget to eat and then appear a bit illogical. Maybe that's why we pulled into the parking lot of **Clasen's European Bakery**, 7610 Donna Drive, Middleton, around 3 p.m. on a weekday and began sniffing for lunch.

"I suppose pretty much of what you have is sweet," we remarked to a clerk, who simply agreed and—to her credit—refrained from adding, "Are you a genius, or what?"

What she did offer was "except for the quiche slices," which is exactly what we suspected, and so we made a beeline to one of the coolers. Inside we found quiche by the pie and slice.

The lovely choices include Garden Harvest, which is just as it sounds—a teasing of tomatoes, spinach, zucchini, onions, mushrooms and other tidbits amid a creamy egg custard and buttery crust.

We added a couple of oh-so-fresh hard rolls—one dill-onion-parmesan, the other a crusty white broetchen (which is German for "small bread"). For dessert: a pastry that was flaky and lightly drizzled with frosting, a fat apricot plopped in the center, its natural sweetness tempered by the dollop of cream cheese beneath it.

Clasen's, owned by the same German family since 1959, produces about 30 kinds of hand-crafted breads and 25 kinds of pastries.

www.beyondthesquare.com 608-831-2032

•

I'm old enough to remember when some people went to airports just to watch the planes land and take off. Heightened security and hefty parking fees have made this harder to do, especially at the busiest departure points.

It's one reason the **Jet Room**, 3606 Corben Court, off U.S. 51 in Madison, is a delight. The bright and friendly restaurant, inside of Wisconsin Aviation, has a wall of windows that make it easy to see private aircraft go about their business.

Much of the traffic is hobby aircraft, but multi-million-dollar business jets make their way here, too. Some swoop in and out with celebrities and sports teams.

Pat O'Malley, a longtime pilot, and wife, **Pam,** have operated the Jet Room since 1997 as a breakfast-lunch place that closes at 2 p.m. The space has a sleek but comfortable feel, with walls and display cases that demonstrate a passion for aviation, and a menu that dispels all those nasty stereotypes about airport food being high in price, low in quality.

A half-dozen versions of eggs Benedict make the food different from that of the average diner. One creative variation contains crab. Another has broccoli and bacon.

Some sandwich names play off the setting. The Seaplane is a tuna melt. The Wingwalker resembles a turkey club. The Crop Duster combines grilled mushrooms with havarti cheese, lettuce and tomato on a grilled kaiser bun.

"People don't realize that we're open to the public," Pat says, because Wisconsin Aviation isn't the place where commercial flights land. Among the restaurant's regulars are retired pilots with "terrific stories."

www.wisconsinaviation.com 608-268-5010

MADISON ROAD TRIP:
A Waddle Around the Capital City

Gail Ambrosius and her heavenly chocolates.

1. Begin the day at **Monty's Blue Plate Diner**, 2089 Atwood Avenue, and scramble up your breakfast rut. Nontraditional choices: potato-zucchini pancakes, breakfast tacos and burritos, omelettes of spinach and feta or pesto and mushrooms. Buy a bag of granola with cashews to go.

Cheery, stylishly retro and open since 1990, Monty's was the start of Food Fight Inc., the umbrella for ten local restaurants, each distinctive in character and cuisine. **www.foodfightinc.com 608-244-8505**

2. A midmorning snack awaits across the street: sinful chocolates from **Gail Ambrosius** (uh-huh, that's her real name), 2086 Atwood Avenue. What's the big deal? Consider the quality of ingredients and imagination—in spices (like saffron-curry-cardamom), fillings (cognac), toppings (fresh rose petals) and shapes (gold-bellied buddhas).

The dairy farmer's daughter, raised near Seymour, studied with a master chocolatier at France's Valrhona Ecole du Grand Chocolat. **www.gailambrosius.com 608-249-3500**

3. Brewing around lunchtime is good grub at the **Great Dane Pub & Brewing Company**, which has three Madison locations, including the former 1850s Fess Hotel at 123 E. Doty Street. Request patio garden seating, if the weather's cooperative, for a quieter interlude.

On staff are five brewers, whose dozen products include Devils Lake Red Lager, a favorite. A simple, tasty, inexpensive meal: soup (try Tomato-Mushroom Bisque, topped with Parmesan) and salad, served with a thick and dense slab of beer bread. That combo is called the Vilas Park. **www.greatdanepub.com 608-284-0000**

4. Time to stroll State Street, beginning at the Capitol Square. At the other end is the University of Wisconsin's **Memorial Union**, 800 Langdon Street, and your reward for all the exercise is a scoop of Babcock ice cream, made at the country's first dairy school.

The campus dairy plant (with a store at 1605 Linden Drive—and shorter ice cream lines in summer) seems to always be experimenting with flavors. Best sellers include Orange Custard Chocolate Chip, but names and combos can get pretty intense (like Badger Blast, a triple-chocolate attack: chocolate ice cream with a swirl of fudge and flakes of chocolate). **www.wisc.edu 608-262-3045**

5. Retrace your steps and land at **The Old Fashioned**, 23 N. Pinckney Street, on the Capitol Square. It is the perfect place for Happy Hour, with a nod of reverence for our unofficial state drink, made one-half dozen ways ("sweet" and "sour" are not two of them).

The laid-back restaurant celebrates the best of Wisconsin's small-town food products, beverages and ways of presenting a meal. Order a Lazy Susan, an assortment of appetizers to spin around the table. Think pickled beets, creamed herring, smoked lake trout. **www.theoldfashioned.com 608-310-4545**

6. Dinner means a tribute to more of the same sensibilities, at **Quivey's Grove**, 6261 Nesbitt Road, southwest of the downtown, in an 1855 stone farmhouse (if you feel like dressing up and getting romantic) or a converted livery stable (for a more communal and casual atmosphere). An underground tunnel connects the two buildings, which look especially spectacular before Christmas.

Entrees are named after local places or important people in Wisconsin history. We never tire of the Popover Glover—a creamy mix of chicken and mushrooms in a delicate popover pastry, named after freed black slave Joshua Glover. Most meals embrace the use of indigenous ingredients. Big and (usually) fruity muffins come with each meal. **www.quiveysgrove.com 608-273-4900**

7. Able to resist dessert? We didn't think so. Order a quick but oh-so-smooth custard, or maybe a sweet-salty turtle sundae, from **Michael's Frozen Custard**, whose Madison locations include 2531 Monroe Street. Check out the flavor calendar for this 18-years-and-counting "Best of Madison" biz at **www.ilovemichaels.com**.

8. Too late to head home? Book a room at the **Arbor House**, 3402 Monroe Street, a B&B with historical and ecological significance. Guests get access to a canoe, bikes and the 1,280-acre UW Arboretum, to work off excess calories. For more about this national award winner: **www.arbor-house.com 608-238-2981**

9, 10, Souvenirs from this trip could include sausages from the Old World wurstkuche at **Bavaria Sausage, Inc.**, 6317 Nesbitt Road (**www.bavariasausage.com 800-733-6695**), and a T-shirt or six-pack of limited releases from **Capital Brewery**, 7734 Terrace Avenue, Middleton. **www.capital-brewery.com 608-836-7100**

Bounty at the Farmers' Market

Wisconsin tends to win most of the best of class awards in the annual U.S. Cheese Championship.

TELL ME ABOUT: Cheese

Follow the trail of cheese, particularly in southwest Wisconsin, and you'll learn as much about pride of place and concern for livestock as quality of product.

For example:

Anne Topham of **Fantome Farm**, Ridgeway, passes up a chance to schmooze with a dozen national food journalists because her nanny goat is in the throes of labor.

Dane Huebner of **Cedar Grove Cheese** in Plain explains that it is environmentally important to purify wastewater—whey and spilled milk—instead of simply spreading it onto farmland as a fertilizer.

Dan Patenaude of **Uplands Cheese Company**, Dodgeville, describes his cows' ideal diet as "kind of a salad bar," high in protein and energy. The company makes cheese about 75 days per year (only when the cows can eat fresh grasses) and has no intention to expand.

All of this talk, and a taste, convinces Franklin Becker, executive chef at Manhattan's longtime and highly regarded Brasserie restaurant, to let the cheeses stand alone.

"A poached egg, with a slice of that cheese, and you're done," he decides, after his introduction to Dante, made with sheep's milk. The chef's job is to "let that cheese shine."

The Dante earned Cedar Grove Cheese top honors in American Cheese Society competition, and Becker will buy Dante and Prairie Premium Cheddar for his restaurant. "Just by itself," he says, a few hours later, when asked to describe how he'd serve Uplands' Pleasant Ridge Reserve, a multiple national and world award winner. This belongs on the cheese course, he says; there is no need to mess with fine quality.

This chef's menus are big on cheeses from France, plus Humboldt Fog, a chevre made in California. Now the lineup will change a bit, all because of a four-day cheese tour, arranged by the Wisconsin Milk Marketing Board.

The event prompts Liz Pearson of *Saveur* magazine to compare Wisconsin to California, which produces more milk and threatens to take the lead in cheese production.

But cheesy competition is not what Liz has on her mind.

"What you have reminds me of the [California] winemakers," she explains, because of the pride and personal stories that are a part of the cheeses and Wisconsin's unified effort to promote them.

Her observations are a reminder that what seems ordinary, locally, may be extraordinary to others, like Karen Hochman.

"Where do I get it?" asks Karen, founder/editor of *The Nibble*, an online (**www.thenibble.com**) assessment of specialty foods and gourmet life. "I'm a real convert."

This was her first trip to Wisconsin, and the New Yorker was reacting to the Timber Lake Wild Horseradish Cheddar, produced by **Meister Cheese**, Muscoda, which also does product development for the gourmet Boar's Head line. "Such exotica in the middle of nowhere," Karen says later, of the quality and variety of artisan products encountered.

The cheesemaker is like a chef who can't taste the results of his recipe for weeks, months or years, notes the 2006 documentary "Living on the Wedge," by Trillium Productions, an independent filmmaker.

And being America's Dairyland is starting to refer to quality as much as quantity, pursued, in some cases, by people who gladly scrap the stresses of white-collar work for the rewards of rural living.

It is about milking just a dozen goats, as Fantome Farm does, for the satisfaction of making fresh chevre by hand: a "slow, gentle, three-day process," Anne Topham says online.

She also explains her satisfaction when selling it: "The people who come every week to the Dane County Farmers' Market have a connection to our farm, to the goats, and to the work of my hands."

Brenda Jensen of **Hidden Springs Creamery**, Westby, has an MBA but prefers rolling hills to urban living. "I wanted to put my arms around something," she says of her decision to make cheese from the milk of 115 sheep. One version contains honey from beehives in the neighborhood. Another has fresh basil marinated in extra-virgin olive oil.

"The farmers care about their animals, so they get good production," asserts David

Leonhardi of the Wisconsin Milk Marketing Board.

The state's 1,200 licensed cheesemakers produce more than 600 kinds of cheese, more than any other state or nation, and win more championship cheese awards than any other state. In 2007, Wisconsin brought home 60 percent of the best of class awards in the U.S. Cheese Championship.

Wisconsin is the only state that has a master cheesemaker program, which follows the European tradition of setting the highest level of training and expertise that can be achieved. Only about four dozen of the state's cheesemakers have earned the master cheesemaker distinction, and they represent about 30 cheese varieties.

Cheesemakers must have a license for at least ten years before being eligible to begin the master cheesemaker program, which involves classroom work and a three-year apprenticeship. The title brings with it the ability to label a specific type of cheese as being produced by a Wisconsin master cheesemaker.

•

A potential headache for U.S. cheesemakers is the European Union's efforts to protect and control the use of some cheese names. It is a way to acknowledge that sometimes names are a specific reference to a geographical area that gives a product its unique character.

Think Roquefort cheese, a type that comes from a specific part of France. In the United States, think Idaho potatoes.

The added value that comes from these PGIs—protected geographical indications—arguably diminishes if any cheesemaker or potato grower can use the label.

"But such protection can also be illegitimate, by unfairly protecting a geographical indication that has become generic," says Rusty Bishop of the University of Wisconsin Center for Dairy Research.

When that happens, he says fair import competition is at risk, and unfair export benefits may develop.

The Roquefort cheese label has been protected internationally since 1951.

Some smaller cheese producers are avoiding complications by assigning one-of-a-kind names to their products.

That's the way to go, says cheesemaker **Sid Cook** of **Carr Valley Cheese**, La Valle.

"When we've worked hard to create our own flavor profiles, the last thing we want is names that compete with European cheeses," he says of his artisanal line.

Artisanal cheeses—those made in small batches by hand—are a part of the specialty cheese market, the fastest growing segment of the cheese industry in Wisconsin, says Peter Leuer of the Wisconsin Milk Marketing Board. It is one reason Wisconsin has so many types of cheese.

Leuer says there were well under 200 cheeses in Wisconsin just 20 years ago.

SOUTHWEST

OTHER TIDBITS

Green County has the most certified master cheesemakers in the country, and thousands flock to Monroe for **Cheese Days** during the third weekend in September, on even-numbered years. **www.cheesedays.com 888-222-9111**

•

California in the 1990s became the nation's leading milk producer, and the state since then has tried to position itself as the heavyweight in cheese production.

Wisconsin produces nearly 2.5 billion pounds of cheese annually, compared to 2.2 billion pounds for California. Wisconsin also is the top producer of organic milk.

•

Two of Wisconsin's best-known products—beer and cheese—are coming together for more than burgers on the grill or a simmering beer-cheese soup.

Seems like the most impressive couples, as in real-life relationships, have good balance. The right twosome is simply a pleasant combination, without the need for excessive camouflage or accompaniment.

One does not overshadow or overwhelm the other. And regardless of whether the result is smooth or bold, it is distinctive.

"Taste a cheese with beer, and you will experience a complement, contrast or even a new flavor combination on the palate," says **Lucy Saunders** of the Milwaukee area at **www.beercook.com**. She has covered the craft beer industry for 20-plus years. "Beer is much less acidic than wine, so pairing beer with cheese is a mostly harmonious match."

Specialty cheeses and craft beers, she notes, are "made from fermented liquids, infused with special yeasts or cultures, and made in many styles, for variety in taste." They are becoming more diverse and less predictable—high-quality variations of classic styles.

Use a plain cracker, nuts or dried fruit to cleanse the palate between pairings. Taste the cheese first, then the beer. What's considered good? As with cheese and wine, quality is a matter of preference. Perhaps you want a particular aftertaste, or a quick explosion of taste.

These beer-cheese pairings, with state-made products, are among those that have been presented to food industry leaders by the Wisconsin Milk Marketing Board, which is funded by the state's dairy producers:

• **Swiss Valley Farms'** Baby Swiss (**www.swissvalley.com**) and Augsburger Golden Lager from Stevens Point Brewery (**www.pointbeer.com**).

• **BelGioioso** Italico (**www.belgioioso.com**) and Gray's Pale Ale (**www.graybrewing.com**).

Kirsten Jaeckle of Monroe's Roth Kase Cheese USA holds an award-winning wheel.

• **Roth Kase** Knight's Vail (**www.rothkase.com**) and Sprecher Brewery's Special Amber (**www.sprecherbrewery.com**).

• **Crave Brothers'** Les Freres (**www.cravecheese.com**) and Tyranena Brewing Company's Fighting Finches Maibock (**www.tyranena.com**).

• **Sartori** Asiago (**www.sartorifoods.com**) and Milwaukee Ale House's Louie's Demise (**www.ale-house.com**).

• **DCI Cheese Company's** Timber Lake Grand Reserve 4-Year Cheddar (**www.dcicheeseco.com**) and the South Shore Brewery Rhoades' Scholar Stout (**www.southshorebrewery.com**).

• **Maple Leaf Cheese's** Jalapeno Jack (www.wischeese.com) and Capital Brewery Maibock (**www.capital-brewery.com**).

•

Free copies of the *Traveler's Guide to Wisconsin Cheese*, which describes and plots dozens of cheese factories (plus breweries and wineries) on a state map, are available by filling out a form at **www.wisdairy.com** or calling **800-383-9662**. To be included, a business must offer a tour and/or have its own retail store.

Pat Boersma believes the food should be the main focus.

BELLEVILLE: No Distractions

The pork tenderloin comes with a mango peach salsa. The duck liver pâté blends spices with cognac and caramelized onion. Veal sweetbreads arrive with a Madeira sauce.

And the bruschetta topping? The base is an herbal spread of cream cheese and mascarpone, followed by a layer of chopped olives and tomatoes, plus a sprinkling of asiago.

This is intimate dining on Main Street, but the Dane County community's population is just 1,910. **Pat** and **Cathy Boersma's** place, **Belle Bleu**, open since late 2006, bills itself as adult casual. That means no diners under age ten.

"We're a distraction-free zone," Pat says. There is no smoking, no football pools or dice shaking at the bar. Look for soft lighting, comfortable seating and an engaging mood (a mix from Tony Bennett to Spyro Gyra to Steely Dan) but "no funeral parlor music."

"Upscale but not uptight" is how the proprietors describe the ambience. Fancy dress is not necessary, but having reservations is a good idea.

The chef makes his own soups, stocks, dressings and breads from scratch. Cathy handles business and front-of-house details. "We want it to feel personal, not corporate," Pat says. He classifies the food as continental: "We're not stuck on one cuisine, or on potatoes and gravy."

So don't expect the menu to stay the same. It depends on available ingredients, the whims of the chef and the weather. Forget pot roast with gravy in summer. "Those big, Gothic meals don't work in the heat," Pat says.

The couple previously operated Bridge Mill Kitchen and Terrapin Station in De Pere; the latter impressed the late Milwaukee restaurant critic Dennis Getto in 1998, who described the sweetbreads as "worthy of any good French restaurant in the world."

Pat and Cathy met while students at the first culinary arts class at Madison Area Technical College. Their purchase and renovation of the Belleville building started off as a hobby project.

The restaurant is one block from the Badger State Trail, and south of town is the trail's 1,200-foot-long Stewart Tunnel (flashlights recommended; walking of bikes required).

Check out the curtain of Mona Lisa beads en route to the restroom. Nice touch. Open for dinner, but "we'll do lunch, too, eventually," Pat says.

Belle Bleu
7 W. Main Street, Belleville
www.bellebleu.net
608-424-1911
•

TIDBITS

Don't expect to dine at Belle Bleu during the annual **Belleville American Music Festival**, in mid-July, because the restaurant temporarily closes, turning into prep and lounge space for the participating musicians.

For more about the event, whose headliners have included Johnny Winter: **www.bamfest.net 608-424-3336**

Organic Valley is one of the nation's largest organic farm cooperatives.

LA FARGE: On a Mission

The family farmer has been designated an endangered species by **Organic Valley**, the nationwide farming cooperative, and the push is on to prevent extinction.

Generation Organic is an ongoing campaign that acknowledges the disappearance of 195 family farms per day for 70 years. The average farmer's age is increasing; more than 60 percent are 55 or older.

"We have worked to protect the bald eagle and the grizzly bear. Now it's time to save the family farmer," says **Travis Forgues**, an Organic Valley member in Vermont, who came up with the project idea.

"The health of our food, our environment and our future generations is at stake."

The co-op's initiative, nicknamed "Gen O," involves a lot of public education on farming as a vital and appreciated profession, the need for diversity and healthy food choices, and guidance for people—particularly younger generations, which Travis represents—who want to consider organic farming.

Organic Valley is the nation's largest co-op of organic farmers. The venture began in 1988 with just seven farmers. Today the total is 1,183 members, and growing.

Headquartered in picturesque Vernon County, where the Kickapoo River flows, the company has grown from simple to savvy. La Farge, population 775, has developed a forward-thinking personality but not lost its down-home hospitality.

This is a company that wants its products in both the school lunch box and the gourmet chef's kitchen.

It has developed the Bovine Bill of Rights, under its Cows Unite campaign, as an attempt to end the use of all things synthetic: growth hormones to genetically modified feed.

"Cows have the right to be cows" is one part of the manifesto. That means being able to graze outdoors, among other things.

The Organic Valley retail product line has grown to include juices and meats as well as dairy products. An eco-friendly $17.5 million distribution center was completed in 2007.

Farm families staff the compact Organic Valley Retail Store, 507 W. Main Street, which sells products at a discount. Tours of the company headquarters, arranged by appointment, can include a stop for lunch at the all-organic cafe—where meal price is based on weight of plate.

Organic Valley Family of Farms
One Organic Way, La Farge
www.organicvalley.coop
888-444-6455

•

TIDBITS

An unusual blend of New Age products and age-old traditions make the annual **Kickapoo Country Fair**, a late July celebration of rural heritage, different from the typical summer celebration of farm life.

The event, hosted by Organic Valley, is a fun combo of workshops about organic cooking and farming, environmental advice, locally grown food and music by local performers. **www.kickapoocountryfair.org 888-444-6455**

*Helen Jo and Grant Zitzmann are farmers
who also staff the Organic Valley retail outlet.*

SIDE DISH: Banana Split Milkshake

More than 400 recipes are on the Organic Valley website, and many of them come from Madison's **Terese Allen**, the company's food editor. This beverage earns a five-star approval rating from consumers.

6 medium strawberries, hulled and cut up
1/2 banana, cut up
3/4 cup Organic Valley Milk or Soy Milk
3/4 cup vanilla ice cream or soy ice cream
2 tablespoons chocolate syrup
Organic Valley Heavy Whipping Cream, whipped (optional)
Chocolate syrup
Maraschino or Bing cherry

Place strawberries, banana, milk or soy, ice cream and chocolate syrup in a deep bowl or the blending container of an immersion blender. Use an up-and-down motion to blend mixture until smooth. (If you are doubling the recipe, use a stand-up blender.)

Serve immediately, topped with whipped cream (if desired), a drizzling of chocolate syrup and a cherry on top.

MINERAL POINT: Cornish Influence

They started out selling them only on Thursdays. Now they are as much a part of the daily menu as burgers at a drive-in restaurant.

The Cornish pasty—a meat pie of cubed steak, potatoes, rutabagas and onions—has been prepared, baked and sold at the downtown Red Rooster Cafe since 1972. It usually is possible to order the pies frozen, for heating at home later, and a vegetarian version is available, if ordered one day before purchase.

"We try to do home cooking," says **Patti McKinley**, who operates the casual eatery with her mom, **Helena Lawinger**. They follow a family recipe, still use lard in the deliciously flaky crust and get fresh pasties into the oven every morning. Then the one-serving pies bake slowly, for at least two hours.

It is easy to order a hearty lunch or dinner at the **Red Rooster** and pay less than $10. The meal-sized pasty costs $6.50.

Daily specials are unpredictable, except for baked chicken and dressing on Mondays; the choice was goulash when we visited. Burgers, reubens and gyros are other options. The dessert case is all about pie, and we snagged a slice of smooth rhubarb custard. Figgyhobbin—a pastry bursting with raisins, nuts and spices—also is a mainstay.

The figgyhobbin has Cornish roots, too, although the cafe's proprietors don't. Are these all homemade desserts? You betcha.

"I think being family-run is important," Patti says, of the restaurant business. She is one of eight siblings, part of a hard-working farm family that made an abrupt change in careers when dad Bill Lawinger, now deceased, bought the former Opie's Confectionery.

The original wainscoting, wood floor and tin roof (at least 15 feet high) remain in this century-old building.

*Cornish pasties are a daily affair
at Red Rooster Cafe in Mineral Point.*

TIDBITS

Mineral Point celebrates its heritage during the annual **Cornish Festival** in late September, organized by the Southwest Wisconsin Cornish Society.

Activities include "sea chanty" singing classes at the Masonic Temple, Kiddleywink Pub night at the Pendarvis state historical site, a celebration of artists and authors with Cornish roots, walking tours and storytelling.

Count on **Shake Rag Alley Arts Center** to present a fun array of workshops, from rug hooking to jewelry making.

www.cornishfest.org 608-762-5718

•

The festival or a restaurant is likely your best opportunity to buy a pasty in Mineral Point. Pasty sales are major church fund-raisers but it can take years to get onto the list for buying them.

"We make 600 to 800 every month," says **Cheryl Smeja**. "You have to know somebody" in order to buy them.

Locals buy them by the dozen, then eat or freeze them—or give them as gifts to out-of-town friends. Church recipes are kept secret; most volunteer cooks get access to only one part of the process. "My job is rolling the crust," says Cheryl. It is someone else's job to crimp the edges, and how you do it is another point of pride and identification among the local congregations.

Stools at the counter are noticeably wider than average. Lace curtains partly cover the storefront window.

Patti, who loves roosters and is proud of her family's work in agriculture, added dozens of figurines and other images of the bird. That includes roosters on wallpaper, which has been around since the late 1970s.

"We baby it," Patti says. "As soon as we see a corner start to curl, we glue it."

Red Rooster Cafe
158 High Street, Mineral Point
608-987-9936

•

MONROE: Lovin' Limburger

Monroe's **Chalet Cheese Cooperative** is the only place in the nation that produces the pungent limburger cheese.

So many people have been quick to assume and judge what they have only smelled. "Probably shouldn't mix it with prescription meds," a co-worker joked.

Frankly, when the layers of wrapping finally were peeled away, it was a bit of a letdown. Limburger has an acquired smell, and the taste is distinctive, but neither is enough to bowl you over.

"Smells like a cheese factory, but not any worse than that," a first-time taster decided.

Limburger sales are picking up in Monroe, as Americans turn on to artisan cheeses and learn to appreciate the respected "stinky cheeses" that have rich histories elsewhere in the world.

Stinky cheese means tasty cheese.

SOUTHWEST

"It sneaks up on you," a couple of us concluded. But that's not necessarily a bad thing.

For just a one-time taste, visit **Baumgartner Cheese Store and Tavern**, at the courthouse square, 1023 Sixteenth Avenue, Monroe. It has been in business since 1931 and is known for its limburger sandwich with horseradish and onion, on rye. 608-325-6157.

Chalet Cheese Cooperative
N4858 County N, Monroe
608-325-4343
•

Wave Kasprzak and Jane Sybers are as busy as they want to be at The Dining Room.

MONTICELLO: Busy as They Want to Be

First, let's address assumptions and stereotypes:

Even though linens cover the tables, you are welcome to dine in jeans, or bike shorts in summer. The limited hours of business, Wednesday through Saturday nights, is not an indication that business is slow. The menu is full of panache and sophistication, despite the rural setting.

The Dining Room at 209 Main here in Monticello, a village of 1,200, is proof that fine dining need not be limited to urban confines. The restaurant has begun its second decade, and it keeps proprietors **Dave "Wave" Kasprzak** and **Jane Sybers** as busy as they want to be.

"I love being in the restaurant business, but we set it up in a way we could live with," Jane says. They don't "pull doubles" (work Saturday dinner hours, then Sunday brunch) because they have vowed to not serve breakfast or lunch.

"If we pushed any harder, we probably wouldn't have survived past two or three years," Jane says. "Or, if the business would have survived, our marriage wouldn't have."

When the couple bought 17 acres of an old dairy farm near Monticello in 1995—so they and their dogs would have room to run—they were still working at fine dining restaurants in Madison. The pace of life was exhausting and frustrating.

How tiring? Wave, then in his late twenties, was willing to discard his chef's jacket for a part-time job as a laborer on a sheep farm. He had worked for restaurants since he was 14 and was close to burning out.

Then came a dare from his mother-in-law, **Ruth Knight Sybers**, who was eyeing a downtown Monticello shot-and-beer joint as a real estate investment: Why not run your own restaurant? Give it a year, she suggested.

Word traveled quickly, and The Dining Room at 209 Main has since developed a loyal following, especially among fine-dining fans who live within a 45-minute drive, from Madison to Janesville to Freeport, Illinois.

It is a convenient stop for bicyclists because of the nearby Sugar River State Trail, which intersects with the 59-mile Badger Trail at Monticello.

"We've had people call to say 'Looking to run a restaurant in Madison?' —and the answer is 'no thank you,'" Wave says. "The dollar signs may be tempting, but the work is not."

He and his wife don't work on Sundays. They'd rather spend that day golfing in summer, watching football in winter. The lifestyle switch also means he has more time to teach martial arts, and she has time to train for triathlons. "It's really been a quality of life issue," Wave says, of the transition. The restaurant kitchen is his domain; she supervises front-of-house operations.

"If you're myopic about work, your world isn't any deeper than that," Jane says.

Wave has begun to spend work hours as a bartender instead of a chef because he trusts the staff that he has trained and is there to assist when needed. The staff includes Jimmy Sandlin, who was hired as a dishwasher at age 14. Now he's in culinary school training.

The restaurant's menu tends to change three times a year, and it is garnished with Asian to Latin influences. Entrees, $18 to $27, include a house salad and make use of locally produced ingredients. That includes Green County's acclaimed cheeses.

Reservations are recommended. One of the restaurant's signature desserts is Sticky Toffee Pudding with Toasted Pecans, which is Wave's interpretation of a London treat, "only with brandy, for a Wisconsin flair."

Occasional, 16-student Tuesday night cooking classes ($50 per class, which includes instructions, recipes and a meal) are scheduled. Rarer and pricier is "Chef for a Day" instruction, which is hands-on instead of observation.

Four students join Wave during "Chef for a Day," arriving at the restaurant at 1:30 p.m. to put together a five-course meal that incorporates a variety of instruction, from knife techniques to sauce preparations. At 5 p.m., one guest for each of the students shows up and the meal is served.

The Dining Room at 209 Main
209 Main Street, Monticello
www.209main.com
608-938-2200
•

Diners can enjoy fine wines and sophisticated cuisine at the Blue Spoon Cafe.

PRAIRIE DU SAC: Blue Spoon Cafe

We're seldom a cheerleader for restaurant chains, but an exception is Wisconsin-based **Culver's**, whose ButterBurgers and custard have been points of pride since the first outlet quietly opened in Sauk City in 1984.

Today more than 350 Culver's exist nationwide, and "drive-through" no longer is synonymous with "mediocre quality."

Now **Craig** and **Lea Culver** are experimenting with a new concept: the quick-casual restaurant that serves fine wines and far-from-ordinary cuisine. It's focaccia instead of buns. "Euro sandwiches" (prosciutto, fresh mozzarella) instead of burgers. Breakfast (eggs Benedict, cranberry-walnut french toast) in addition to lunch. Gelatos instead of custard (but there is custard in the pancake batter).

This is the **Blue Spoon Cafe**, and it is a cautious endeavor that has slowly gained a following since its Prairie du Sac opening in 2001. Fast-lane growth is not the goal; the second Blue Spoon, in Middleton, didn't open until 2007.

The setting, in Prairie du Sac, is a pleasure because customers can face the Wisconsin River and dine outside. Eagle spottings are commonplace during winter.

The 60 to 80 wine selections concentrate on the U.S. but also come from around the world. Near the entrance is a wine table, with close-out specials of $10 or less per bottle. Monthly tastings lack pretentiousness (example: "MMM . . . Wines that begin with 'M'").

The gelato, made in small batches, can be purchased by the scoop or quart. Expect a dozen choices, which may change throughout the day, and more than 100 varieties overall.

"We're continuing to experiment with the concept" of quick-casual, says **Mike Boss**, director of operations/development.

Blue Spoon Cafe
550 Water Street, Prairie du Sac
2831 Parmenter Street, Middleton
www.bluespooncafe.com
608-643-0837 608-824-1810

•

TIDBITS

What's the difference between ice cream and frozen custard? Culver's custard is premium ice cream with a bit of egg yoke solids, which enriches the flavor and texture. By law, frozen custard needs a butterfat content of at least 10 percent.

If you don't know one freeze from another, take this advice from the Food Network (www.foodtv.com):

"Ice cream is basically a frozen custard that is made from eggs, dairy and sugar. Gelato is similar to ice cream except that it has more egg yolks and contains less air. It's a much denser product and contains more fat.

"Sorbets and granitas contain no dairy. They are made from a simple syrup that is flavored, usually with fruit and a few spices and herbs. Their textures differ because of how they are prepared.

"Sherbet is basically an ice milk and is a cross between ice cream and sorbet."

PRAIRIE DU SAC: Fruit of the Vine

Charles O'Rear and Daphne Larkin of California traveled 80,000 miles in two years to gather material for a book about the best wines in the United States, and their research was a celebration of people, place, passion and product.

"Like people and wine, vineyards can have personality," they wrote. "Often grape growers treat their vines like children—they watch them grow, know how they behave and enjoy what they give." They were referring to a picture of a patch of grapevines in winter, "Vicki's Vineyard," at **Wollersheim Winery** near Prairie du Sac.

Wollersheim, the state's first commercial winery, was established in 1972. Its award-winning products include Prairie Fumé, a semi-dry white that has earned gold or "best of" ratings in Texas, California, New York, Florida, Michigan and Ontario.

Prairie Fumé, first made in 1987, is produced on a hill that overlooks the Wisconsin River. The winery's 25 acres of French-American and American hybrid grapes are grown where European vintners settled more than 150 years ago.

Guided, one-hour tours of Wollersheim are offered several times daily, except on major holidays. Tours end with wine tasting and are filled on a first-come, first-served basis.

Wollersheim's annual and free Nouveau Beaujolais tasting typically occurs on a Saturday in November. The dry red is described as the perfect holiday wine, "meant to be enjoyed young," and a good match for the Thanksgiving turkey.

The winery's annual open house occurs on a weekend in March, and activities include grapevine pruning and cooking with wine demonstrations.

Wollersheim Winery
7876 Highway 188, Prairie du Sac
www.wollersheim.com
800-847-9463

•

TIDBITS

More than 30 wineries exist in Wisconsin. The best place to sample them in one spot is the Wine Garden during the Wisconsin State Fair in August.

To learn more about **Wisconsin Winery Association** members, consult **www.wiwine.com** or **608-443-2465**.

Tom Gresser serves great local beers and encourages thoughtful conversations.

ROXBURY: Watch Your Mouth

The jukebox got yanked because it was a cause of irritation and disagreement, as in "turn that up," "turn that down" and "who played this?"

Then the pool table was removed. "Always a source of conflict or argument," the barkeep concluded.

During football season, after a transient band of unruly Badger fans annoyed the regulars, the television was tossed. "I'm going to do it tomorrow morning, while I'm still mad," the owner announced. He already had curbed smoking and tightened the noose on vulgarity.

"Would you please watch your language in here?" was the first warning, and if the swearing continued, the request would be repeated, nose-to-nose with the offending customer. Behavior, and clientele, soon changed.

So what is left at the **Roxbury Tavern**, in an unincorporated town whose only other draws are St. Norbert's Church and the **Dorf Haus** restaurant?

"We drink good beer and talk to each other," says **Tom Gresser**, the owner, who laughs far more easily than all this may indicate.

Among the regulars are farmers, doctors, teachers, lawyers, factory workers and

retirees. Some of them plot political campaigns or events. Jim Hightower has been here. So has Congresswoman Tammy Baldwin.

"We tell Tom that he needs to put lines on his bar napkins, so we can read what's been hatched" the day after taking notes, says Gail Lamberty, who has helped organize "Voices of the Progressive Traditions" and Fighting Bob Fest, tributes to Robert La Follette's progressive politics.

Tom recalls refusing to post a County Board campaign poster in 1980 because "I didn't want to alienate anybody." Things have changed, but "I try to not argue too much politics—hell, there are still Republicans coming in here."

He dilutes the Roxbury's reputation as just a place for liberals by sometimes bringing in musicians on Sunday afternoons—or organizing a couple of hours of James Joyce readings, to mark the anniversary of *Ulysses*, while customers eat Irish stew or steak-and-kidney pie.

He takes pride in presenting a comfortable space for everyone: single women, same-sex couples, races other than Caucasian and—yes—conservatives. Benefit concerts have helped local charities. A wake for his beloved canine companion, Sam, included bluegrass music, a retired minister's eulogy and $1,800 raised for a veterinary medicine program at the University of Wisconsin.

The annual Geezers New Year celebration involves dinner and live music, but the tavern closes at 10 p.m.—one hour later than usual.

On tap are four kinds of beer, three from little **Lake Louie Brewing**, in nearby Arena. Sugar-rimmed goblets are filled with Spanish coffee: add rum and Kahlua, top with whipped cream. The drink arrives flaming.

Put away any thoughts of ordering a Bud Light. There is none here.

On the menu are bison burgers and chicken reubens, an assortment of beef burgers and soups made on the premises. Wednesday is Spaghetti Night, with vegan, vegetarian and meat-eater varieties.

Not bad for a joint whose kitchen isn't much bigger than a closet and has no oven.

Add Taco Tuesdays, plus Cajun/Creole food on Thursdays and Saturdays, African peanut stew on occasion. Staff make their own fries and freeze cubes of tea for iced tea, so it won't taste watered down.

Add respectable local food suppliers—**Wyttenbach Meats**, **Carr Valley Cheese**, **Willow Creek Farm**, **Lodi Coffee Roasters**, **Weber's Lodi Bakery**—and you have the makings for a pub with memorable grub.

So the Roxbury Tavern isn't typical, although it may look that way from the outside.

Tom knows the place needs paint, and he credits St. Vincent de Paul in Prairie du Sac as a great place to shop for decor.

Tom paid one customer for a framed collection of antique fishing lures, another for a framed assortment of marbles. "When you want it back, just pay me back," he says.

A hammock hangs from the ceiling. So does a canoe and Mexican flag. An old poster of a Muslim art show is "a little display of our tolerance." Two clocks show the time in west and east Roxbury (locals claim there is a ten-minute difference).

Elsewhere, magazines are scattered. A half-dozen copies of the *New York Times* arrive on Sunday mornings; most are picked up by regular customers.

When Tom bought the Roxbury Tavern in 1989, it was "an average country tavern—softball, horseshoes, a lot of beer and a little food." He was 40 years old, had just returned from a West Coast hunt for horticulture work, and was not in the mood to work for someone else at an entry-level wage.

Four sisters who grew up on a farm near Dane—Rhonda, Christine, Lisa and Michelle Meier—help Tom run the Roxbury. They make blueberry and apple-cinnamon pancakes for up to six dozen people on Sunday mornings, using organic flour that is freshly milled on the premises. Friend Lisa Lutz, who conducts cooking classes locally, has helped Tom refine the food, and the styling.

An elegant, framed certificate—whose nine signatures include Ellen Kort of Appleton, Wisconsin's first poet laureate, and Forevertron artist Tom "Dr. Evermor" Every of Baraboo—unabashedly established the Roxbury Rectangle in 2001 as a local version of New York's legendary Algonquin Roundtable.

Painted rocks by artist JoAnne Robarts jazz up the Roxbury. They include one that looks like a hamburger. "Featuring the 2½ -pound hamburger," Tom proclaimed, in a tavern advertisement. "Bet you can't eat it."

Historian Jack Holzhueter, also the organist at St. Norbert's, found his way to this tavern "early on," in search of lunch. Now he's an ardent fan who describes the business as highly revered and much appreciated.

"My life would be less rich without it," he insists. "I hope I don't outlive the Roxbury Tavern."

Roxbury Tavern
8901 Highway Y, Roxbury
608-634-8434
•

Brewmasters Tim Wauters and Tom Porter create handcrafted beers that taste great and have clever names at Lake Louie Brewing, Arena.

TIDBITS

One of the hottest microbrew labels in southwest Wisconsin is **Lake Louie Brewing**, a tiny business on a half-acre pond near Arena, population 685. Products include Warped Speed Scotch Ale, Coon Rock Cream Ale and Mr. Mephisto's Imperial Stout. Free tours on Saturdays, by appointment. **www.lakelouie.com**, 608-753-2675.

Mindy Segal of Chicago's HotChocolate gets cooking in Sauk City.

SAUK CITY: Cheese to Please

Some of the finest professional chefs in Wisconsin and beyond are making their way to Sauk City, population 3,100 in Sauk County, to cook for an appreciative crowd.

The **Carr Valley Cooking School**, on U.S. 12, is a way to make everybody more aware of the dozens of cheeses made by a fourth-generation business that began in 1902.

As if the products need more attention: **Carr Valley Cheese** in the past four years has won more than 170 national and international awards. Many of the accolades go to artisan—small batch—varieties that aren't made anywhere else.

"These are the people we already do business with," says **Sid Cook**, regarding the chefs who are brought in to cook. "We thought [the classes] would be good for marketing" the cheeses as well as the chefs.

Sid, the mastermind behind Carr Valley and its products, is a certified master cheesemaker whom others describe as a rock star in his profession.

"My goal is to produce magnificent cheeses," he told me. "To me, it doesn't matter which state produces the most." We were discussing the tussles that Wisconsin sometimes gets into with California and New York about cheese production and variety.

Marisa, Sid's teenage daughter, is at the Sauk City retail outlet, behind the cash register. Eager to share product samples, she explains the history of the business and the difference between cheeses, two of which are named after her.

At the back of the store, dozens of wheels of mixed milk Marisa age in a temperature-controlled cooler. Cave Aged Marisa has earned international attention. The cooler's glass panels face almost three dozen cooking school students in the adjacent kitchen demo area, so there's always a clear reminder of what brings them together.

On a Sunday afternoon, it is standing room only in the demo area, as Mindy Segal, owner of Chicago's HotChocolate restaurant, shares baking advice. Two of her recipes use Carr Valley Cheese: a turnover with Cave Aged Cheddar, apples and pecans; and Swedish Farmers Cheesecake, which calls for Swedish Farmers Cheese.

Students get advice, recipes and a portion of whatever the cook prepares. Usually, that means a meal, served on linens and with proper tableware. The classes are attracting average cooks as well as professional chefs who want to learn new techniques from respected peers.

Mindy, a longtime and high-end pastry chef, worked at Charlie Trotter's and Spago restaurants in Chicago before venturing out on her own.

"This won't be a profit center for us," Sid acknowledges, without regret. But the gatherings have value in other ways. That includes a chance to interact with great chefs and eat what they prepare.

Class registration is required. Cost averages $45. Carr Valley is headquartered in LaValle and also has retail outlets in Mauston and Fennimore.

Carr Valley Cooking School
807 Phillips Boulevard (U.S. Highway 12), Sauk City
www.carrvalleycheese.com
800-462-7258

•

Carr Valley, Sauk City, offers samples of many cheeses.

TIDBITS

Anna Wolfe, editor of *Gourmet News*, based in Maine, during a Wisconsin cheese tour described the culinary kitchen at **Carr Valley** as the start of a smart trend for cheesemakers.

The caliber of the Carr Valley kitchen, its cooking classes for the public and the high-end chefs recruited as instructors make a winning combination, Anna said. She also considers it smart marketing: The average person can learn how to cook with Carr Valley cheeses, and exposure with notable chefs is a bonus.

•

Another award-winning cheese manufacturer with cooking on the front burner is **Roth Kase USA**, headquartered in Monroe, whose Culinary Education Centre typically is used for corporate events or rented to groups.

Large windows in the professional kitchen provide a clear view of the hundreds of washed rind specialty cheeses that are shelved, washed and turned daily as they age. The kitchen gives professional chefs an easy way to "taste and work with our cheeses in a professional kitchen setting," says **Kirsten Jaeckle**, director of marketing. Cooking classes are a possibility for the future.

GranQueso, a Hispanic/Portuguese type of cheese, is among the Roth Kase products that are award winners. The company has ethnic versatility; its other big cheeses include Grand Cru Gruyère, which has a Swiss heritage, and the Italy-influenced Mezzaluna and Fontina.

Visitors, from behind observation windows, can watch cheese being made. Check out the discount bin at the store before heading home; over-stocks and imperfectly shaped cheese wedges mean great quality at lower costs. The factory, retail store and culinary facility are at 657 Second Street, Monroe. **www.rothkase.com 608-328-2122**

Justin Trails Resort offers farm-fresh food in a peaceful country setting.

SPARTA: Changing Gears

Sixty years on Earth, 40 years of marriage, 20 years in business. This is how **Donna Justin** explained her reasons for celebrating, in autumn 2007. She and husband **Don** own and operate **Justin Trails Resort**, about 225 acres near Sparta, a third-generation dairy farm that has been transformed to cater to romantics, nature lovers and silent sport enthusiasts.

We traveled the 5.5 country miles south of I-94, between La Crosse and Tomah, after dusk but had no problem finding the property. Donna urged us to sneak out to the sumacs, away from the yard and building lights, for total darkness and a stellar view of the stars. Had it been a moonlit night, a quiet hike would have been an attractive option, just as cross-country skiing and sledding on the tubing hill might be on full moon dates during winter.

Come daylight, breakfast at the Lodge (a converted machine shed) begins with homemade granola, yogurt and a bowl of fresh fruit; ours was topped with blackberries, picked on the farm. Donna's culinary trademark is her mandarin orange muffins, which also contain chocolate chips; a basketful was on the table.

Then came fresh vegetables, thinly sliced and grilled, plus scrambled eggs seasoned with chili powder and cumin. Don cooked, and right outside of our breakfast booth was a flutter of hummingbirds, dipping into their own breakfast: the nectar of a feeder.

Guests can head to the nearby Elroy-Sparta trail for bicycling, or kayak and canoe on the La Crosse River, but Justin Trails also has reasons to stay put. You can walk the former cow paths and other hiking trails, past patches of goldenrod and fields of soybeans. Or absorb the panoramic view of Leon Valley, from the top of Gerry's Peak, and add your initials to the carvings on the limestone rocks.

The animals attract attention, too. Exercise Heidi and George, the Siberian huskies. Feed Dusty and Rusty, the friendly llamas. Find the barnyard cats. Then test your golfing skills, but leave the clubs at home.

The resort has two 18-basket courses for disc golf. The game is like traditional golf, but players use Frisbee-like discs, not clubs and balls, and aim for chain link baskets, not holes in the ground. Yes, there is a water hazard—a conservation pond that has been around since 1961. A forest, cornfield, narrow passageways and abrupt elevation dips and spikes are other obstacles.

"We gave up farming because we were getting old," Donna says, with a grin. Ten miles of groomed trails for cross-country skiing were their first diversion for overnight guests, and the area continues to attract ski race trainees.

"Summer became the off-season," Donna explains, until the 1.5- and 3.5-mile disc golf courses were designed. The diversion has been a hit with families, people new to the game and serious competitors. The Professional Disc Golf Association has held tournaments here.

The Justins have worked hard to respond to what their customers want, be it a fireplace and whirlpool bath for two, or pet-friendly accommodations. Unusual dietary restrictions are accommodated; lunch and dinner can be arranged; breakfast can be delivered to a guest's room.

A converted granary and a log home both are big enough to accommodate a family. The proprietors give one-hour guided property tours aboard their ATV, or guests can do self-tours of the grounds on foot or mountain bike. A masseuse is on call. Online are the farm's global positioning system coordinates, as well as driving time estimates and directions.

It all was enough to lure *West Wing* actor Martin Sheen and his wife, Janet, whose roomy accommodations are called the Presidential Suite. Room rates of $115 to $325 per night include breakfast. Trail passes are $5 per day, and it is fine to buy one without staying overnight.

Justin Trails Resort
7452 Kathryn Avenue, Sparta
www.justintrails.com
800-488-4521

•

TIDBITS

The only smoking allowed at **Justin Trails** is "in your vehicle."

The Justins sell their granola (made with organic oats, sunflower seeds, dried cranberries, nuts, coconut, honey, peanut butter and seasonings) by the bag: 12 ounces for $5, 3 pounds for $20. Also for sale are personal care and edible products made by family businesses in Wisconsin.

•

Rolling hills and Amish farms are roughly 15 miles south of Justin Trails. Particularly picturesque is the curvy County D, between Cashton and La Farge, in Monroe and Vernon counties. Several farmers use small, wooden roadside signs to announce their specialties: handcrafted furniture, bakery, produce, woven rugs, quilts.

For a more formal tour of the area, contact **Kathy Kuderer** at **Down A Country Road**, two miles east of Cashton on Highway 33. **www.downacountryroad.com** **608-654-5318**

The tour cost is per family car or van, and tour reservations are required. No tours are given on Sundays.

Rosie Zimmer's Local Choice means products grown by the area's farmers.

SPRING GREEN: Staying Close to Home

At this grocery, most of what can be bought has been grown or raised within an hour away.

Spring Green's **Local Choice Farm Market** gives farmers the opportunity to enhance visibility and product sales all year, even in winter, when only one weekly farmers' market operates in nearby Madison.

Consumers gain reassurance about food quality because they know the birthplace of their dairy products, meats and produce. "People are happy to know their products are free of chemicals, and they may know the farmers" represented at the store, says **Cheryl Hoeper**, store manager.

"Someone may walk in and ask, 'Are these Mike's apples?'" she says, as an example. "They are happy to have access to food from people" they know and trust.

"There is a feeling that agriculture no longer supports the local community" because so much of farming has become industrialized, says **Rosie Zimmer**, a Local Choice owner, with husband **Gary Zimmer**. "In this system, we help our community" because the concerns of both farm and urban people are addressed.

Her spouse is president of Midwestern Bio-Ag, a longtime producer of organic fertilizers and livestock minerals.

Local Choice's 30-plus agricultural producers, whose names and locations are pinpointed on a Wisconsin map in the store, each agree to follow sustainable farming practices. Many products, but not all, are certified organic.

Farmers are quizzed before their products become a part of the mix. What do you do to keep your animals healthy and comfortable? What do you do to keep your soils mineralized?

"You will find everything you need for a week's worth of groceries, a camping trip in the woods or for a picnic," a Local Choice brochure states. The business also sells sandwiches and picnic lunches, a good match for American Players Theatre patrons.

The business, so far, has been a delicate balance between stocking local products and fulfilling customer requests. Some of the condiments and snack foods come from a regional distributor of natural/organic foods.

Prepared foods—from fresh bakery to jams—come from certified commercial kitchens.

Rosie's fiber arts studio and sales area occupy about one-third of the space in the store. The weaver says she may relocate as the food inventory expands.

One of the first things a customer sees at Local Choice is a list of new items, which changes weekly. It is not a consignment operation. When Local Choice decides to add a product, Rosie says, "we buy a small quantity," add a profit margin, "and see how it goes." Kimchee from a farm in Viroqua, for example, may not be a quick success like the pies and scones from **One Sun Farm** in La Farge.

Meats and poultry are in freezer cases, but customized orders can be delivered fresh (with enough notice). Smoked trout spread and granola share space with cheeses and other dairy products in a refrigerated case. Organic turnips recently were priced at $2.25 per pound—it is not warehouse pricing.

Rosie shrugs when cost is mentioned. It all depends upon the product, she says, and customers from the Chicago area consider Local Choice's organic prices to be reasonable. Harder to quantify are the long-range health benefits of following a diet that is chemical free and mineral enriched.

"Farm animals tend to be fed so much better than humans," she says, because of emphasis on a mineral balance in diet.

Fridays tend to be big sales days at Local Choice because that's when several farmers make product deliveries. Wednesday is "spinach day," because that's when it is brought from a farmer's hoop house—and it goes fast.

So far, it seems like a win-win situation for the Zimmer family. Their son's **Otter Creek Organic Farm** products have an automatic market. That includes the basil pesto and sun-dried tomato flavored cheeses that **Cedar Grove Cheese** makes with milk from the Zimmer farm.

Another branch of the family business is **Gorman's Locker** in Lone Rock, certified to do organic meat processing. That is the only type of meat processed.

To Rosie, Local Choice does not replace but supplements the seasonal farmers' markets. "The winter months determined who our base customers are," she adds.

Local Choice Farm Market
140 S. Winsted Street, Spring Green
www.localchoicefarmmarket.com
608-588-2321

•

TIDBITS

Within a backyard block of **Local Choice** is a much-loved business that is one part funky cafe, one part gourmet grocery, one part used-book library, and one part boutique and gift shop.

The Spring Green General Store—a sweet baby blue on the outside, with a long porch for lingering—used to be a cheese warehouse. Inside are surprises, be it the Cambodian Yellow Curry with Pineapple Salad, the Mexican Polenta Lasagna or the Egg Foo Yung Scramble (for breakfast).

It is not unusual to hear live music on Saturday afternoons. Poets and other artists share their original works on the first Monday of the month. Biggest event of the year? BobFest, always on the Sunday before Memorial Day, is a love fest of Bob Dylan music. **www.springgreengeneralstore.com 608-588-7070**

•

Furthermore, we'd be remiss to ignore the most popular local brews, produced by **Furthermore Beer**. Almost as good as the flavor are the names: Fatty Boombalatty, Three Feet Deep. **www.furthermorebeer.com 608-588-3300**

TOMAH: Mr. Ed Serves Mankind

It's a half-hour wait for a table at 6:30 on a Friday night, and we're only at the halfway point in our travels, so we ask to eat at a barstool table. "Sometimes they say that's OK," says Rhonda, pleasant, but showing a slight frown, "and sometimes it isn't."

Tonight it's fine, and our high-top perch is near the buffet tables. It's $8.95 for the broasted chicken and fish (served fried, broiled), a buck less if you don't want the salad bar.

Into our bowls go chunks of iceberg lettuce and shredded cheese, pickled beets, bright green peas, gelatin with whipped topping, pasta salad with imitation crab, mini-marshmallows and rice mixed with pineapple and a creamy dressing.

The plates are slightly, but noticeably, smaller than average. The crowd is a mix of hard-bodied types, from nearby Fort McCoy, and locals with baseball caps that advertise New Holland, the Packers and a love of hunting.

The waitresses are friendly and accommodating. Bar patrons scoop free popcorn into plastic baskets. Smokers are embraced, not chastised. A sign says potato cheese soup, but this batch is long gone.

On the walls is artwork of Native Americans and splashes of warm, southwestern colors. The exterior looks like a giant log cabin, a beacon in the middle of this town of 8,500.

Little is extraordinary about the setting, cuisine or clientele. The owner, though, is another story. **Mr. Ed's Tee-Pee Supper Club**, on the main drag of downtown Tomah, is run by Ed Thompson, who has sometimes generated more interesting headlines than his big brother, former Governor Tommy Thompson.

Ed has been busted for his nickel video poker machines, has been stabbed by the local butcher, has run for governor on the Libertarian ticket, has been dubbed the Billy Carter of Wisconsin (remember former president Jimmy's little brother?).

The New York Times seems to love this tale of two brothers.

"Ten years ago this month, Ed Thompson was divorced, broke and living with a dog named Ace," Dan Barry wrote, in 2001. "But he knew that if he followed through on his darkest impulses, it would be headline news: 'Governor's Brother Takes Life; Was Colorful.'"

A year later, Matt Bai profiled Ed for the same newspaper and wrote:

"Ed isn't just the owner of the Tee-Pee, a solid steakhouse with a tin Indian mounted out front. He's a local icon and caretaker. Each year, he serves up free Thanksgiving dinners for more than 1,000 area residents. He drives home drunks and takes in stragglers; his staff at the Tee-Pee includes an ex-con and a guy who was homeless and now sleeps upstairs."

The total fed on Thanksgiving now exceeds 1,400, and Ed says that's his way to give back to his community, which has tolerated his dark side. He says he gave up drinking and smoking in 1997.

"It's like my church," Ed says of the Tee-Pee. "It's where I can serve my fellow man as best as I can."

He has saved the business twice, buying it out of bankruptcy in 1990, selling it a year later, then rescuing it again, in 1993.

"The Tee-Pee has its own spirit," he says, with pride. "It reaches out to everybody," regardless of occupation, education or income.

Mr. Ed's Tee-Pee Supper Club
812 Superior Avenue, Tomah
608-372-0888
•

SOUTHWEST

Pickled beets, slaw and other salads fill the plates at Mr. Ed's Tee-Pee Supper Club.

A typical bucolic Wisconsin summer farm scene.

WISCONSIN DELLS: Down on the Farm

Three miles north of the over-the-top attractions that define and fuel this city is an anomaly that quietly defies vacation stereotypes here.

The **Thunder Valley Inn** is about gut emotion instead of glut experience, life at a slow pace instead of lightning quick thrill rides, subtle influences instead of sensory overload.

"Being by a tourist town, the people are already here, and they don't all want to go down a waterslide," says **Anita Christopherson Nelson**, to explain why her seasonal restaurant and bed and breakfast survives. (It typically opens in mid-May and closes in mid-October.) She and her daughters have operated the inn and presented old-fashioned threshing dinners (with live Scandinavian music) for almost two decades.

"Many people search for the real things that make Wisconsin special, and the family farm is something we have that is special," she explains.

Her intent was to "be natural, real and Scandinavian." To compete, she knew the inn's food, music and hospitality would have to be authentic. Daughters **Kari** and **Sigrid** (now in their thirties) help prepare meals as well as sing and yodel. They play their fiddles for guests, too, or are accompanied by their mother's piano (she is a former music teacher).

"We didn't have much money to work with, but my husband—bless his heart—said you'll never be satisfied unless you try this," Anita recalls.

Today the family and other employees also give bread-making lessons; conduct farm tours; tell Ole and Lena jokes; and serve smorgasbord breakfasts and dinners of slow-roasted beef, hand-peeled potatoes, strawberry-rhubarb jam, Scandinavian almond cake and more. Visitors also have animals—chickens to kittens—to watch and feed.

"It has not been a big money maker, but it has given our children a way to learn how to live with people and share their talents," Anita says.

For guests who choose to spend the night, accommodations are comfortable but not lavish. It's in the European style, the innkeeper says, where it is more important to make a personal connection than to offer whirlpools and fireplaces.

More than 250 teenagers from around the world have lived with and worked for the Nelson family during the past half-century, through Future Farmers of America, 4-H and other youth exchanges.

"The cows don't teach them much English, so in the summer they waitress or bus tables," Anita says. They also get exposure to pop culture—the waterparks and other attractions that make up American vacations.

The hardest experience for the Nelsons was when 36 cattle were lost in a barn fire in the 1980s. The family considered not rebuilding.

"But our boys (Peter and Nels) wanted to milk, and they love the land," Anita explains, so the family milks 275 cows on its 600 acres.

When the barn was rebuilt, the Nelsons had a viewing room attached to the 16-stall milking parlor, with handicapped access.

"This is our future," Anita says, noting that her own energy for operating the Thunder Valley Inn (two miles away) sometimes wanes. She considers the roomy viewing room—which has a kitchen, piano and dining area—one way to continue teaching urbanites and younger generations about rural living.

Don and Anita Nelson married in 1960, after growing up on farms a couple of miles apart in the town of Newport. Their sense of home, culture and commitment continues to be strong in this rural Norwegian community.

The local farmers fought in the 1980s to have a Wisconsin Dells landfill located elsewhere, and in 2000 to stop Perrier from setting up a water bottling plant in adjacent Adams County.

"We could make a lot more money if this area were not rural," Anita says, "but there are some things that you can't figure in dollars and cents."

Thunder Valley Inn
W15344 Waubeek Road, Wisconsin Dells
www.thundervalleyinn.com
877-254-4145

•

A ride along the Mighty Mississippi ends a summer day in a pleasant way.

ELSEWHERE IN THE SOUTHWEST

Rudy's Drive-in, 1004 La Crosse Street, is a third-generation business in La Crosse that began as a little box of a root beer stand in Chippewa Falls in 1933. The carhops wear roller skates, the atmosphere screams 1950s, and "cruise nights"—for classic cars and those who love them—are Tuesdays in summer.

It's chili dogs and burgers in baskets, root beer by the float or gallon. Open seasonally, March to October. **www.rudysdrivein.com 608-782-2200**

•

Another swell way to spend a sultry summer night is aboard the **Julia Belle Swain**, which docks at Riverside Park in La Crosse. A gentle river ride on this steamboat—one of only five left that transports passengers on the Mississippi—is big on nostalgia and local history.

We ran into a group celebrating a fiftieth anniversary, which was an especially excellent match for the entertainment, accommodating staff and filling, hot buffet. Hearing the steam calliope, operated via an antique keyboard, feels like an authentic slice of riverboat life.

Overnight cruises also are possible, with lodging at port city hotels (Prairie du Chien; Winona and Wabasha, Minnesota; Lansing and Dubuque, Iowa).

The first *Julia Belle Swain*, afloat from 1913 to 1931, was named after a boat builder's granddaughter. The second, which is the La Crosse boat, was christened in 1971. **www.juliabelle.com 608-784-4882**

•

What's the best-known place for breakfast in Lone Rock? If you're a pilot, the answer is **Picadilly Lilly Diner**, E2513 Highway JJ, near Tri-County Regional Airport, Sauk County.

How close is it to the airport? Well, you can almost taxi your plane to the restaurant door. That makes it interesting for everybody.

This is where pancakes are bigger than plates. Biscuits and gravy ("lotsa sausage," the menu promises) also is popular and massive. It's $2.50 for one-fourth of an order, which should tell you something.

So the food is hearty, business is good, and there is a nice mix of locals and pilots. Owner Eileen Hamburg says the diner was a weather station until the late 1970s, and today some of the original weather-spotting equipment is in the EAA AirVenture Museum, Oshkosh.

Closing time at the restaurant is 2 p.m. daily. Call ahead if you're bringing a party of six or more. **608-583-3318**.

•

Popcorn wasn't on the menu, but it reportedly was brought as a gift for the host, during that first Thanksgiving in Plymouth, Massachusetts. So the popular contemporary snack also is one of the oldest documented American foods.

One of Wisconsin's most prolific producers of the product is Grant County's **Rural Route 1 Popcorn**, which puts together its merchandise at 105 E. Tama Street, Livingston, and sells it at 101 Highway 18, Montfort.

The **Elmer Biddick** family had long grown seed corn but decided to diversify by growing popcorn on 25 acres in 1983. Today white and yellow gourmet popcorn kernels grow on several hundred acres.

Most popular specialty product: Ivory Almond K'Nuckle, which is popcorn and almonds, covered with white fudge. A slew of other popcorn blends and flavored popcorn can be sampled at the Montfort retail outlet and purchased by the pound.

Popcorn also can be ordered online, by phone or through fund-raising events. The products come in tins, tubs and microwavable packets.

www.ruralroute1.com 800-828-8115. The Montfort shop, which also stocks home furnishings and gifts, is open daily, except for major holidays—including Thanksgiving.

•

"Nice 'shrooms" would be pleasant and appropriate commentary if you're in Muscoda, particularly in mid-May. That is when the Grant County community of 1,400 celebrates its abundance of light and sponge-like morels. The sale of more than 2,000 pounds of the delicate fungus is not unusual during the annual **Morel Mushroom Festival**, on the weekend after Mother's Day.

'Shroomers are rewarded for collecting the biggest, smallest and most unique morel mushrooms. Fried morels go on sale at 10 a.m. and how long they last depends upon availability. Muscoda earned the title of Wisconsin's Morel Capital in 1982. **www.muscoda.com 608-739-3182**

•

One great brewery, with two brewery tours. **New Glarus Brewing Company**, 119 Elmer Road, in spring 2008 opened its new 75,000-square-foot, 100,000-barrel plant about one mile south of the brewery that has been in operation since 1993.

Co-owner **Deb Carey**, whose husband, **Dan,** is the brewmaster, likens the new building's mood to a little German village. It sits on a hill that overlooks New Glarus, one of Wisconsin's best Euro-styled communities.

Both brewing facilities are on Highway 69. Both are worth a tour because of the difference in architecture, technology and what is brewed. The creator of our much-loved Spotted Cow and Fat Squirrel produced beer under 20 labels in 2007. The brewery continues to add new labels.

SOUTHWEST

Dan and Deb Carey on the bottling line at New Glarus Brewing Company.

The tendency is to offer the tour for free, then charge a bit for the beer tasting. **www.newglarusbrewing.com 608-527-5850**

•

Norwegian men were busy building wagons in the late 1800s, so local tobacco warehouse owners had a shortage of workers at harvest time. When wives were asked to help sort tobacco, they agreed, on one condition.

The women wanted one break in the morning and another in the afternoon, to tend to chores at home—and sip a cup of coffee.

That's how the story goes in Stoughton, and that's why the Dane County community bills itself as the birthplace of the coffee break. **The Coffee Break Festival**, on a Saturday in August, has become an annual event. The day begins with free coffee and doughnuts. **www.stoughtonwi.com 888-873-7912**

•

It is logical that the hometown of the coffee break also would contain the **Koffee Kup**, 355 E. Main Street, the oldest restaurant in Stoughton, around at least since 1912 and doing business in an 1891 building. Beer as well as coffee is on the menu.

One board lists types of pie and other desserts. Another has soups of the day and the daily specials. We've noticed that prices on a board don't always match what's on the menu, but they're within a dime or so.

The crowd is a wonderful mix of ages and collar colors. Customers look content; some linger.

The daily special, at $5.95 when we visited, was chicken and ribs. Too much, we decided, because of all the extras: soup, salad, potato, hot vegetable and dinner roll.

By 1:30 p.m. on a weekday, only four of six soup choices still were available. That included chili, which added 30 cents to the bill.

A bottomless cup of coffee has long been 50 cents at the Koffee Kup. Pie flavors, which vary with the season of year, include Fruit of the Forest (an assortment of berries) and Festival of Fruits (strawberry, rhubarb and apple).

Owners **Kendall** and **Trish Gulseth** also introduced the Garbage Omelette, a three-egg masterpiece that envelops ten other ingredients (cheeses to meats to fresh vegetables). It is topped with chili.

"I ate the Garbage at the Koffee Kup," customer T-shirts used to proclaim. **608-873-6717**

•

People who seek fortification while pedaling the 32-mile Elroy-Sparta bike trail need not veer far from this abandoned railway passage, which snakes through three tunnels of rock.

Right next to the Village Park in Norwalk is **Stony Creek Cafe**, 104 Railroad Street, whose pizzas and eggplant strips are popular menu items. There is no need to leave your bike unless you need an indoor break; just order from the take-out window and bask in the sun. **608-823-7227**

•

Heavenly bread, when you're in Sinsinawa, means loaves of cinnamon, zucchini, raisin and a host of other bakery that seems blessed as well as tasty because it comes from the kitchen at **Sinsinawa Mound**, 585 Highway Z, Grant County.

The work begins at dawn and ends long after sunset. A staff of four dozen serves up to 700 people per meal, too, but meal access requires registration at a gathering—retreats to meetings—being held on the grounds. Some ingredients come from the Sinsinawa Dominicans' gardens.

Hundreds of loaves are baked daily—and even more leave this religious community during holiday bazaar time, when Catholic churches sometimes sell these products in addition to what their own members bake. Caramel rolls, one dozen to a plump clump, sell for $5. Fruitcake is $6 per pound. Bread is $3 or $4, depending upon type and size.

Online orders are accepted, or take a tour of the grounds, walk the labyrinth and end up buying a loaf at the pretty gift shop. Private overnight retreats can be arranged. **www.sinsinawa.org 608-748-4411, ext. 116**

•

Last, a good word for a burger that doesn't involve meat. The Walnut Burger has been served at the 1871 **Trempealeau Hotel**, 150 Main Street, Trempealeau, since 1986.

The burger is made with ground California nuts, with tamari adding a delightful flavor to the hearty mix. It has gotten so popular that it's also sold in frozen four-packs at grocery stores. Retailers include natural food stores.

The walnut burger's addition to the menu was a (successful) attempt by owners **Jim** and **Linda Jenkins** to introduce vegetarianism and widen food choices for their overnight guests and other customers.

Also on the menu are Walnut Balls, an appetizer that resembles meatballs. It is served with salsa and honey mustard sauce, for dipping.

The business, near the Mississippi River, is a logical stop for bikers on the Great River State Trail. The sleepy town rocks when the hotel schedules music. A large lawn and screened porch overlook the river.

Want more than a meal? The hotel has rooms, suites and a cottage for rent. **www.trempealeauhotel.com 608-534-6898**

•

Susie Gilbertson and Rick Becker are hard at work at the Grumpy Troll, Mount Horeb.

ROAD TRIP: Fortification Along the Bike Trails

More than 100 bicycling trails exist in Wisconsin, and many are "rails-to-trails" railroad track conversions that twist along farmland, forests, small towns and waterways.

State-maintained trails that are at least 2 miles long are described at **www.dnr.wi.gov**. Among the newest is the 40-mile Badger State Trail, which heads from Madison to the Illinois state line. This route's intersection with the 41-mile Military Ridge, 23.5-mile Sugar River and 34.4-mile Capital City trails makes it a tremendous conduit for getting acquainted with southwestern Wisconsin.

1. **Seeking like-minded travelers?** Stay at **Earth Rider**, 929 W. Exchange Street, Brodhead. It is a bike sales/repair/rental shop and five-room hotel, just off the Sugar River Trail. www.earthridercycling.com 608-897-8300

2. Coffee break time. Indigo Coffee & Tea, 300 S. Main Street, Verona, presents a fine and funky array of Fair Trade crafts as well as food and beverages. Sandwich combos are inventive (panini with avocado, tomato, cheddar and green chiles). For kids, and Elvis fans: organic peanut butter and bananas. Breakfast burritos, slices of quiche, stuffed croissants and wraps all come with a side of fruit.

Best cool-off choice: the Purple Monster, a smoothie with blueberries, pomegranate, bananas and yogurt. **www.indigocoffeeandtea.com 608-845-6800**

3. Bikes and bikers. Riley Tavern, 8205 Klevenville Riley Road, Verona, is amidst farmland and prairie. Known best for the Sunday breakfasts of specialty pancakes and tasty Bloody Marys.

Rest a spell on the porch, pat the agreeable family pooch and watch the world rotate. This can be the slow lane at its best, although lively bikers (as in Harley) love it here, too. **608-845-9150**

4. Time for some suds. Grumpy Troll Restaurant & Brewery, 105 S. Second Street, Mount Horeb, respects martinis as well as beer brewed on the premises. Ask for a Blue Mounds Mudslide, from the Grumpy Martini list, if you must—but the rotating list of brews includes two 2007 world medal winners: Curly Scotch Ale and Maggie (an Imperial Indian Pale Ale).

The dozen types of taps sometimes include a barrel-aged brew. Walleye, by sandwich or plate dinner, is served daily and tastes great when pan fried. The rest of the menu runs from salads to steaks. **www.thegrumpytroll.com 608-437-2739**

5. Sweet tooth. Sjölinds Chocolate House, 219 E. Main Street, Mount Horeb, is the place to satisfy your sweet tooth in an exotic manner. Pastry chef Tracy Thompson serves chocolates from around the world, plus her own caramels, truffles and pastries. Expect mochas, lattes and obscenely decadent hot chocolate. **608-437-0233**.

6. More suds. New Glarus Brewing Company, at Highways 69 and W, New Glarus, produces Spotted Cow (slightly fruity) and Fat Squirrel (hazelnut taste). Wisconsin Belgian Red, with a pound of Door County cherries per 750-ml bottle, earns awards internationally. Tours, tastings available in the newly expanded brewery. **www.newglarusbrewing.com 608-527-5850**

7. Baked delights. New Glarus Bakery, 534 First Street, New Glarus, is slightly off the path but worth the diversion. Business began in 1910, specializing in Swiss treats, lovingly made. Order hand-rolled pastry horns (filled with almond paste or ground nutmeats) or hand-cut *lebkuchen* (honey sticks). Devour buttery *gipfelq*

(like a croissant) and pack away a loaf of *alpen* (wheat sourdough).
www.newglarusbakery.com
866-805-5536

8. For a tour of the Big Cheese, manufacturer **Roth Kase**, and access to specialty cheeses at factory outlet prices, visit Alp and Dell, 657 Second Street, Monroe. The cheese store, adjacent to the factory, sells dozens of varieties.
608-325-3355

9. Fine dining possibilities—explained elsewhere in this book—include **Belle Bleu** in Belleville and **The Dining Room at 209 Main**, Monticello. It is fine to come as you are. Just make sure to make a meal reservation.

Angela Anderson has got the goods at New Glarus Bakery.

TELL ME ABOUT: Brats

Back where we grew up, the ultimate food compliment—regardless of weather or time of year—came down to these words: "That's a good brat."

You'll find brats cooking almost every weekend in Sheboygan County, at taverns, churches, bowling alleys and parks. I can think of a half-dozen grocery stores with outdoor booths for service clubs to sell brats. I know of at least one brat maker that has a drive-through window.

The most typical fundraiser meal is a hamburger or brat on a hard roll (preferably from **City Bakery**), a heap of warmed German potato salad and a ladle of baked beans. Add a can of pop, a slice of home-made pie and the tab still is under $10.

So brats are everywhere, and that makes us pretty picky about how they're prepared.

There's an art to grilling brats, and it's worth knowing about.

What's a good brat? It's more than a zesty sausage that's plopped into a bun. The German sausage that helps shape Wisconsin's personality generates a lot of debate among the people who love to eat it.

For example, what's the worst thing you can do to a bratwurst?

A. Boil it before grilling it.

B. Pan fry it instead of grilling it.

C. Prick it with fork tines before boiling or grilling it.

D. Sear it like a steak.

All these choices have their advocates, but chef **Mike Zeller** of **Johnsonville Sausage**, the nation's leading brat manufacturer, isn't afraid to provide the definitive word. "Some folks think brats should be grilled like a steak—seared quickly to seal in the juices. That's wrong," he says. "Searing makes the brats split open and the juices leak out."

So what's the proper way to cook a bratwurst? "Don't be in too big of a rush; they need 20 to 30 minutes to cook thoroughly. Make sure the fire's not too hot. And turn them frequently," advises Mike, who was born on a Sheboygan Brat Days weekend.

More specifically, charcoal grill operators should let coals turn to white ash—"until you can hold your hand over them for three to four seconds"—before putting the sausages on the grill. Then turn them every five minutes.

Mary Lou Haen of the Sheboygan Jaycees (which has sponsored Brat Days since 1953) probably would agree. She proclaims this in *Wisconsin Food Festivals* by Terese Allen: "Bratwurst cannot be boiled or microwaved! Use tongs when turning the brats over the coals. You don't want to lose any of the savory juices encased in the sausage by pricking them with a fork."

Grill them to a deep brown color (not burnt), she says. If you're not ready to immediately serve them—on hard rolls, never a generic, cheap, mass-produced hot dog bun—"there is a Sheboygan-approved method for holding bratwurst: Simmer two cans of beer with one cup butter and a thinly sliced onion. The brats can be kept hot in this mixture until ready to eat."

For brat purists, that's probably all you need to know. But other folks have a big itch to get creative, either with brat recipes or brat ingredients.

Cream of bratwurst soup, anyone? We've seen that as a choice at a rural Lions Club soup luncheon.

Brat tacos? Brat egg rolls? Those have been among the unusual food choices at Brat Days, which lures up to 80,000 people, depending on the weather.

And the word "brat" certainly no longer refers to only pork sausages with secret spice concoctions (often including ginger, nutmeg, coriander, caraway, garlic, salt, pepper, whatever). Butchers make chicken and turkey brats, no salt brats, jalapeno brats—the list is long.

TIDBITS

The best time to visit Johnsonville, a tiny town that contains little besides a volunteer fire department and Laack's dance hall, is on the first Sunday after Independence Day, for the **Johnsonville Sausage Fest**.

Take Sheboygan County M, off Highway 23. Hundreds of locals gather for breakfast, then an outdoor church service, polkas, beer and brats of all flavors.

A jolly and charming event, the festivities go on outdoors, under tents and inside the firehouse until 7 p.m.

•

Johnsonville Sausage Company donates the first 150,000 brats served during the **World's Largest Brat Fest**.

A big brat donation is part of what the event gains by adding "Johnsonville" to the festival's official name. But if organizer **Tim Metcalfe** of **Metcalfe Sentry Foods** has his way, he'll purchase additional brats (at cost) from the sausage maker.

The event's next goal is to sell almost 19 miles of brats (lined up end to end) and get the Guinness folks to confirm it as a world record. As of 2008, the self-proclaimed record at Brat Fest is 191,712 brats.

You need hydraulic equipment to lift the 6,000-pound lid that covers Johnsonville's Big Taste Grill, which the company routinely rolls into major events, such as this one. The grill heats 750 sausages at a time, or 2,500 per hour. There is room for 12 grillers, who stand on a 4-foot walkway. One-half ton of brats can be stored in the equipment's refrigerated area.

The whole setup, when covered and on the road, looks like a semi carrying a vat of milk. It has been to Times Square and the Pentagon (to raise money for families of Sept. 11 victims), Super Bowls and the Kentucky Derby.

Proceeds from the annual Johnsonville World's Largest Brat Fest, a Memorial Day weekend event at the Alliant Energy Center's Willow Island in Madison, benefit local charities. More than 70 nonprofit groups have been helped since the event began in 1983. **www.bratfest.com**

•

The competition gets intense within the **Wisconsin Association of Meat Processors**. Annual brat judging is split into four categories: cooked specialty bratwurst (**Hoffs United Foods,** Brownsville, east of Waupun, was grand champion in 2007), fresh specialty bratwurst (**Viking Village**, Reedsburg, was tops), precooked bratwurst/uncured (**RJ's Meats**, Hudson) and smoked bratwurst/cooked and cured (**Lake Geneva Country Meats**, Lake Geneva).

A perfect day in Wisconsin: gorgeous summer sun and hot, juicy grilled brats.

All kinds of small towns are in on the act.

•

To learn more about the sausage and the people with a passion for them, check out these websites:

www.bratwurst.com
Johnsonville Sausage, the nation's top bratwurst manufacturer. 888-556-2728

www.usingers.com
Usinger's is a Milwaukee company that is proud of its elfish image, and of not changing its family sausage recipes—created in 1880. More than 70 kinds of sausage are made, yachtwurst to knackwurst, and the company has been described as the Cadillac of sausage makers. **800-558-9998**

www.klements.com Milwaukee-based **Klement's Sausage Company**, established in 1956, has the contracts to provide sausage for Milwaukee Brewers, Milwaukee Bucks and Minnesota Twins games.

Klement's is the home of the goofy-looking and much-loved **Racing Sausages. 800-553-6368**

Klement's Racing Sausages get the Milwaukee Brewers fans on their feet.

CEDARBURG: Long on Shortcake

Strawberry lovers can indulge their sweet passions at the Cedarburg Strawberry Festival.

Hearing that more than 800 people were waiting in line for pancakes would be enough to make you change your plans for breakfast, under normal circumstances.

But when the destination is downtown Cedarburg during the last weekend of June, you might reconsider. The pancakes are topped with strawberries and whipped cream, and the line forms way before the first plate is served.

About 100,000 berry lovers head to the historic community of Cedarburg to indulge in fresh berries in many ways. The quality, number and diversity of artwork, crafts, food and music make the event a pleasant way to spend an afternoon.

It has become a bigger challenge to meet the demand for berries by the quart, by the wine bottle or in smoothies, slushes, shortcakes, sundaes, schaum tortes and—you betcha—strawberry-flavored beer and brats. Seeing plastic containers with a California-based Driscoll's label was our first clue that not all sold here is locally grown.

The festival's coordinator says organizers work hard to maintain good integrity of the berries, but not all vendors are in the sprawling event's jurisdiction of Washington Avenue, which is the main drag downtown. So if buying local products matters to you, make that your shopping district for this event.

The festival is all about berries because Cedarburg historically had an abundance of strawberry farms nearby, but the landscape is changing. A housing development replaces Jerome Fechter's 30-acre berry farm on Highway 60; the retiree had raised berries for three decades.

Wisconsin has about 100 commercial strawberry growers using about 1,200 acres to raise the fruit. It is unusual for a farmer to devote more than 20 acres to the berry, because the harvest is labor-intensive, says Anna Maenner of the **Wisconsin**

Fat ripe strawberries tempt the festival visitor.

Berry Growers Association.

"The number of producers stays pretty constant," she says. Although there are many types of strawberries, Anna says she can tell the difference between ones grown in California and Wisconsin.

"We grow different varieties," she explains. California, which produces 80 percent of the nation's crop, specializes in hybrids that will stay firm and hold their color as they are transported long distances. Wisconsin berries tend to be smaller, but have exceptional flavor.

Vincent "Bud" Schmit, who operates **Schmit's Farm Produce** near Mequon, is responsible for gathering the thousands of quarts of berries for Cedarburg's festival. He says the fruit comes from four or five growers, all in Wisconsin and Michigan.

"The consumer buys with their eyes," he notes, a nod to the challenge of growing good-looking berries, a volatile crop whose health is at the mercy of the weather and good timing when picking. Bud's strawberries are raised for the Cedarburg festival "and not much else."

Then his attention turns to vegetables, particularly his 250 acres of sweet corn, some of which are ready for harvest in early July because the corn is grown under plastic.

Much of it is taken to West Allis in early August for the popular Lions Club booth at the Wisconsin State Fair. Bud's bounty also is sold at five roadside markets in northern Milwaukee and neighboring communities.

Cedarburg Strawberry Festival
www.cedarburgfestivals.org, www.ozaukeetourism.com
800-403-9899

•

TIDBITS

The big shindig for Cedarburg as autumn approaches is the Wine and Harvest Festival, in mid-September along Washington Avenue downtown. The star is **Cedar Creek Winery**, which is based in the community.

•

The **Wisconsin Berry Growers Association** maintains an online list of members that sell berries or allow the public to pick their own. For more: **www.wiberries.org** 920-478-3852. Typically, as the harvest ends in southern Wisconsin by early July, berry picking is beginning or at a peak farther north.

•

Oliebollen seems like such a friendly word, and you hear a lot of it during **Holland Festival**, an annual celebration in Cedar Grove since the 1940s. It takes place in late July.

Locals haul out their wooden clogs, to scrub and dance down Van Altena Avenue during the festival parade. Kids race in wooden shoes. Visitors can watch the shoes be carved by hand and buy a pair that are custom-fit to their feet.

Thousands of oliebollen—slightly warm, sugar-coated and raisin-filled treats that look like doughnut holes—are deep-fried from noon to night. They're addictive, but don't think about the literal translation: oil balls.

Another ethnic food choice: *woosterbroojes,* meat-filled dough (think pig-in-the-blanket). **www.hollandfestcom** 920-668-6523

EAGLE: Old Time County Fair

Fair season seems to peak in August, led by the kingpin of all, the Wisconsin State Fair in West Allis. Add the month's county fairs, and there is enough cotton candy to coat Stoughton. All right, maybe just your front yard.

Least well known but most quaint is the one-day **Old World County Fair** near Eagle, at the Old World Wisconsin state historic site in mid-August. Interpreters at this 576-acre outdoor museum of living history reproduce an 1860s event that is largely about home cookin' and blue ribbon bakin'. They base their work on documentation of the 1858 Walworth County Fair and passages from *Farmer Boy* by Laura Ingalls Wilder, says Jennifer Van Haaften, curator of interpretation.

Staff members make breads, cakes, pies, cheeses and preserves for exhibiting and place their recipes next to their entries. Judges don't award ribbons but talk about the history of these finished products, and their ingredients.

For sale are fair dinners: ham and turkey, baked beans, pickled beets, steamed or baked potatoes, jams, jellies and three kinds of pie—pumpkin, minced meat and vinegar. Vinegar? "It looks like a lemon meringue, but we use cider vinegar instead of lemon," Jennifer says. It all is a reminder that cooking with the seasons and using local ingredients are not new concepts.

Old World Wisconsin also presents **Four Mile Dinners** in September, after-hours events that help explain what it was like to be guests at a stagecoach inn. The cost is $50, and only ten people are accommodated per event "because we only have so much room around the dining table."

Visitors take a horse-drawn carriage ride to the inn and participate in kitchen chores. They also play parlor games before eating their meal from basic, ironstone dishes. Roasted chicken is seasoned with rosemary and sage from the kitchen garden, and mashed potatoes may have lumps. It is not gourmet cooking, but a relatively accurate representation of how people dined in the 1870s. No alcohol is served because the inn—one of more than 60 historic structures in the historic farm and village—has a dry history.

Old World Wisconsin
S103 W37890 Highway 67, Eagle
www.oldworldwisconsin.org
262-594-6300

•

SOUTHEAST

Fields Best sells vegetables grown at Michael Fields Agricultural Institute.

EAST TROY: Fertile Fields

The **Buy Local, Buy Wisconsin** initiative has spread statewide, and the goal is to spend at least 10 percent of your food budget on edibles produced close to home.

"Local" is defined as within 100 miles, and a longtime leader in this effort—way before the good-intentioned hype became fashionable—is the **Michael Fields Agricultural Institute**. The nonprofit ag researcher and mentor has existed since 1984 and today is the steward for 1,000 acres, about 600 acres of which are sublet to a dairy farmer.

Marsh, woods and prairie buffer strips also are under Fields's watch.

Nine-month programs teach farming as a second career and coach young adults about gardening. Shorter workshops focus on culinary tours, youth education, urban agriculture or a course that students design themselves.

Food system work—through crops, policies and research—takes up much of the rest of the staff's time. The average person is welcome to visit and walk field roads over roughly 100 acres, following the tree line and Honey Creek past patches of flowers and ponds, crickets and grasshoppers, berries and greens, a crop of corn and parcels of wildflowers.

Seasonal cooking classes occasionally occur in one of two commercial kitchens. Guided tours of Nokomis Organic Bakery, on the grounds, and the ag operations are possible for groups that make reservations.

This is a place to learn, instead of being amused. Materials at the institute remind us that food, on average, travels 1,494 miles before it is eaten. Development projects, in Wisconsin alone, destroy 25,000 acres annually.

Michael Fields Agricultural Institute
W2493 County ES, East Troy
www.michaelfieldsaginst.org 262-642-3303

•

TIDBITS

The institute celebrates the bounty of autumn during its annual **Harvest Festival** in early October. This is the only organized opportunity for the public to see what Michael Fields is about.

The day includes farm and garden tours, an explanation of research activities, an antique tractor show and activities for children. Admission is free. Lecture topics are diverse, such as home-brewed beer and renewable energy.

•

Open on weekdays all year is **Fields Best**, W2463 County ES, a small food and gift shop with in-season fruits and veggies for sale. **Nokomis Organic Bakery** uses the building's commercial kitchen to produce tasty wheat/garlic/basil bread, various cookies (cranberry walnut is the most popular) and other baked goods (Sunshine Bars, which taste like moist granola bars, use orange juice and honey as sweeteners).

•

Fields Best, the institute's for-profit branch, also is a vendor at the **Milwaukee Public Market**, 400 N. Water Street.

Also in the area, tucked across from the East Troy Railroad Museum and electric trolley rides, is **Lauber's Old Fashion Ice Cream Parlor**, 2010 Church Street, which has been in business since the 1920s. The jukebox plays 78s. The ice cream menu takes up four pages. Tons of memorabilia will yank you back to simpler times. Open seasonally. **262-642-3679**

•

In 2005, the *Wall Street Journal* pronounced it the best pie in America.

"It was a wonderfully rustic pie, with hearty chunks of apples, that retains both a crunchiness in the crust and a tenderness in the filling," the newspaper concluded.

The Elegant Farmer, in Mukwonago since 1970, produces 250,000 of these pies per year. The secret is in the wrapping: Each pie is baked in a paper bag. That means the apples steam and hold their shape, instead of turning into mush, and the top crust tastes like a sugar cookie with crunch.

"We didn't expect that," says **John Bauer**, who with brother **Mike Bauer** and **Keith Schmidt** owns the Elegant Farmer. The pie recipe, first tested in 1990, came from a Texas cookbook and has been revised along the way.

People who ride Wisconsin's century-old electric trolley from East Troy get a charming surprise at the halfway point in their journey: the trolley stops at the Elegant Farmer, where there is time to disembark, sample products and shop.

The specialty food store is part of a former dairy farm, where retail sales began in 1947 from a simple roadside produce stand. Today, about 30 of the remaining 55 acres is orchard.

John is proud of the deli's signature ham, which is injected with apple cider. Homemade caramel corn and cheese corn, from-scratch salads, salsas and a line of bakery items are made on the premises. "We strive for homemade, quality products," John says.

A big chunk of the business is wholesale, from Chicago to Milwaukee.

If not riding the rails to the store, drive to 1545 Main Street, Mukwonago. **www.elegantfarmer.com 262-363-6770**

The Elegant Farmer, Mukwonago (page 127), has wonderful breads and baked goods. In 2005, the Wall Street Journal *proclaimed their apple pie the best in America.*

ELKHART LAKE: A Naturally Sweet Deal

It is early November, **Richard Wittgreve's** harvest has just ended, and his product is likely not on your pantry shelf. He grows 20 acres of sorghum, more than anyone else in Wisconsin, enough to produce 2,350 gallons of syrup.

During Depression years, it was not unusual for a farm family to grow its own little patch of sorghum and use it as a natural sweetener. Juice squeezed from the sorghum cane would be boiled until only pure, amber syrup remained.

That's also how Rich processes his crop, only vats and bulk tanks (which in another life held fresh milk) move the sorghum from one state of consistency to the next. The enterprise is awash with reclaimed materials: a 1950 boiler from a cheese factory, fueled with scrap wood from shipping crates, turns the processing room into a sweet-smelling sauna.

The syrup is stored in barrels, like honey, and later packaged in 4-ounce to 5-pound jars. Some bakeries order the sorghum by the pail or barrel. Rich also sells sorghum-coated popcorn.

All the work is done by Rich and his friend **Warren Kalk**, who toil until midnight on some days, until the cane is all harvested or frost sets in.

Sorghum mills, which Rich contends were almost as commonplace as cheese factories, vanished after World War II, as refined sugar became more plentiful and people lost enthusiasm for labor-intensive sorghum processing. About 500 people produce sorghum nationwide, and about 90 percent are hobbyists. Our guy is an exception: this is his largest crop, followed by hay and pumpkins.

The nutrient-rich sorghum syrup was used in baking, as an ice cream topping, and to flavor baked beans. It is not as thick as molasses, which is a sugar industry byproduct, and not as sweet as maple syrup. Like honey, sorghum will crystallize over time, but a microwave or pan of hot water will restore its original form.

Rich first grew sorghum in 1985, after the death of his grandfather, who routinely supplied the family. "I used the wrong seed," Rich recalls. "It froze before it was ripe." But he persisted, and the next year's crop was more resilient.

The U.S. sorghum belt, says the National Sorghum Producers Association, extends from the Rockies to the Mississippi River and Texas to South Dakota. So Elkhart Lake, in this case, is slightly off the map.

Rolling Meadows Sorghum Mill
N9030 Little Elkhart Lake Road, Elkhart Lake
920-876-2182
•

Fountain Prairie Inn & Farms helps others develop respect for the land.

FALL RIVER: Taking the High(land) Road

It was **John** and **Dorothy Priske's** thirty-fifth wedding anniversary, and they had chosen to spend part of the day with us, driving around their farm in Columbia County, trying to explain what makes all the work worth it.

Their truck bounced down a long swath of newly cut pasture, then veered through a sea of tall grassland that almost reached the vehicle's windows. It is hard to know where the pasture ends and 60 acres of restored prairie/wetlands begin.

When John shut off the motor, all we heard was a happy chorus of twitterings, which was the point of our little trip. "Meadowlarks and bobolinks—we see a lot of them," he says. "It wasn't that way before," when the Priskes farmed 900 hogs and grew corn.

Back then, a diet of 90 percent corn fattened the animals for market quickly, and insecticides followed the corn planters to keep the crop free of pests and natural diseases. It was an efficient operation, but around 1999 the Priskes decided it wasn't enough to satisfy their soul.

They wondered about their two farm dogs that died of cancer within a six-month period. They took a trip to New Zealand and were amazed at the quality of meat from animals that were grass-fed and brought to maturity slowly.

So when the Priskes returned to Wisconsin, they devised a plan to duplicate this type of farming, slowly transforming cornfields into a nutritious mix of tall-growing grasses.

The 280 acres of **Fountain Prairie Inn & Farms** today include lush pastures for about 300 head of Highland cattle, a heritage breed—one that has not been manipulated genetically through generations. Chefs at restaurants from Madison to Sheboygan and Brookfield to Wisconsin Dells serve the dry-aged beef from this farm.

"The Highland is a show stopper," says Dorothy Priske, because of its reddish brown coat, long hair and long horns. Visitors like the looks of the cattle, so the animals are a draw for Dorothy's farmstead bed and breakfast.

The five guest rooms in her 1899 Victorian farmhouse are quiet and lovely, typically decorated with quilts and wallpaper from the era. Only the Suite Times has a private bathroom, which contains a two-person whirlpool, but having a slew of modern amenities is not the point when staying here.

It delights the proprietors when they are able to reconnect people with the land and enhance their understanding of how food gets to the table. They are evangelists for the slow food movement, which is all about returning to the way food used to be raised and prepared, in response to corporate food production practices.

"Are we really farmers or environmental activists?" John asks rhetorically. "I guess we're both." To some neighbors, they also were odd, as in "What happened? You used to be good corn farmers."

The transition has been a huge step for the Priskes, who are not flashy risk-takers but are accustomed to challenges. "When you're out on the deep end, there aren't a lot of people with you," John notes.

They were raised on Wisconsin farms, and John long ago sold melons at the Merrimac Ferry boarding point. "That's how I bought my clothes for school in the seventh and eighth grades," he recalls. "We were self-sufficient and dirt poor," he says of the eight siblings in his family, "but we always ate well" and knew the taste of good food.

Fountain Prairie Inn & Farms
W1901 Highway 16, Fall River
www.fountainprairie.com 920-484-3618
•

Nostalgia is everyday business at Schreiner's.

FOND DU LAC: Turn the Clock Back

We can't decide what is best about **Schreiner's**, a beloved restaurant that was born during the Depression, in 1938.

Maybe it's the waitresses, who wear white uniform dresses and aprons, nylons and sensible shoes. Maybe it's the counter seating in the dining room, which has a good view of the cooks at work.

Or maybe it's the way nobody blinks an eye if you order clam chowder for breakfast. "If it's ready, we'll serve it," the menu says.

It doesn't matter that Fond du Lac can't harvest its own clams; this chowder is sold by the frozen quart as well as the steaming cup. The same can be said for the chicken dumpling soup, but it's the chowder that Schreiner's deems "famous".

Ritz Nut Torte, made with Ritz crackers, goes over often and well. So do the individual Jell-O salad molds. And the multigrain granola with sliced almonds and honey. The from-scratch roast beef hash. The slow-cooked hot beef with rich, brown gravy. Order a smoked liver sausage on caraway rye, or fried liver with onions. Neither makes you an oddball here. Soak in the once-common, now-nostalgic ambiance as you savor the home cooking.

For dessert? Maybe it will be sour cream raisin pie, walnut pie, pineapple crisp or chocolate éclairs. It all depends upon the day and the whims of the baker.

Stone Cellar Brewpub, Appleton, introduced a European pilsner beer in honor of Schreiner's seventieth anniversary in 2008.

Schreiner's Restaurant
168 N. Pioneer Road, Fond du Lac
www.fdlchowder.com 920-922-0590

•

The table is set for gracious dining at Ten Chimneys.

GENESEE DEPOT: Le Cordon Lunt

Actor **Alfred Lunt** knew how to work the kitchen as well as the stage, and his meals were productions full of personality and style. The Broadway legend, who died in 1977, was a graduate of Le Cordon Bleu, the Paris cooking school.

His recipes, typed and placed in a three-ring binder, were stashed in a secret closet concealed by a movable library wall. Much of what the household cherished, like letters and family photos, were also kept safe there.

The goods were discovered more than a decade ago, as the **Ten Chimneys** estate of Lunt and **Lynn Fontanne** (his theatrical partner and wife) in Waukesha County was being saved from destruction.

"We had other priorities," recalls Sean Malone, Ten Chimneys Foundation president. At the top was raising $12.5 million to save the longtime retreat, now a National Historic Landmark and open to the public for tours.

A volunteer eventually began turning the dozens of recipes and tidbits of advice into digital files. Mr. Lunt had long been working on a cookbook, but the order of his material needed to be arranged.

The food files have been matched with charming photos of the Lunts, taken over many years by Warren O'Brien, whose work shows the couple entertaining, relaxing and at work in the garden and kitchen.

The result was a whimsical "hybrid cookbook" that can be appreciated for its lovely photography as well as for its culinary history and contents.

Notations tend to be conversational. Recipes are untested by Ten Chimneys. "The most passionate of cooks were clamoring for the book," Sean says. "So we thought, 'Why not let them do the testing?'"

Anecdotes and feedback from cookbook purchasers are encouraged. Reader commentary will be a part of the book's next edition.

The recipes tend to be uncomplicated. Alfred's Carrots and Mint is simply chopped fresh mint leaves that are added to cooked carrots. Occasionally, the "something extra" will keep guests guessing, because of an ingredient's removal right before a meal.

Mr. Lunt put dill pickle slices into canned tomato soup, for example, and added whole allspice to simmering clam chowder. "You'll find you're quite pleased with yourself, and your guests with you," a note from him unabashedly states, with regard to the latter concoction.

Alfred's Eggs Madrid, "a luncheon or late supper dish," is a ring of scrambled eggs on a round serving dish, filled with creamed chicken and surrounded by tomato sauce, all served hot.

"The majority of recipes . . . would not come under the heading of 'haute cuisine,' but they are tasty, economical for the most part, simple to make, and though familiar to some may not be to others," Mr. Lunt wrote.

Details about the actor's passion for the kitchen is a part of the Ten Chimneys tour, offered seasonally, and *The Tester's Edition of Alfred Lunt's Cookbook* is sold in the gift shop.

Ten Chimneys
S43 W31575 Depot Road, Genesee Depot
www.tenchimneys.org
262-968-4110

•

TIDBITS

The elegant **Ten Chimneys** estate can be toured on Tuesdays through Saturdays, May until mid-November. Reservations are needed. On the property are a three-story house, eight-room cottage (a former chicken coop), Swedish-style log cabin, creamery, greenhouse, barns/stables, pool/poolhouse and other smaller buildings. Together they have ten chimneys.

The couple at this property entertained some of their era's most celebrated performers, including Katharine Hepburn and Noel Coward. Starting in 1924, Ten Chimneys was considered a summer playground and retreat for these and other actors. The Lunts made it their retirement home in 1960.

When all the talk about great food in comfortable surroundings makes you hungry, head to the sunny **Corner Stone Restaurant**, S43 W31343 Highway 83, Genesee Depot.

On the creative menu: french toast with a topping of hazelnut liqueur and berry sauce, plus pecans. Mexican Fondue is a chicken-chili sauce, for dipping tortilla chips and andouille sausage. Sandwich choices include the Pot Roast Melt and Olive Grilled Cheese, but the Monte Cristo is the house specialty.

Dinner is another story, and it often is accompanied by music on Saturdays. **262-968-3093**
www.corner-stonegeneseedepot.com

Creative fare at Corner Stone

SOUTHEAST

KENOSHA: Timeless Supper Clubs

Wisconsin loves its supper club heritage, and two of the greatest names in the business are ten miles from each other in Kenosha County, on a road that hugs the Lake Michigan shoreline. So it's easy to immerse yourself in the culture for a weekend and have two different experiences.

We love the neon signage of a giant martini glass outside of the **HobNob**, 227 Sheridan Road, which opened in 1954 and is operated by **Michael** and **Anne Aletto**. Inside, the feel of classic elegance is immediate and nostalgic.

Dine on a Friday or Saturday, and your meal will be accompanied by light jazz or piano tunes. Steaks, seafood and other entrees come with a salad, soup and potatoes, but a more contemporary "bistro" fare also is offered

The collection of alcohol has grown to feature 2,000 bottles of wine, plus an extensive array of cognacs.

"Swanky" is a way the HobNob describes itself, and we'd be surprised if you'd disagree. This is a place to celebrate an anniversary that ends with a zero. Casual attire is acceptable. Arrive before sunset, and take a good look at the Great Lake that is steps from the restaurant door. Linger with an ice cream drink after the meal.

www.thehobnob.com 262-552-8008

•

Further south is **Ray Radigan's Restaurant**, 11712 Sheridan Road, Pleasant Prairie, a converted farmhouse with fine food and a sometimes lippy staff. The business has been around since 1933.

We were chided, briefly, for arriving five minutes later than our reservation time. This is a tight ship with pride in creating soups to biscuits from scratch, and it demonstrates a fussy attitude about meats and other ingredients.

The outside still looks like a simple white house, and the interior is more like a home than a business. Out of all the slogans in the world, second-generation owner **Mike Radigan** chooses this one: "Where a steak still really means something."

"Everything is still done the Old Man's way," the website says, and that includes homemade relishes, which many supper clubs have dropped, or added to salad bars. At Radigan's, start off dinner with a tray of raw and pickled relishes, homemade kidney bean salad and cottage cheese that is good enough to be carted away by the pint. It's a tradition that used to be an automatic part of the meal. Now it's $3 per person.

What else? Herring in a cream-onion marinade has been a longtime specialty. So has the calf's liver, with sautéed onions, plus schnitzels and steaks.

www.foodspot.com/rayradigans 262-694-0455

Kohler Food & Wine Experience is culinary theater for foodies. On stage is Walter Scheib, White House chef for Presidents Clinton and Bush.

KOHLER: One Fine Autumn Stew

We are busy eating frittatas with diced butternut squash, leeks and grated cheese. It is day one at the annual **Kohler Food & Wine Experience**, and coming next is oxtail, tender and gravy-rich, served with a puree of potatoes and fava beans.

"Best broth of any cut of meat in the world," the chef asserts, but he considers veal shank an adequate substitute. There is time to sip the accompanying glass of Chianti. It is not quite 11 a.m., and the topic is the foods of autumn.

Pacing is everything. The advice, calories and spirits will continue past dusk. More than one dozen chefs, each presenting at least three recipes, are the meat of this three-day event that is co-sponsored by *Food & Wine* magazine in late October.

One chef after another tries to outdo his peers, with regard to flavor, fusion, food quality, fruits of the vine. Overhead mirrors and video screens make it easy to see whatever is being whisked, chopped, garnished.

The audience gets recipes and samples and sits close enough to call out questions. Even the biggest setting (in a heated tent that can hold more than 200 people) seems intimate. Many fans line up for cookbook autographs afterward.

This is food theater at its best, delivered by respected regional and ethnic chefs and culinary celebrities who have included icon Jacques Pépin, Chicago's Rick Bayless and White House maestro Walter Scheib. Spirits add another dimension to these lessons, both at the food demos and during specialized beverage tastings. Tequila, vodka and cognac are as likely subjects as pinot gris and shiraz, or whiskey vs. whisky.

Cheese maven Laura Werlin, author of *The All American Cheese and Wine Book*, has been a perennial favorite for explaining cheese types, flagging notable new cheeses and matching cheeses with wines.

The conversations need not be pretentious. Consider this observation, from Laura: "Bleu cheese and red wine are like a train wreck in the mouth."

The cost per one-hour seminar averages $30, so it is pricey (and unwise, gastronomically, to expect to attend a daylong string of the events). Admission to a few of the events is free.

About two dozen seminars occur per day. Many overlap. It is rare for one to be repeated. Purchase tickets early; half the choices might be filled before the gathering begins.

It also pays to waddle to a free product sampling area that showcases artisan cheeses, jams, meats, treats and hot beverages. Aisles at the nearby Woodlake Market also tempt shoppers to taste dozens of gourmet products.

Call it educated indulgence. Here you may learn that a sampling of SarVecchio engages the tastebuds, not your sense of hearing at a symphony. And a savvy palate, for food or wine, requires patience as well as alertness.

"Wait for it, wait for it," wine distributor Gary Binter advises, during a session to understand components of wine. "Let the wine feel all parts of your mouth, and then think of what you're *not* tasting."

Much of it is all in good fun. "You don't have to cross-examine a wine to enjoy it," the teacher suggests.

There are more beverage events than food-wine pairings. Sometimes couples split, temporarily, to investigate personal interests—say, Chilean wines vs. how to cook bratwurst.

The Food & Wine Experience unofficially kicks off the culinary season in Kohler, a town best known for its plumbing fixture factory and the American Club, the Midwest's only five-diamond AAA resort.

"No man is an island in himself, and that is even more so in the kitchen," culinary kingpin Jacques Pépin once told dining companions in Kohler. "Enjoy your food and wine—this is what life is all about."

Kohler Food & Wine Experience
late October, multiple Kohler locations
www.destinationkohler.com/foodandwine
800-344-2838, ext. 756

•

TIDBITS

Wisconsin's newest outlet for little luxuries, the **Craverie Chocolatier Cafe**, opened in late 2007 in Kohler's fashionable Shops at Woodlake.

You can come here for breakfast or lunch, but our bet is that your eyes remain fixated on dessert: the golden Danish that is filled with blueberries and cream cheese, the silky white chocolate rum raisin gelato, the dark chocolate brownies that almost drip with gooey caramel, the divine raspberry lemon cake.

The smallest gems of extravagance take up the most space under glass. Handmade chocolates, about 30 types, sell for $1.20 to $2.35 each. At the high end, a 10-piece box of Terrapins (most of us know them as turtles) sells for $24.95. Time the visit right—or wrong, we suppose—and you'll watch the candy, pastries and other treats being made. So aroma is not the only temptation.

A unique and proprietary blend of Swiss chocolates is at the heart of this confectionery line, says Ulrich Koberstein, director of culinary arts at the American Club. He and his staff developed the Craverie concept and menu. The final judge throughout the process, however, has been Herbert Kohler Jr., who heads Kohler Company, and in 2003 was approached about investing in a Wisconsin chocolate shop. He preferred to develop his own.

Work began to create the perfect Terrapin, a combination of chocolate, caramel and pecans. After about 18 months and 400 recipe variations, the product was finished. Today there are four versions: Original, Cranberry, Java and Nutty.

"Then it was a question of how many types of chocolates do we need to open a shop," Ulrich says. In the works for 14 months was a line of ganaches— candy filled with a mix of flavored chocolate and heavy cream—and chocolate toffees, shaped like little mountains with a snowy topping of white chocolate.

The Craverie concept is about providing both indulgences and healthful dining options, so the Lean side of the menu lists salads, soups and other choices by calorie and sodium content.

Kohler Original Recipe Chocolates are on sale online; consult **www.kohlerchocolates.com 800-778-5591**. No preservatives are used, so the chocolates should be consumed within a month of purchase. (As if you can resist them!)

SOUTHEAST

LAKE GENEVA:
The Lap of Luxury

Inside Gilbert's are 13 hand-carved fireplaces.

It was the afternoon of New Year's Eve when I blew into **Gilbert's**, kind of like a hopeful lunatic, peeking through a kitchen door to see if I might take a look around.

This was a spontaneous stop, during a research trip for another topic—winter lodging—and just hours before the restaurant's busiest night of the year. The kitchen crew fetched **Sherry Mizialko**, one of the owners, who understands the allure of this location, a hilltop mansion built in 1885.

This certainly isn't the only awesome house on Lake Geneva's Wrigley Drive, but the copper roof, gingerbread trim and slender tower are standout features.

Many diners in this Victorian house will have a splendid view of Geneva Lake. Thirteen hand-carved fireplaces and a wide mix of woods, mahogany to walnut, coax guests to feel pampered. Within the decor are other fine details: rugs are Oriental, chandeliers are Austrian-cut crystal, woodwork is hand hewn.

Chef **Ken Hnilo**, a Kendall Culinary School graduate, also sets the bar high with his menu, which changes daily. Winter choices, when we last looked, included Irish organic salmon with seared Canadian foie gras.

Meats are free range. Fish is line caught. Food that is treated with chemicals or genetically modified is avoided. Herbs, when in season, are picked daily from the kitchen garden.

Numerous private and group dining spots exist in the 30-room house, which was built for a millionaire industrialist. The biggest surprise, though, is that the cherry staircase leads to a four-bedroom suite (with kitchen, plus cozy fourth-floor loft). The

TIDBITS

Chef **Ken Hnilo**, who formerly worked at the award-winning Charlie Trotter's in Chicago, occasionally conducts hands-on cooking classes for up to 20 people at Gilbert's. He also periodically presents multicourse tasting events during the restaurant's Women's Weekend getaways.

Owners of Gilbert's are **Ken** and his wife, **Danielle**, plus her parents, **Sherry** and **Dan Mizialko**. The restaurant is named after the son of Ken and Danielle.

•

What was for dinner on New Year's Eve, when we visited? Pickled herring (for good luck!) with micro-cress salad started out every meal. Then came three courses of delectable choices, each matched with wine:

- Organic beef tenderloin tartare with micro-salad, Italian white anchovies and truffle coulis;
- Butter poached lobster with New Zealand white asparagus, lobster risotto and lobster nage;
- Pumpkin cheesecake napoleon with cinnamon panna cotta, chai ice cream and dark cherry compote.

Cost? About $150.

privacy and dynamite views make this a terrific girlfriend getaway for special occasions.

Sherry says it's not unusual for a wedding party to book this Aerie Suite along with the wedding reception.

Gilbert's
327 Wrigley Drive, Lake Geneva
www.gilbertsrestaurant.com
262-248-6680

•

The Red Circle Inn is the oldest restaurant in the state.

NASHOTAH: A Marathon Run

We were glad to head to this town of 1,266 for New Year's Eve, to meet three couples I've known since the 1970s. Our fine dining destination was the homey **Red Circle Inn**, touted as Wisconsin's oldest restaurant.

It was an appropriate match for a group of dear friends who value the history among them.

The Red Circle opened as Nashotah Inn in 1848, which is as long as Wisconsin has been a state. Bavarian immigrant Francis Schraudenbach built this place of respite near the intersection of two burgeoning stagecoach roads in what today is Waukesha County.

About 40 years later, beer baron Frederick Pabst bought the property and changed its name; "red circle" referred to a colorful part of the Pabst brewing trademark. Bar furnishings remain from that era, although the inn burned in 1917.

Today the owners are **Norm Eckstaedt** and **Nico Derni**, who say at least two important business conversations took place at a round table that remains in the main dining room. It reportedly is where the first Milwaukee Road streamliner design was sketched in the 1930s, and where baseball owners in the 1950s agreed to move the Braves from Boston to Milwaukee.

Such history lessons are fine, but is the food any good? Of course. The menu is big on steaks and seafood. One signature entree that also was on the New Year's Eve menu: Beef Wellington Perigourdine, a thick and juicy tenderloin baked in puff pastry.

Expect to pay $20 to $30 for a hearty entree, which includes soup or salad. Staff attention to detail and high-end ingredients make this more of a gourmet dining experience than traditional supper club fare.

The restaurant, which is open only for dinner, is four miles north of I-94 on County C.

Red Circle Inn
N44 W33013 Watertown Plank Road, Nashotah
www.foodspot.com/redcircleinn
262-367-4883
•

Want skates with that order?

OSHKOSH:
Drive-In and Skate Out

Ardy & Ed's Drive-In, within sight of Lake Winnebago and U.S. 45, on the southern outskirts of Oshkosh, has been in business since 1948. A blast of orange signage suggests that it used to be an A&W, which the owners confirm.

Ardy Davis, whose husband, **Ed Timm,** died in 1979, recalls peeling and blanching 100-pound sacks of potatoes. "You'd have to make them every day," she says. French fries remain on the menu, but now they come frozen, bagged and precut.

What makes Ardy and **Steven Davis's** drive-in unusual are the roller-skating carhops. "Their idea," Ardy says, and it came up after the parking lot turned from gravel to blacktop in 1985. The girls, "even the little ones," can deliver seven or eight mugs of root beer at a time, Ardy says, with amazement. It is not unusual for '50s and '60s music to play in the background. Customers can order indoors, too, but the diner-like seating is minimal—and it's more fun to watch the roller queens at work.

"A brat patty—now that's Wisconsin," a friend from Minnesota remarked, when scanning the menu. "And when's the last time you saw a pizza burger at one of these places?" The latter is a burger filled with mozzarella and topped with pizza sauce. Sandwich buns come from **Schoenberger's**, a local and longtime bakery. Ice cream was locally produced, too, until the company was sold to Manitowoc's **Cedar Crest**.

Ardy & Ed's typically is open from March 1 to October 1.

Ardy & Ed's Drive-In
2413 S. Main Street, Oshkosh
www.foodspot.com/ardyandeds,
920-231-5455

•

You can shop for unusual gifts while waiting for your lunch.

PEWAUKEE: Always a Beautiful Day

A couple of blocks from the pretty downtown of this Waukesha County community—where the beach and lakeshore seem to almost touch Woodland Drive—we found a sign that says Welcome to Heaven.

The sign hangs from a wall of a two-story house, whose orange awnings and exterior trim remind us of a Creamsicle. In summer the yard is full of flowers and potted plants that are for sale.

Customers of **It's a Beautiful Day Cafe** take a seat in the shade outside or mosey into a cheery room with pink walls, where a wallboard proclaims: "Today's Special: Acceptance and Love."

Upstairs is a boutique of little luxuries: delicate shawls, fun jewelry, mugs, gifts for yourself or others. Downstairs, a guitar, drum set and music stands have been pushed to one side of the room. They come out on Wednesdays and Fridays, when locals and the occasional touring musician come to perform in early evening.

Folk, jazz, blues, soft rock—it all has found a place here. There is no cover charge; the owners simply pass a hat for donations.

Tasty fare and a colorful restaurant—It's a Beautiful Day Cafe.

The number of coffee drinks rivals the list of food choices. Offerings are neither over-the-top unusual nor predictable. The breakfast parfait contains yogurt, granola and dried cranberries or cherries. The egg sandwich comes with a side of applesauce. Mixedberry french toast can be ordered with a side of Canadian bacon but not bacon strips.

That's just a part of breakfast. Lunch means salads, sandwiches and an occasional soup, if **Deb Aukofer** has time to make it. She, husband **Dan** and daughter **Angie Aukofer-Parker** are the co-owners.

Baked goods represent three generations of women, Dan says. That includes the Italian cookie, a little butter cookie whose recipe comes from Deb's Sicilian grandmother.

It's a Beautiful Day Cafe
316 Oakton Avenue, Pewaukee
www.restaurant.com/beautifulday10
252-691-2233
•

RACINE: CHARTER CHATTER

The Great Lakes Sport Fishing Council lists about 50 charter fishing captains in Wisconsin, plus five clubs for charter fishermen.

Each captain has a specialty, typically salmon and trout, and most home ports are along the 300 miles of Lake Michigan shore. Some operations, like Fishing Charters of Racine, have been around for decades.

"The structure of the lake bottom outside the Racine harbor includes a variation of depths, with three different reefs," say the captains of Fishing Charters. "While constantly on the move with voracious appetites, the fish are attracted by these reefs, which provide good feeding grounds."

The company contends that Wisconsin's southernmost 25 miles of Lake Michigan produce 38 percent of all fish caught on charters in the state.

Racine since 1975 has hosted the annual summer Salmon-a-Rama, which reeled in 750 fishermen from 11 states. In 2007, the name changed to **The Big Fish Bash**, and the 1,521 contestants represented 18 states.

The event is a fishing tournament with more than $100,000 in prizes—plus bands and beer; activities for children; and pool, dart and cribbage tournaments for adults. The 2,780 fish entered in competition weighed a total of 25,202 pounds.

TIDBITS

Walleye Weekend, around since 1978, turns Fond du Lac's Lakeside Park into a big blowout of activity that is capable of amusing all ages along Lake Winnebago. Walleyball is softball, not volleyball. Count on the Lakeside Evening Kiwanis to sell fried walleye fillet sandwiches and dinners that also include potato salad, cole slaw and rye bread.

Why Fond du lac? One of the good corporate citizens is Mercury Marine, the outboard motor and inboard engine manufacturer, which decided to introduce the National Walleye Tournament. The event in 2007 was a live release competition for teams of fishermen, with $13,000 in prizes, paying down to seventy-fifth place. The three-day festival includes the second Sunday in June and typically brings 100,000 visitors to Fond du Lac.

www.fdlfest.com 920-923-6555

SIDE DISH: SKILLET FISH—ITALIAN

1 small onion, sliced
2 tablespoons margarine or butter
1 pound fish fillets
¼ cup lemon juice
½ teaspoon oregano leaves
2 cups sliced zucchini
1 cup sliced fresh mushrooms
½ cup chopped tomato
½ cup shredded swiss cheese

In large skillet, cook onion in margarine or butter until tender. Add fish, lemon juice, oregano, zucchini and mushrooms; cover and simmer 10 minutes. Top with tomato and cheese; cover and simmer 2 minutes, or until cheese melts. Serve immediately. Serves four.
—*Recipe from Fishing Charters of Racine*

SOUTHEAST

How big do they get? In 2007, Michael Troppmann of West Allis caught a 24.4-pound rainbow trout in the boat division. Nathan Radke of Racine brought in a 22.9-pound Chinook salmon while fishing on shore, a near-match for the 23.2-pound Chinook that Steve Monosa of Racine captured while off-shore.

Great Lakes Sport Fishing Council
www.great-lakes.org
•

The Big Fish Bash
second full week of July
www.bigfishbash.com
•

Palate-pleasing plates for the purists at Il Ritrovo.

SHEBOYGAN: The Culinary Edge

Sheboygan is turning into one of the state's culinary heavyweights, and we're not just talking about char-grilled brats. The land of deep fried wonders and thick swirls of butter—on your burger and atop your baked beans—is luring foodies as well as lovers of the lakeshore.

Leading the charge, downtown, is **Stefano Viglietti**, whose **Il Ritrovo** pleases the pizza purists. This casual restaurant is one of the few U.S. members of the Verace Pizza Napoletana Association, which makes Neapolitan pizza in the authentic Italian way. That means several things, including the use of a specific type of Italian tomato, but no tomato sauce.

The restaurateur also operates the more upscale **Trattoria Stefano**, and his fans include *Travel + Leisure* and *Food & Wine* magazines. It is not unusual for clientele to drive from the Fox Valley, or beyond, just for dinner.

Stefano has earned the respect of his competitors in nearby Kohler, which routinely include him as a cooking instructor there.

His presentations are savvy but not pretentious. When talking about having breakfast for dinner, the chef is not lazily flipping eggs, firing up the toaster and

Jeremy Williams presents a luscious cottage pie.

making small talk. He is explaining frittatas and casually suggesting that the average cook could make the eight-egg dish 50 ways.

Stefano has added English cuisine to his repertoire, too. His **Duke of Devon**, reminiscent of neighborhood pubs on Great Britain's Devon Coast, busts stereotypes. The cottage pie, bangers and mash are neither bland nor predictable.

Why England? It is **Jeremy Williams's** homeland, and this native of Great Britain's Devon Coast is Stefano's brother-in-law.

Stefano says he was stunned by the quality of England's food during his first visit to the country. At its best, "I would put it up to any other meal I've had in Italy," he told foodies during a cooking seminar.

The best is what Stefano and his executive chef, **Jason Richardson**, want showcased in Sheboygan. That means using quality, organic and locally produced ingredients in recipes that otherwise appear humble and ordinary.

Diced root vegetables and ground beef are simmered in red wine to make the luscious Cottage Pie, topped with Yukon Gold potatoes, mashed with plenty of butter.

The Ploughman's Lunch contains cheddar, brie and Stilton cheese from England, as well as ham from Berkshire hogs. Also on the menu are curried chicken and vegetables, seafood rolls, steak and mushroom stew.

A half-dozen types of beer from Fuller's, the oldest brewery in Great Britain, are on tap or sold by the bottle.

Duke of Devon
739 Riverfront Drive, Sheboygan
920-458-7900

•

Trattoria Stefano
522 S. Eighth Street, Sheboygan
920-452-8455

TIDBITS

Stefano also operates **Field to Fork**, a downtown Sheboygan market/deli that sells products from Italy and local farmers. **920-694-0322**. It is adjacent to the acclaimed **Il Ritrovo**, 515 S. Eighth Street, **920-803-7516**.

The chef acknowledges that his business challenges are logistics and time. "I'm tired of the phone ringing," he says. "Sometimes things sound good but don't get going. Deep down, I'm a cook and I want to make food. The calls annoy me."

His reference is to the task of communicating with dozens of farmers per week. Although he could do business more easily with just one large-scale food purveyor, Stefano has resisted the temptation, in his effort to patronize the products of local farmers.

Fine local and Italian artisan products fill the sales cases at Field to Fork.

You will be richly rewarded for your search for Majerle's Black River Grill.

SHEBOYGAN: Worth the Hunt

Same city, different direction: Hard-to-find Majerle's Black River Grill on the southern outskirts of Sheboygan puts together a terrific lunch in nice surroundings.

The log cabin is near Kohler-Andrae State Park, and just down the road from the amazing James Tellen Woodland Sculpture Garden; **www.kohlerfoundation.org/ tellen.html**. Garden admission is free.

The Friday special was a perch sandwich, on a toasted hardroll, and a cup of split pea with ham soup—made on the premises. To wash it down, order the Black River Lemonade; strawberry slices and a splash of grenadine add color and flavor.

Majerle's Black River Grill
5033 Evergreen Drive, Sheboygan
www.blackrivergrill.com
920-803-5115
•

Fresh mozzarella is salted at Baker Cheese Factory, near St. Cloud.

A Tasty Guide for Travelers

ST. CLOUD: The Fun Factor

A distinct childhood memory is of a spectacular blaze that I could almost feel from my bedroom window. That was when the Hulls Crossing Cheese Factory burned to the ground, in the early 1960s. It was just one dip in the road away from our farm.

Soon afterward, my dad started hauling milk to **Baker Cheese Factory**, in the town of St. Cloud, a family business surrounded by fields of corn and hay—not far from Eden, the hometown of Milwaukee Brewer retiree Jim Gantner.

Stacked steel cans filled with fresh milk from several dairy farms would fill the little box of a truck that my dad drove. I could never make a full can budge, even during my muscle-building, hay-wagon-unloading teen years.

But sometimes I'd go along for the ride anyway, perfectly useless as a laborer but always mindful that I might get a soda or candy bar from Tony's, a bar across the road from the factory. The heavy cans of milk would be hoisted onto a conveyer of rollers, then dumped into a tank, sent to a sanitizer and reappear magically—hot, clean and ready to restack onto the truck, for exchange with farmers the next day.

The work was all done by hand. Occasionally the empty cans would get clogged or go clanking onto the concrete floor, if a helper (my brother Fred) didn't time it right and stayed a little too long at Tony's. That wouldn't brighten the mood of anybody involved.

It's easy to assess the work and dynamics decades later. At the time, I was a clueless little girl who simply saw the ride as a chance to increase her sugar level and play with the cheesemaker's daughter, **Mary Baker**.

Now we both have entered middle age, and much about life has changed, but Baker Cheese thrives. A fourth generation of the family is involved, and production has grown in many ways.

The factory produced cheddar longhorns, daisies and 80-pound blocks when Frank Baker started the business in 1916. About 15,000 pounds of milk per day were being processed by the 1930s.

Today 1.3 million pounds of milk from about 100 farms arrives daily, and it is converted into mozzarella string cheese, a product that won the company first place in 2007 American Cheese Society competition.

Some of the cheese appears in grocery stores under the Baker Cheese label, but more is private-label work that is shipped nationwide for the country's best-known cheese manufacturers.

"I always had a lot of pride in our company, and what my grandpa (Frank Baker) did," says **Brian Baker**, son of **Dick Baker**, both avidly involved in the business.

This company was the first string cheese manufacturer in Wisconsin, in the late

1970s, and the item remains one of the strongest-selling snack cheeses "because of the fun factor," Brian says.

You can peel strings from the one-ounce sticks of mozzarella because of the cheese's makeup. Think about hot pizza: The mozzarella "stretches" as you break away with the first bite.

"Thirty years ago, string cheese was a novelty," notes Brian. "In the early 1980s, it was a niche market. Now it's a solid market as a snack cheese."

Today Wisconsin has dozens of cheese plants, instead of hundreds, but production has increased. Much of the Baker operation has gone high-tech, too. The cheesemaking system is automated, packaging capabilities have increased, milk receiving and storage stations are enlarged.

Tony's is gone, which likely ensures higher productivity. And those steel cans? They've become flower hold-

Baker was the state's first string cheese manufacturer.

ers and decoupage decor, reminders of harder times and bygone lifestyles.

Baker Cheese contains a small retail outlet that carries cheeses made on the premises and at other factories in the area. String cheese is sold prepackaged or in bulk orders by the pound. Bulk purchases can be arranged as bite-sized nibblets or one-ounce sticks.

To place an order: **920-477-7111**. Cheese and sausage gift box assortments are described online.

Baker Cheese Factory
N5279 Highway G, St. Cloud
www.bakercheese.com
920-477-7871
•

ELSEWHERE IN THE SOUTHEAST

Honey Acres, a five-generation beekeeping business that began in 1852 when C.F. Diehnelt moved to Wisconsin from Germany, is a sweet success on 40 acres at N1557 Highway 67, Ashippun.

Honey of a Museum exhibits teach how beekeeping has changed, how honey is made and how honey is used. The Tower Gift Shop offers samples of honey products and sells many types of honey by the jar and as fruit bars, candy and mustard along with beeswax candles and other items.

www.honeyacres.com 800-558-7745
Admission is free, but groups should make an appointment for tours.

•

Chuck and **Sue Holzwart** in 2000 opened a cafe at their **Whispering Orchards** apple farm, W1650 Highway MM, Cleveland. The place is a big hit, especially during breakfast. The apple pancakes and apple dumplings draw a crowd, and specials sometimes include potato kugel, plum bread french toast, fruit crepes and toppings of peaches and fresh cream.

So it's more than hearty farm fare. The Holzwarts operate farmland formerly owned by Chuck's grandparents. He and Sue started selling apples from their garage and just moved along from there.

On the property are more than 1,300 apple trees, some of which are more than a century old. The family harvests 20 kinds of apples, operates their own cider mill and sells crafts to food and beverage products in a gift shop. A black goat watched from the rooftop of a farm building when we visited. Other critters can be fed and photographed.

Most diners take an upstairs table, and the servers get a good workout, since the kitchen is downstairs. Expect taxidermy, too: the collection includes a black bear, peacock, red fox and beaver.

920-693-8584

•

The **Fireside Dinner Theatre**, 1131 Janesville Avenue, Fort Atkinson, started out as a pyramid-shaped restaurant in a cornfield in 1964, and its reputation for fine dining prompted a quadrupling in size by 1972.

Since 1978 the destination is a much-loved showstopper, too, capable of accommodating several thousands of guests per week. Many come for a filling buffet (or plated meal with gourmet flair) and feel-good entertainment. Professional actors, singers and dancers—many from New York—audition for the productions, which range from the comedy *Barefoot in the Park* to Christian, holiday and

Broadway-name musicals.

Also at the Fireside are five shopping boutiques, selling everything from fresh bakery to imaginative gifts for gardeners.

www.firesidetheatre.com 800-477-9505

•

Wisconsin is best known for its German heritage, but the Racine area is home to one of the nation's largest Danish enclaves. These families have helped popularize the kringle, a flakey and oval pastry that is filled, typically with fruit preserves, nuts, cream cheese or chocolate.

No one in Wisconsin makes more kringle than **O&H Danish Bakery**, which immigrant **Christian Olesen** started in 1949. Today it's a fourth generation family business that includes a Kringle of the Month Club.

The 12 flavors in 2008—cream cheese, black forest, maple walnut, turtle, blueberry, cinnamon roll, raspberry, almond, apple, pumpkin caramel, cranberry and pecan—represent less than one-half of the kringle combinations that O&H produces. Choices vary a bit each year.

"We come up with new flavors and let our customers taste-test them," says Eric Olesen, a third-generation co-owner with brothers Michael and Dale. Key lime, introduced in 2004, has since become a popular seasonal product, sold in July. Mango didn't go over, "probably because we're in Wisconsin."

O&H sells more than 2 million kringle per year. Production is a three-day process, done by hand. The dough rests overnight, twice, before baking.

"When people are faced with a decision about what they want to put in their mouth or spend their money on, they're going to make sure there is value in it," Eric says. "We work very hard in our bakery, making products that focus on quality."

www.ohdanishbakery.com 800-709-4009

•

"Upper crust" refers to the top of a hierarchy, but in Watertown everybody has access to the **Upper Krust Pie Shop**, 1300 Memorial Drive, for sweet and savory fare.

Dozens of dessert pies, Amish Custard to Very Berry Rhubarb, can be ordered by the full size or as "minis" that are shipped in sets of three. At the restaurant, you can try 'em by the slice—an appropriate way to end a meal of quiche or pot pie.

Too much? Angel food cake with raspberry sauce is another dessert option. So the menu isn't all about pie, but that's what makes this stop unusual. It seems like anything you're hankering for that involves a flakey crust is possible here, especially if you order it at least one day in advance.

www.upperkrustpieshop.com 920-206-9202

•

Belly Flops, when you're shopping, are misshapen jelly beans that are sold at a deep discount at the **Jelly Belly Center**, 10100 Jelly Belly Lane, Pleasant Prairie. A gift shop is inside of the candy manufacturer's warehouse distribution center.

Free tours occur daily, except on major holidays. Visitors can sample sweets before they buy. The Jelly Belly, which comes in 50 flavors, is but one of 100-plus candies made by Jelly Belly Candy Company.

www.jellybelly.com 866-868-7522. The warehouse, located at the intersection of Highways 31 and 165, is near I-94 in Kenosha County.

Belly flops at the swimming pool were never so fun as these.

Simce 1941, Miesfeld's has given brat lovers a reason to fire up the grill.

ROAD TRIP: Packing a Great Picnic in Sheboygan

Sometimes it's better to be alone, you know? Take a hike, pick a park and picnic table, to vanish from life as you know it from 9 to 5.

The perfect picnic, in Sheboygan, requires more than one-stop shopping. So make your list, and don't forget the charcoal for the grill, hey?

1. Start out at the **Miesfeld's Triangle Market**, 4811 Venture Drive, the only meat market we know of that has a drive-up window. Efficient and high-quality, but typically shadowed by brat giant Johnsonville, which cranks out sausage just a few miles west.

The brats have earned top State Fair honors, but offbeat alternatives include garlic brats, jalapeno brats, chicken brats, Cajun brats and no-salt brats. Want to go cold? Buy a snack bologna or summer sausage. And don't forget the cheese; the assortment is fine. **www.miesfelds.com** 920-565-6328

2. Next stop is the **Charcoal Inn**, 1637 Geele Avenue or 1313 W. Eighth Street, which produces a potato salad worth bragging about, and the portions are generous. A single order is enough for two, usually. May as well add an order of baked beans, delivered with a dollop of butter swimming on the top. We love butter in Sheboygan! 920-458-1147 or 920-458-6988

3. Don't forget the bread. City Bakery, 1102 Michigan Avenue, wins the "best of" voting for hardroll, which isn't a lightweight category of competition in this city. The bun is fresh but slightly chewy, and a crucial part of the grilled meat sandwich ensemble.

Pick up a long john or cruller, why don't you—as a treat for slogging through all this shopping? 920-457-4493

4. Add a refresher. Z-Spot Espresso & Coffee, 1024 Indiana Avenue, presents all-natural fruit smoothies to temper the heat. Make mine a Hawaiian Vacation, one-half pound of pineapple, bananas and mango, plus yogurt and apple juice. www.zspotespresso.com 920-4576-6690

5. Sample a dessert. Gosse's, 1909 Union Avenue, can provide a nice square of torte for dessert, and there likely will be several choices—poppyseed to banana split. Expect a graham cracker crust, topped with a cream cheese/whipped topping combo. From there, anything goes. 920-457-8696

6. Cheese please. Gibbsville Cheese Co., W2663 Highway OO, Sheboygan Falls, is a short drive to a sleepy town and a family-run factory that has produced tasty cheddars, Colby, pepper cheese and curds for decades. The cheesemakers used to be the sales clerks, too. Best buy for the adventurous: mystery cheese.

Don't visit the retail outlet from June to August; no cheese is made then. www.gibbsvillecheese.com 920-564-3242

7. To simplify, head to **Woodlake Market**, 795 Woodlake Road, Kohler, for the widest variety of upscale and down-home foods and beverages around. It is appetizing, one-stop shopping and a part of the **Shops at Woodlake**, near the American Club. www.destinationkohler.com 920-457-6570

8. Prime picnic locale: Kohler-Andrae State Park, 1020 Beach Park Lane, Sheboygan, on Lake Michigan. Just don't let the sand from the dunes season your meal. www.dnr.state.wi.us 920-451-4080

9. Too full to stagger home? Rates at the **Harbor Winds Hotel**, 905 S. Eighth Street, Sheboygan, are reasonable. Walk the boardwalk along nearby Lake Michigan for exercise. www.stayinsheboygan.com 920-452-9000

A time-honored Wisconsin tradition: the Friday night fish fry (which is typically cod)

TELL ME ABOUT: Fish

A significant percentage of lake perch served at fish fries comes from Europe or Asia, says a researcher at the University of Toledo, and this is a part of what fuels UW-Milwaukee's work to raise yellow perch in a controlled environment.

The challenge is to "keep the product authentic but enable the commercial production of it," says J. Val Klump, director of the Great Lakes Wisconsin Aquatic Technology and Environmental Research (WATER) Institute.

"The yellow perch market tends to be insatiable," he says. "If we can find a way to produce them, the demand will be there."

The Lake Michigan perch population took a nosedive in the 1990s, dropping 95 percent from its high of 24 million. Zebra mussels, other invasive species, lake current changes and overfishing accounted for the change.

No commercial fishing of perch is allowed on Lake Michigan, says William Horns, Great Lakes fisheries specialist at the DNR. The Green Bay and Lake Michigan perch populations are considered separate, he adds, for purposes of management and because ecosystems are different.

Val predicts more than half of the fish we eat will be raised in controlled environments in 20 years, as a response to the anticipated collapse of the world's seafood population by 2048 and heightened concerns about world security issues.

"Much of what seafood we eat is imported," says Fred Binkowski, senior scientist. "We don't know where it's growing, what it's eating" or what additives may be introduced into the diet.

•

Milwaukee's WATER Institute raises and studies yellow perch from North Carolina, Chesapeake Bay and Lake Winnebago. Each stock is kept separate, to maintain genetic integrity, but there also is cross-breeding, to produce yellow perch that are fast-growing and more disease-resistant.

The researchers are able to raise yellow perch to market size in 12 months, roughly one-half the time that is typical. The 14,000 yellow perch so far raised to market size at the WATER Institute tend to head to **Schwarz Fish Company** in Sheboygan, for filleting and sale. The WATER Institute has been known to keep a stash, too, for serving the occasional dignitary.

Great Lakes WATER Institute
www.glwi.uwm.edu
414-382-1700

•

TIDBITS

Consider the makeup and mutation of a long-lived Wisconsin tradition: the Friday night fish fry. The fish most likely is cod, caught thousands of miles away, not lake perch or bluegill. It is a fish that marine biologists worry could become extinct in 10 or 20 years, if overfishing and methods of fishing do not change.

Only 10 percent of the world's supply of large predator fish—which includes cod—remains.

Americans are eating more seafood because of the reputed health benefits. About 80 percent of the seafood we eat is imported. In this part of the Midwest, about 75 percent of the fish we eat are ocean species (orange roughy, Atlantic cod, haddock). Orange roughy, a long-lived species, is in severe decline because the fish are caught before they have reached reproductive maturity. Sharks, groupers, Chilean sea bass, imported shrimp, farmed salmon, and many species of tuna are critically endangered because they are overfished.

More fish are caught than can be replaced, the National Environmental Trust and others have concluded. That is partly because fishing vessels have become high powered, with onboard refrigeration and sonar technology. Fishing cables that are miles long contain thousands of baited hooks.

So although it is easier to find fish and catch them, about 20-25 percent of every commercial catch is discarded because the fisherman doesn't have a license to keep it, or it has no great sales value. This "by-catch" is thrown overboard, the fish dead and dying. Other animals get caught in the nets as well. As a result, the fish supply dwindles and the ocean habitat gets knocked around, putting ecosystems—close to home, as well as far away—at risk. Because waterways are interconnected, there is a domino effect.

Conserve Our Ocean Legacy, a nonprofit environmental campaign, blames overfishing, pollution and the proliferation of invasive species (alewives, sea lampreys) for the depletion of fish in the Great Lakes. "We need to prevent the same disaster in our oceans," the literature says.

Wisconsin Department of Natural Resource's Bill Horns says Lake Michigan "is dramatically different than it used to be," and he mentions 160 new and exotic species of lake life, which have changed the dynamics of the environment. A success story is the whitefish population, which nose-dived in the late 1950s but hit a record high 40 years later. Salmon stocking also has worked well, Bill says.

"But we haven't restored the lake trout, after 50 years of trying," he acknowledges, noting the fish's abundance in the early 1800s. The amount of natural production, versus stocking from fisheries, is slight.

He is optimistic about the future of lake perch, saying the population probably will bounce back "at some point," but notes that—even in the best of times—Wisconsin imported more of the fish than it caught. Most of the freshwater perch has come from Lake Erie, he says, and that ecosystem is a lot different from Lake Michigan's.

•

You can get a wallet-sized card from the Blue Ocean Institute that lists "ocean-friendly" fish caught sustainably. It also rates different species by their healthiness for consumers, that is, which species are of concern because of contaminates like mercury, heavy metals and pcbs.

For more on sustainable fishing: **www.blueocean.org/seafood**

MILWAUKEE:
Ethiopian Influence

"I like to cook, and when I cook, it is good."

That is how **Mulu Hailu Habtesilassie** sums up her work at **Alem Ethiopian Village**, one of downtown Milwaukee's newest ethnic alternatives. She and brother-in-law **Zerihun Bekele** are working a little magic inside of a former Latino cafe.

While customers wait for dinner, they learn about the proprietors' native land, which is the oldest independent country in Africa and one of the world's oldest nations. Ethiopian photos and indigenous crafts—basketry and wall weavings, tell part of the story.

Then comes the food—tender from slow cooking, with exotic spices that tantalize and surprise.

Sarabjeet of Uganda serves injera to scoop up traditional fare at Alem Ethiopian Village.

Sometimes the flavor is cardamom, garlic, ginger, onion—or a mysterious blend that Mulu brings from her homeland excursions, or buys from a relative who operates a spice shop in Minneapolis.

"It is good, healthy food," she says. "Much comes from organic stores," and the dishes are traditional, family recipes—like *yebeg alitcha*, a lamb stew, and *yemiser wot*, lentils that simmer in a red pepper sauce.

"Pepper" typically means rich flavor, not tongue-burning heat. Entrees arrive on communal platters, with the spongy injera flatbread used to scoop up food in lieu of silverware.

First-timers should consider the combination platters, which allow sampling of four or five entrees for one price. It is unusual for a dinner to exceed $12, and lunch fare is even less expensive. So the meal is a deal, especially in downtown Milwaukee.

"I cook like I am going to eat it," Mulu says, with a laugh. She moved to Wisconsin

Mulu Hailu Habtesilassie cooks with a tantalizing mix of spices.

in 2003, to join family and friends here, then married Solomon Habtesilassie. They were a good match because of, among other things, Mulu's love of cooking and Solomon's desire to open a restaurant.

The latter actually was his mother's dream, but she became ill and died in 2005. Her name? Alem, just like the restaurant.

This is a modest business with hope and passion but not extraordinary financial means. Business comes as a response to flyers that are posted around town and word-of-mouth advertising from satisfied customers.

About one year before the introduction of Alem, friends opened the **Ethiopian Cottage** at 1824 N. Farwell Street, on Milwaukee's east side. For more: **414-224-5226**.

Mulu is glad to share those details; the friendship is of more value than the competition.

Alem Ethiopian Village
307 E. Wisconsin Avenue, Milwaukee
414-224-5324
•

MILWAUKEE: Old World Third

Old World Third Street—the city's first German retail district, on a cobblestone street, with a mix of architectural styles—is rich with ethnic diversity and pride of Wisconsin heritage. For example:

Old German Beer Hall, patterned after the Hoffbrauhaus in Munich, serves Bavarian beers and food (think casual, like warm and soft, German-style pretzels). Best novelty: the Shot-Ski, five shot glasses affixed to a ski; five people try to down an anise-like Killepitsch, or other liquor, in unison. 1009 N. Old World Third Street. **www.oldgermanbeerhall.com 414-226-2728**

•

Milwaukee Brat House, new as of spring 2008, specializes in sausage sandwiches, including bratwurst, and cheese platters. "We are military veterans, patriots, New Yorkers, free masons and Irish boxers," a Craig's List employment ad stated. "Do you fit in?" 1013 N. Old World Third Street. **www.milwaukeebrathouse.com**

•

Usinger's has manufactured sausage since 1880. There is nothing fancy about the sausage shop, which is a part of the charm, and wall murals show the jolly elves hard at work (they are, elsewhere in the building). Product variety will make you smile and wonder (can you say "mettwurst" and "kishka"?). Price discounts likely. 1030 N. Old World Third Street. **www.usinger.com 800-558-9998**

•

The Spice House, a second-generation family business, began in 1957. Spices from around the world are ground and blended by hand and in small batches. Check out the Milwaukee Iron Seasoning—with garlic, various chilies and more—created to honor Harley Davidson's ninety-fifth birthday. 1031 N. Old World Third Street. **www.thespicehouse.com 888-488-0977**

•

Tutto means "everything" in Italian. Expect a fusion between Italian and American cuisine: fries with Parmesan, calamari with a sweet sauce of sesame. The restaurant-bar emits a classy vibe, regardless of whether the TV screens show the Super Bowl or Academy Awards. 1033 N. Old World Third Street. **www.tuttomilwaukee.com 414-291-5600**

•

Mader's opened in 1902 and has earned many accolades during its first century: most famous German restaurant on the continent, world's largest store of Hummels (see the second story gallery). Entrees include pork shank, rouladen, schnitzels. The sauerbraten is marinated ten days before roasting. 1041 N. Old World Third Street. **www.madersrestaurant.com 414-271-3377**

Old World Third Street offers plenty of European—and Wisconsin—flavor.

The **Chocolate Tree** sells bulk chocolate made at **Ambrosia Chocolate Company**, in business in Milwaukee since 1894, but now an Archer Daniels Midland subsidiary. The products are a good match for bakers and candy makers, although fudge and other ready-to-eat treats also are sold. 1048 N. Old World Third Street. **414-271-3371**

•

Wisconsin Cheese Mart is a specialty cheese store in the neighborhood. Much of the merchandise comes from cheesemakers around the state. In the mart's Old World Third Street Basket are cheeses as well as products from some of the aforementioned businesses. 215 W. Highland Avenue. **www.wisconsincheesemart.com 888-482-7700**

•

One of our all-time Milwaukee favorites in this vicinity is the **Calderone Club**, 842 N. Old World Third Street, a longtime family business that serves scrumptious Italian food at reasonable prices. We've loved the gigantic, crispy-thin pizzas ever since we had our first bite in the 1970s. **414-273-3236**

For more about all of these places: **www.oldworldthird.org**

Breakfast can be imaginative as well as hearty and delicious at Heinemann's.

MILWAUKEE: How Times Change

Here is how the Milwaukee news story began:

"There are times when some men are simply dazzled by women.

"And there also are times when many men enjoy watching them, pinching, tickling or otherwise doing their best to charm them right out of their wits.

"Without fear of contradiction, in fact, it can be stated that most all men like women. At any hour of the day or night, too.

"Sad, but true, however, is the fact that there are exceptions.

"For example, how about at lunch during the peak of the Thursday rush in the men's grill at **Heinemann's** restaurant downtown?

" 'The answer is no, absolutely no,' said **Thomas Burns**, the president of the restaurant chain, when six women—two of them with their children—plunked themselves down in booths normally reserved for men."

The restaurateur, a son-in-law of the founders, went on to declare the infiltrators as "blatant militants," "trash" and "fascists."

Heinemann's opened as a candy store in 1923, morphed to include bakery, then became a restaurant. For 40 years it had a men's-only grill at 102 E. Wisconsin Ave. (until a successful women's rights court challenge in the 1970s). That high-profile location no longer is a Heinemann's, but there is one only three blocks away, at 411 E. Wisconsin.

Times have changed for the better, and the bright and cheerful Heinemann's chain today is welcoming and busy. It is not unusual to wait for a table on weekends; locals especially love the breakfasts.

On that menu are attractive items that aren't over-the-top. We've tried the grilled coffee cake (with cinnamon, raisins), cranberry pancakes (oatmeal and triple berry are other eye-catching choices), and eggs and asparagus (on toast, with hollandaise).

Creativity shows up elsewhere, too, as in the Strawberry Health Shake, which blends strawberry banana yogurt, bananas and orange juice. Worth a visit is the website, just for the daily bakery schedule. The goods—Apple Raisin Bread to 5-Chip Cookies—are made at a central Heinemann's commissary.

A fourth generation is involved in management at Heinemann's, so it's likely to continue as a family business, and that's a very good thing.

Heinemann's Restaurants
www.heinemannsrestaurants.com
•

333 W. Brown Deer Road, Fox Point
414-352-2244
•

317 N. 76th Street, Milwaukee
414-258-6800
•

411 E. Wisconsin Avenue, Milwaukee
414-224-7800
•

18000 W. Bluemound Road, Brookfield
262-792-1500
•

5601 Broad Street, Greendale
414-423-6200
•

2717 N. Mayfair Road, Wauwatosa
414-774-5200
•

Wendell McLester and granddaughter Lauren McLester-Davis enjoy fresh frybread.

MILWAUKEE: HISTORY LESSONS

The easiest food to find, during Milwaukee's annual Indian Summer Festival, is one with a versatile set of uses but a heartbreaking history.

Indian frybread—puffy and sometimes slightly sweet—works as a dessert (with cinnamon-sugar), holds a meal (like a sandwich) and suffices as a dip for sauces (like a tortilla). It is best when eaten freshly fried.

The addition of beans, meat and cheese—served openface—turns the bread into Indian tacos.

The frybread has Navajo roots, although many other tribes have adopted it as their own. It is a symbol of survival and captivity, invented when Native Americans were forced onto reservations in the 1800s.

The makings for frybread—powdered milk, baking powder, lard, flour, salt and sugar—were among the few foods within reach of the hungry. So tribes used these meager government rations and found a way to put them to good use.

The **Indian Summer Festival**, with a gorgeous Lake Michigan shoreline as its backdrop, celebrates and explains the diversity and commonalities of Native American culture in Wisconsin.

Authentic tribal villages are re-created. Storytellers share wisdom and lore. The festive and sacred, traditional and contemporary blend as one event that educates while it entertains. Participants wear authentic, colorful costumes as they dance, pray, explain their heritage and demonstrate artistic skills.

Cultural areas are considered sacred, so no alcohol is served within designated parts of the festival grounds.

Food vendors have names like **Frybread Express, Spring Creek Bison, Turkey Tee Pee** and **Whitefeather**. Look for wild rice in soups and casseroles and sold uncooked by the pound. Hull corn soup, buffalo jerky, venison brats and walleye filet sandwiches are other choices that are atypical for a festival setting.

Indian Summer Festival
Henry A. Maier Festival Park, Milwaukee
first weekend in September
www.indiansummer.org
414-604-1000
•

There's plenty of color and pagentry as well as wonderful native foods at Milwaukee's Indian Summer Festival.

MILWAUKEE AREA

TIDBITS

Indian Summer Festivals Inc. also presents the **Winter Pow Wow** in early March at Wisconsin State Fair Park, West Allis. Activities are similar to the summer event, but they occur in a smaller setting indoors.

•

Milwaukee calls itself the City of Festivals, for good reason.

A series of summer ethnic and specialty festivals shows off a wide tapestry of cultures—just as Summerfest, the world's largest music festival, embraces a diversity of music styles for 11 days (including the Fourth of July. **www.summerfest.com**

All events, typically on a Thursday through Sunday, occur at the lakeside Maier Festival Park. Some are the largest of their kind in the nation, if not the continent. In the lineup are:

- **PrideFest** (for the gay, lesbian, bisexual and transgender communities), June, **www.pridefest.com**

- **Polish Fest**, June, **www.polishfest.org**

- **Festa Italiana**, July, **www.festaitaliana.com**

- **German Fest**, July, **www.germanfest.com**

- **African World Festival**, August

- **Arab World Fest**, August, **www.arabworldfest.com**

- **Irish Fest, August, www.irishfest.com**

- **Mexican Fiesta**, August, **www.mexicanfiesta.org**

For more about other Milwaukee festivals: **www.milwaukee.org** **800-554-1448**

MILWAUKEE: The Chef's Choice

The conversation begins like this: "My daughter-in-law is the one who cried as she ate her scallops here. Really."

It is a sincere, gushing compliment and the chef, **Sanford "Sandy" D'Amato**, murmurs something we can't hear. No one is going to announce to you that he and wife Angie own the place. They mingle casually with customers. Quality of food and service has long been among the best in the nation.

Sanford Restaurant was the family grocery store for 80 years. It's also the building where the chef was born, and the D'Amatos live across the street from where they work. The area feels more like a neighborhood than urban hub.

"You kind of learn your path as you go along," Sandy says, as he nears 40 years of work in restaurants. "I'm really happy with the path I took. When I moved back to the Midwest, it was to open a restaurant" because work in New York City convinced him it would be too expensive of a proposition there.

So Sandy has been in charge of the cooking, Angie runs the front of the house and the James Beard Foundation recognizes the work of both. Sanford in 2008 was a semifinalist for Outstanding Service in the Beard awards (the Oscars of the restaurant biz), and Sandy was an Outstanding Chef semifinalist (the top award bestowed to a chef nationwide).

It's far from the chef's first accolade. Sandy won Beard's Best Chef Midwest in 1996 and has previously been a semi-finalist for the national honor.

Good service, he says, "is something you should never feel conscious of —it shouldn't be something that hits you in the face." He compares it to watching a great movie, then trying to figure out what made it so. "Was it the wine? The dessert? No, it was everything."

Sanford is due for a change in appearance, he says, something he and

Sanford's presents a buttery cranberry-walnut tart.

Angie undertake every eight or nine years. Extreme changes are not what this is about, because it will always be important for the restaurant to feel like home, in spirit.

"We want it all to fit in with our food and service," Sandy says. "Welcoming, comfortable—yet feeling that you've gone to another place."

The little black dresses and dark coats and ties, which customers tend to wear, work well against the white walls. A narrow passageway, which leads to the restrooms, passes the small kitchen, where staff can be seen diligently at work.

At your table, lift a delicate silver bell, to discover the butter underneath. Containers of long, slender breadsticks suggest artistry as well as sustenance.

"The restaurant is entertainment," Sandy observes, "and you're only as good as your last show." The chef is speaking of food quality and leisurely pacing, not theatrics or pretense. Dinner easily lasts two hours.

Cooking with fresh ingredients of the season is Sanford's priority, so we choose the four-course seasonal menu ($49) when dining in winter.

The order for dessert is taken first because from-scratch preparation takes time. We select a cranberry-walnut tart with buttery crust and butter pecan ice cream. The entree? Grilled organic king salmon, served on scalded rapini (like a leafy broccoli), with saffron lima bean broth.

It's all good, so good.

The second entrée at our table is—what else!—grilled scallops, which arrive firm, plump and flavorful. We don't cry, but we think about it and instead end up with grins.

Sanford Restaurant
1547 N. Jackson Street, Milwaukee
www.sanfordrestaurant.com
414-276-9608

•

TIDBITS

Ten years after the 1989 opening of **Sanford Restaurant**, Angie and Sandy introduced the more casual **Coquette Café**, 316 N. Milwaukee Street, in the city's Third Ward, a district of boutiques and entertainment.

Dream Dance serves "new Wisconsin cuisine."

French ale washes down flatbread pizza topped with smoked salmon, house-made sausage, tapinades and fresh cheeses. Expect the extraordinary elsewhere on the menu, like the Danish meat patty, topped with picked beets and marinated cucumber, or the leg of lamb sandwich.

Newest is the D'Amatos' **Harlequin Sweet & Savory Bake Shop**, at the same address as Coquette. "The only thing we didn't make [at Sanford] was our bread, so that's how [the bakery concept] started," Sandy says.

A morning specialty is warm buttermilk doughnuts, with raspberry filling. For lunch: a Usinger's all-beef hot dog in a seeded egg bun. French pastries, artisan breads, soups and sandwiches are handmade, on the premises.

www.harlequinbakery.com, **414-291-9866**
www.coquettecafe.com, **414-291-2655**

•

Six Wisconsin restaurateurs were among the 20 semifinalists for Best Chef Midwest in the 2008 James Beard Foundation Awards competition.

They are **Tami Lax** of **Harvest**, Madison; **Shinji Muramoto** of **Restaurant Muramoto**, Madison; **Jason Gorman** of **Dream Dance**, Milwaukee; **Adam Siegel** of **Bartolotta's Lake Park Bistro**, Milwaukee; **Thomas Peschong** of **The Riversite**, Mequon; and **Jim Webster** of **Wild Rice**, Bayfield.

U.S. Senator Kohl is a longtime fan of Branko Radicevic's restaurant.

MILWAUKEE: An American Classic

"My buddy," explains the solo diner, after finishing an early supper. The restaurateur grins and puts on his trademark beret, then poses for the camera with his friend.

Branko Radicevic has no need to advertise what his family serves at **Three Brothers**, a Serbian restaurant in Milwaukee's Bay View neighborhood. Recipes have withstood time: some are more than 200 years old. Meals are not rushed: the *burek*, a buttery phyllo dough pie, may take an hour to prepare. Customers, including this one—**U.S. Senator Herb Kohl**—are loyal.

"One of my favorite places," says Herb, an unassuming presence at a quiet corner table. He has eaten here for at least 30 years and says he prefers burek with a cheese filling. It also can be made with beef or spinach/cheese, and each pie is enough to feed two hungry people.

Our country has no shortage of exceptional restaurants, but few earn the rank of "classic" from the James Beard Foundation, which since 1997 has acknowledged the culinary excellence of longtime, family-owned enterprises.

Only four to eight businesses per year earn an America's Classics award, and

Three Brothers is the only honoree—so far—in Wisconsin. Branko earned the award in 2002, and you can find it on a wall at the restaurant, if you look diligently.

Meals arrive on china, but few pieces match. Tabletops are an ordinary kitchen laminate. On a wall, behind the bar, is a faded mural of the Grand Tetons, artwork that predates the restaurant. Three Brothers is in its third generation of family ownership, in business since 1950.

"Quality is not achieved through haste," notes the restaurant menu. Among the other entree choices: *chevap chi chi* (a Serbian beef sausage) and *sarma* (pickled cabbage leaves filled with beef and rice).

"Roast leg of lamb is a newer recipe," Branko says. "We used to do the whole lamb, but people said it was too greasy."

He describes Serbian cuisine as simple: just a few ingredients of high quality, with a smart use of spices such as paprika, black pepper, saffron.

Someone from the family always cooks. Tonight it is his wife, Patricia. Branko, in his eighties, trims the meat and buys the produce, "but only after I see it."

His father, a wholesale wine merchant in Yugoslavia, landed in a German concentration camp during World War II and later fled to the U.S. The restaurant name reflects the hope that his three sons would join him.

Branko arrived in 1959 and was an international banker on the East Coast until his father became ill. "By cultural tradition, the eldest son takes over," he explains. The restaurant's upstairs has been his home for more than 30 years. A son and one of three daughters also help run the business.

Three Brothers is open only for dinner. Most entrees are under $20.

Three Brothers
2414 S. Street Clair Street, Milwaukee
414-481-7530

•

For more about the America's Classics awards, consult **www.jamesbeard.org**. James Beard was a celebrated chef, food writer and culinary mentor who died in 1985.

TIDBITS

Within Milwaukee's Bay View neighborhood is an endearing enclave of fiercely independent businesses that define and sustain the area. Two are named **DeMarinis**. Italian food, same family, sore subject, and we don't care to go into the details here. Let's just say that the feud goes back to the mid-1990s, when brothers **Dom** and **Phil** opened their own restaurant, around the block from the original DeMarinis.

Dom and **Phil's DeMarinis**, 1211 E. Conway Street, has a beautiful view of downtown Milwaukee. With big bay windows and the outdoor patio, seating is prime for watching the fireworks that accompany Milwaukee's summer lakefront festivals.

Now a third generation (sisters Lucia and Anna-Maria, in their thirties) has gotten involved in the sit-down restaurant, known for its thin-crust pizza, Italian sauce and sausage sandwiches ("not as much of a fennel, black licorice flavor" in the sausage).

The original restaurant is **Mama DeMarinis**, 2457 S. Wentworth Avenue, a corner bar whose Italian offerings include traditional and vegan choices. That includes vegan pizza, with vegan sausage and vegan cheese. This DeMarinis is run by **Rosie** and **Josie**, sisters of Dom and Phil.

"I haven't spoken to them since 1996," Lucia, daughter of Phil, says of her aunts. She acknowledges the novelty of having two restaurants with the same family name in such close proximity.

"A lot of people just like to see the difference between the two of us," she says. "It's a conversation piece."

Although Dom died in 2003, his name stays on the business, and Phil says his sisters came the funeral. "He was more easy-going than I was," Phil says. "He made amends."

A one-hour wait for seating is not unusual at either location, and both may remind you of *Cheers*. There are deep loyalties, friendships and, yes, rivalries.

414-481-1770 (**Mama**) and 414-481-2348 (**Dom** and **Phil**)

Also a short walk away: **G. Groppi Food Market**, 1441 E. Russell Avenue, which sells imported and domestic specialty foods, especially Italian meats and pastas. Order a hot panini sandwich; you won't be disappointed.

The promise "Original Store—Original Italian Sausage Recipe" refers to longevity of business and tradition. The market has been around since

The deli is delectable at G. Groppi's Food Market.

1910 and today is owned by **Nehring's Family Markets**.

Most significant is its namesake. **Giocondo** and **Giorgina Groppi** used to just sell fresh produce from their home. Then came the sausage recipe and bigger market inventory.

Groppi's was known as a place to talk politics as well as buy fresh mozzarella. The owners' twelve children included Father James Groppi, the rambunctious civil rights leader and Catholic priest (until he married activist Margaret Rozga in 1976).

Siblings **Louis** and **Tom Groppi** kept the family market in operation until 2002, when they tired of competing with bigger supermarkets. The Nehrings, whose other specialty stories include **Sendik's** in Shorewood, took over ownership in 2003.

www.ggroppifoodmarket.com 414-747-9012

MILWAUKEE:
Two for Tea?

Watt's Tea Room features very civilized plates of finger sandwiches, desserts, and tea.

I am in downtown Milwaukee, "taking tea," and doing a miserable job of it. An attractive, two-piece, antique tea strainer reveals my ignorance about how to keep the teapot's tea leaves out of the teacup.

A woeful confession that I am a dope doesn't faze my server, who demurely ignored my stubborn struggle until I asked for assistance. "It happens all the time," she says, breezily. "Let me get you another cup." Which she does, and the afternoon tea resumes without incident.

Delicate finger sandwiches—a peppery cucumber, a spread of chopped olives, tuna and chicken salads—arrive with a pot of Evening in Missoula, an herbal blend that includes chamomile, wild cherry bark, red clover and star anise. Fruity blends, blacks and a green are other tea choices.

Next comes a delicate selection of sweets: a cranberry scone, chocolate truffle torte and slice of Sunshine Cake. The cake is the signature dessert that has been made here, from the same recipe, for more than 100 years. It tastes wonderfully light, with a slightly citrus French custard filling and boiled, whipped frosting.

There is something nostalgic about the cake, the relaxed pace, the graciousness of staff and the harpist's gentle background music. **Watts Tea Room**, on the second floor of a downtown Milwaukee shop that since 1870 has specialized in fine tabletop products, harkens to a time when quiet conversation and leisurely dining were commonplace and valued.

Especially when shopping. Long gone are most department store restaurants, where friends could break up the day and compare purchases over lunch or a cup of something hot, especially on a wintry day.

Also exceeding rare, and sometimes less revered, is the restaurant that preserves its past instead of reinventing itself through trends. The Sunshine Cake is one example. Another is the English muffins, made from scratch with buttermilk daily, and shipped overnight to adoring fans as far away as New York City. The muffins are on the breakfast menu.

"The whole concept of shopping, then breaking away to take a breath, has changed," laments **Chrisanne Robertson**, vice president and fine crystal buyer at **George Watts & Son**. She also is a watercolorist with degrees in art history and printmaking.

Chrisanne in 1974 visited Watts Tea Room for the first time, after her family moved to Milwaukee from Los Angeles. She was in her early teens and already had developed a taste for sophistication and elegance.

Within ten years, she was working for George Watts, an employer whom she describes as "extremely approachable" but having "a larger-than-life personality."

The proprietor, who died in 2005, was accustomed to speaking his mind, even when it was unpopular. He hired and promoted African-Americans as his salesmen in the 1940s, lashed out against McCarthyism in the 1950s, campaigned unsuccessfully to run against Governor Tony Earl, and collected 44 percent of the vote when running against Milwaukee Mayor John Norquist in 2000.

But her boss also learned to bend as times changed. He added wines to the tearoom menu, even though he was a Christian Scientist and did not drink alcohol. The shop, which specializes in "some of the fine museum pieces of the future," also carries Fair Trade merchandise and supports the work of emerging local artists.

It is an effort to unite the world, acknowledge traditions and maintain respect for the world's finest china, crystal and other tableware, much of it handmade. Wedgewood, Waterford, Lenox, SteubenGlass, Royal Worcester, Swarovski and Moser are a few of the product lines.

"We like the ambiance," says Darlene Jirikowic of Milwaukee, while finishing lunch with her mother, Grace Jirikowic, of Bayfield, and preschool son Riley. Darlene has been coming to the tearoom since her oldest child, now an adult, was a toddler.

"I have always been treated very well here, no matter how young my children have been," she says.

For Chrisanne, it's all a matter of identifying and celebrating the planet's uniqueness. "When I travel," she says, "I seek that which is different. It's exceedingly rare to see something other than the homogenized" businesses and "canned strip mall experience" that can be found just about anywhere.

George Watts & Son, Inc.
761 N. Jefferson Street, Milwaukee
www.georgewatts.com
800-747-9288

•

Three generations have made the holidays sweet and nutty at Quality Candy.

ST. FRANCIS:
Sweet Success

There is time to shop before I meet **Margaret Gile**, so I eye her merchandise and decide which extra calories should go home with me. It is not an easy decision, but I eventually get my reward.

It is an exquisite piece of fairy food, also known as angel food or sponge candy, an instant reminder of childhood and Christmas. This version has a double-dousing of chocolate, and inside is a light and sugary mix that vanishes soon after it hits the tongue. There is a hint of molasses, but no gummy or brittle texture.

This seasonal confection has been made by **Quality Candy** for 90-plus years. The third-generation family business since 1960 also has owned **Buddy Squirrel**, the state's largest retail nut and popcorn operation.

The company is headquartered at St. Francis Industrial Park, near Milwaukee's Mitchell Field airport. Retail outlets extend from Racine to Milwaukee's Bayshore Town Center, then west as far as Madison.

Scraps of paper with handwritten recipes for butter almond toffee and candy with cream centers are framed on the walls here. Visitors see them during tours of the production area.

The handwriting belongs to Margaret's grandparents, Joseph and Lottie Helminiak, Polish immigrants who began this business venture on the cobblestone streets of Mitchell Street in 1916. It was an ice cream parlor, too, and everything—from candy canes and taffy to ice cream and sauces—were made from scratch. Chocolates with a flavored cream center became their specialty.

Premium ingredients were a priority from the beginning, says Margaret, who since 1998 has been president of Quality Candy/Buddy Squirrel. One of the biggest challenges came during World War II, when butter and sugar were rationed and "supply and demand were not working in their favor."

The business survived, but that's when ice cream products were dropped. The two-person operation eventually turned into a 200-employee enterprise that has had three homes in 90 years. The latest is a former bicycle warehouse that was deliberately designed to accommodate tour groups.

Margaret says the average employee has worked here at least a dozen years. One spent 54 years at Quality Candy before retirement.

"We learned early to respect it as a business," Margaret says, of her introduction to candy making during girlhood. "It was not just candy as a treat."

She speaks lovingly of the "wonderful colors and enticing smells" of her family's business, the kind employees who welcomed her into the workplace, the huge and heavy pots of caramel and cream.

"It's a very happy industry," Margaret says.

The products are sold online, and wholesale customers make up half of the business. They include Macy's, Bloomingdale's, Neiman Marcus and Dillard's. A Buddy Squirrel mascot shows up at charitable events.

Quality Candy/Buddy Squirrel
1801 E. Bolivar Ave., St. Francis
www.qcbs.com
800-972-2658

•

TIDBITS

Tours of **Quality Candy/Buddy Squirrel** candy and nut production occur January through October. The cost is $2 per person; children must be at least ten years old. Reservations are necessary, and minimum tour size is ten. Not traveling in that large of a pack? You may well be able to join another tour group.

The production facility has a retail outlet that sometimes carries candy and nuts at a discount.

The business hosts an open house from 10 a.m. to 4 p.m. on the Sunday that is two weeks before Easter. People stand in line to get free samples and watch candy/nut production.

Penzeys can enhance your spice cabinet.

WAUWATOSA: The Spice King

Turning the average home cook into a gourmet chef is not **Bill Penzey's** goal. He'd rather help you use food to make a connection or strengthen a bond.

"People cook because of the relationships in their lives, not to be *Iron Chef* cooks," says the founder of **Penzeys Spices**, which in 2008 tripled the size of its Milwaukee-area headquarters. The company began in 1986 and has about three dozen retail outlets nationwide.

What do you make when cooking for only yourself? Let's say salad. The number of ingredients in a meal tends to increase when the audience is your lover or a group of friends, or associated with an event that invites celebration or comfort.

Bill says "Love to Cook, Cook to Love," a slogan designed for his company's magazine, pertains to the entire business. "You need to see the value that comes from cooking," he says.

He talks of a childhood friend, John Tillison, who is at work for Penzeys in Shanghai, looking for providers of garlic and ginger. The job is to examine more than product taste.

"A lot of people say they have a good quality product," Bill says, "but it's almost impossible to produce something of good quality without caring about what you do, viewing the work you do as an extension of who you are."

So the friend, traveling with his ten-year-old daughter, sizes up work environment and leadership as well as products that are for sale.

What happens when the boss walks into the production area? Do employees avoid eye contact, or smile? Work faster, or stop to greet their visitors?

"People who are not being treated well don't care" as much about work quality, Bill asserts.

You could say that the company's story begins at the dawn of history.

"It's not about us being experts," Bill says, but about helping the average cook feel comfortable with seasonings that gained respect thousands of years ago. "Anytime you make spices complex, people tend to feel overwhelmed."

He refers to "the tyranny of the new—attempts by the media and others to spin and muddy the global spice world by concocting convoluted recipes or products with names like "grains of paradise, or something else that seems dreamy."

The average food magazine talks down to its readers, Bill believes, and phrases like "test kitchen" sound off-putting. "This isn't a test," he says.

So he's a believer in good cooking but not pretentious image. He bristles, for example, at the suggestion that his Penzeys outlet at Manhattan's Grand Central Terminal may appear too plain.

"What makes you think we should market ourselves as the Jetsons?" Bill responds.

That also is why he chooses to concentrate on seasonings, instead of adding bread makers, other kitchen equipment or gimmicks (like neckties with chili pepper designs) to the product line.

He is similarly wary about adding cooking classes. "We'll see what we evolve into, but classes work to make cooking seem more complex" than necessary. "Just hang out with people who cook" and see how they do it, he advises. "Just add flavorings to foods you enjoy—that's where we're at."

Some sort of tomato-based sauce, put over pasta, is what he tends to cook for his own family. The sauce likely will include fennel, oregano, basil and garlic—and the meal dates back to his time as a college student in Madison.

The average Penzeys customer spends $18.68 on his ever-growing world of seasonings.

He sells four kinds of cinnamon, for example, and hires staff who are knowledgeable about explaining the differences. In his office is a cinnamon stick from Vietnam that is at least two feet long, but cinnamon from China is the company's best-seller. (Cinnamon from Ceylon and Indonesia is also sold.)

Bill is in this business because of his parents' influence. They supplied restaurants with coffees, teas and spices, and they operate the **Spice House** in Wauwatosa.

A sister, **Patty Erd**, and her husband, **Tom,** operate Spice Houses, too, but in other Milwaukee (and Illinois) locations.

"Different approaches," Bill says, with a shrug. The businesses are separate from Penzeys, but the family supports one another.

Cultural influences, he says, encourage home cooks to enlarge their spice cabinets. He mentions cumin, commonplace in Mexican cooking, but new to many in the U.S. "If you're ever jaded with life in general, spend some time with saffron," he suggests.

"Now we're back to what's normal" compared to the 1950s, when many U.S. household spice shelves contained little more than salt and pepper.

World War II, Bill notes, temporarily halted the spice trade, because ships were used for military purposes. So cooking habits changed.

As more women entered the workforce, they had less time to cook. And with the invention of TV dinners, they found less reason to cook.

Plant tours of the new 300,000-square-foot Penzeys Spices are expected to begin in fall 2008. A retail store already is open. The Nutmeg Room eventually will offer "a nibble" of food that involves Penzeys products.

The company also produces *Penzeys One World of Flavor*, a bimonthly magazine about "cooking and caring," available by subscription, with newsstand sales to begin in March 2009.

Penzeys Spices
12001 W. Capitol Drive, Wauwatosa
www.penzeys.com
414-760-7307

•

WEST ALLIS:
Delightful Diversity

Sample foods from dozens of nationalities.

Amusing mismatches are evident in every direction. A woman wears a bright Ukrainian costume and eats Thai food. The garb of another says "China," and she's shopping for an Egyptian souvenir.

On a child's plate of sweets are kolaches from Poland, gingerbread from Germany, baklava from Greece. He adjusts a sombrero and digs in. When the music begins, segues from hula to polka, Celtic tin whistle to Native American drum all happen with minimal effort.

Sushi or sauerbraten? A jig or square dance? All is possible at **Holiday Folk Fair International**, an annual festival that involves about 60 ethnic groups, each eager to demonstrate the music, crafts and culinary traditions of their native lands.

The event began during World War II, when volunteers met at the International Institute of Wisconsin, "to prove that people of different ethnic backgrounds, religions and political persuasions could work together in harmony." The first folk fair set out to prove that "an island of intercultural friendship and unity in a world at war" could thrive.

There were two entertainers that first year, 1944: a Mexican singer and Polish accordion player. The event lasted seven hours and drew a crowd of 3,000. Now the Folk Fair lasts three days, and annual attendance since 1973 has exceeded 50,000.

Thousands of children learn about the world as they hop from one exhibit booth to another, to get their Folk Fair "passport" stamps. Adults learn the art of Norwegian scissors cutting, Japanese bonsai and other longstanding ethnic artistry. To say this is a melting pot is an understatement. Cornucopia of goodwill and respect is more like it.

Holiday Folk Fair International
Wisconsin State Fair Park, West Allis
www.folkfair.org 800-FAIR-INTL
•

Mille's Italian Sausage has been the longest running vendor at Wisconsin's state fair.

WEST ALLIS: Take Me to the Fair

Early August is the time of year when **Amatore "Matt" Mille** heads home and fires up the charcoal grill. Home is Milwaukee, Matt makes Italian sausages, and his cooking is no little backyard barbecue, although this is a family reunion.

Sister **Toni** comes from New Jersey; brothers **Mike** and **Mark** are in Milwaukee. Their children and grandchildren—the youngest are five-month-old twins from Chicago—arrive from other directions.

A **Mille's Italian Sausage** stand has been at the Wisconsin State Fair since 1932, longer than any other food vendor. It has involved five generations of the Mille family, and it is difficult to find this particular sausage during other times of the year.

"We work so hard for those 11 days—12 to 15 hours a day," says Matt, who is in his sixties. "It's dirty work, but I wouldn't miss it for the world."

Grandparents **Amatore** and **Antonette Mille** opened one of Milwaukee's first pizza places in 1947, at 82nd and Greenfield, across from the fairgrounds. As their state fair sausage stand grew in popularity, so did the amount of ash and smoke from the grill, which caused competing vendors to complain. That prompted Mike Mille Sr., Matt's dad, to create a vertical grill, where the sausages would cook on long spits that were alongside— not above—the coals. The juices no longer dripped into the fire, the smoke cleared, and the sausages still are prepared this way, dozens browning at one time.

The sausage is Antonette Mille's recipe, produced for more than 50 years through **Klement's Sausage Company**, only for the fair, Summerfest and a couple of Milwaukee car races.

During the state fair, several tons of sausage will be served in Italian rolls from **Peter Sciortino's Bakery**, a longtime fixture on Milwaukee's Brady Street.

"Sharp or sweet?" is what the family of servers will ask, a reference to two types of peppers that can be added. It is not unusual to have 16 bushels, which are freshly pan-fried, when the workday begins at 6 a.m.

The menu is not complicated: sausage sandwiches, beverages and cannoli (also

MILWAUKEE AREA

from Sciortino's). That's it.

"From the earliest years, Grandma and Grandpa always stayed focused on selling the best possible Italian sausage sandwich," Matt writes in his 2006 book, *Eleven Days in August: A Chronicle of Summers*.

"They had many opportunities to make more money by adding other high-margin products or by cutting corners on quality here or there, but they never went down those paths."

The sausage recipe was a long-time experiment that eventually was perfected and has long been left alone. Fennel is a part of what makes it unique, and the family is considering commercial sales that would be in addition to occasional events.

Matt tried it long ago, carting a sausage booth to festivals and fairs as far away as Calgary. The money was all right, he says, but the satisfaction just wasn't the same.

Herb Kohl's Milk House serves 160,000 glasses of flavored milk during the fair.

"It's a homecoming," Matt says about returning to the city that he left about 30 years ago. "It's about going back to family and a part of myself."

He describes this working vacation in Milwaukee as "a dramatic change" from the rest of his life, which involves business suits and corporate worlds, to sell and market information technology in New York City.

His father died in 2000, a few weeks after the State Fair. That could have ended this family affair, but it hasn't. Food fads—on a stick or atop a tray—come and go, but Mille's endures without a need for change.

"There are more food providers," Matt observes, "but there is still an emphasis on quality and uniqueness of products" at the State Fair. The event "doesn't really change much from year to year, and that's a good thing."

Wisconsin State Fair
Wisconsin State Fair Park, 640 S. 84th Street, West Allis
www.wistatefair.com
800-884-FAIR
•

ELSEWHERE IN MILWAUKEE

All participating growers farm within 35 miles of **Fondy Farmers' Market**, 2200 W. Fond du Lac Avenue.

"Some of our farmers' ancestors were the original homesteaders of southeast Wisconsin," says a market brochure. "Others come from a long family tradition of farming in southeast Asia. They raise many hard-to-find Asian varieties of produce, as well as traditional favorites."

Convenience stores easily outweigh groceries in central Milwaukee, and a goal is to make it easier for low-income residents to buy healthful food at a reasonable cost. In 2003, Fondy Food Center (which operates the market) made it possible to pay for purchases with food stamps. Cooking tips and demos occur on some Saturdays.

Fondy Farmers' Market has fresh local foods, and suggestions for how to serve them.

The Fondy market is open from mid-May to mid-November, but sometimes only on Saturdays. Hours depend upon time of year.

www.fondymarket.org 414-933-8128

•

The **Milwaukee Public Market**, open since 2005, is a fine and fun mix of organic and specialty foods. In summer, outdoor vendors include local arts and craftspeople, creating an almost festive atmosphere.

Cooking classes—in the **Madame Kuony** demo kitchen, on the former warehouse's second floor—are led by some of the area's most celebrated chefs. The area also is an apropos location for noshing on market purchases, like reuben soup from the **Soup & Stock Market**, steamed tamales from **El Rey** or hand-dipped chocolates from **Kehr's Candies**.

www.milwaukeepublicmarket.org 414-336-1111

Coast, along Lake Michigan, is a great place to enjoy the view with your Happy Hour.

Many chefs present cooking classes that involve a harvest of fresh ingredients, but it's rare for the class to literally reach out to the farm. That's what **Dave Swanson** of **Braise on the Go** does. He has a traveling culinary school.

Class settings will incorporate locations relevant to what is in season, from an orchard to a farm to a rural bed and breakfast. Dave's routine tends to begin with a 30-minute farm or facility tour, then a two-hour cooking demo with food sampling. The classes are relatively small—a maximum of 20—and content depends upon the setting and lessons.

Dave's training included time at Le Cordon Bleu in Paris. His employers have included Le Francais in Wheeling, Illinois, and Sanford in Milwaukee.

"Subtle flavors in balance" is how Dave defines his style of cooking. He is drawn to the word "braise" because the technique is one of the first that culinary students learn, and it is at the core of good cooking.

www.braiseculinaryschool.com 414-241-9577

•

One of the best locations for Happy Hour in downtown Milwaukee is **Coast** restaurant, 931 E. Wisconsin Avenue. Time it right, and you'll see the Milwaukee Art Museum's Calatrava "wings" in a slow flutter at closing time (5 p.m., except Thursdays).Order a drink of at least $4 and you will receive a complimentary hors d'oeuvre from the bar as a reward. We're not talkin' stale chips and dip: Think mini crab cakes, hibachi beef sticks, bruschetta bites and calamari.

Samplers also have been a hit with us here. They include flights of mini martinis and a trio of soups.

www.coastrestaurant.com 414-727-5555

•

One of Milwaukee's finest restaurants, **Dream Dance**, is inside a casino and until 2008 was a chore to find. Head upstairs and look for the entrance between the bingo hall and buffet.

Now the gem at **Potawatomi Bingo Casino**, 1721 W. Canal Street, has moved to the first floor because of the casino's $240 million expansion. Look for the big wood and leather dream catcher, plus one of copper-painted steel, with globes of many colors.

The new décor is big on metallics and dark woods. Chef **Jason Gorman's** menu continues to be called "the new Wisconsin cuisine," and a wild game section will be added (kangaroo, ostrich, pheasant—more than the venison that has long been an entrée choice).

What to expect? Culinary playfulness that works: Sprecher Root Beer Venison Rossini (with butternut squash pancakes) as an entrée, Lobsterwurst (lobster/ shrimp/scallops with brat-like seasonings, plus mascarpone pierogi and Tahitian vanilla butter sauce) as an appetizer.

The restaurant says its wine list—850 selections, and growing—is the largest in the state and sold at retail pricing levels.

Being considered: the addition of a "chef's table" and program in which you become "chef for a day" and help Jason prepare a meal. The students would get their own chef's coat and have five friends join them for dinner.

The casino expansion also results in the opening of two new restaurants (**Ru Yi**, with Asian cuisine, and an American food restaurant) and a food court. Casino space triples, to about 750,000 square feet.

www.paysbig.com 414-847-7883

•

"Sabor," in Latino cultures, means "good flavor" and "churrasco" means "barbecue." Stretch that to "churrascaria," and we have an all-you-can-eat meal based on succulent, barbecued meats.

Throw out that image of flipping burgers on the Weber grill. At Milwaukee's **Sabor**, 777 N. Water Street, this meal turns into a festive and near-constant procession of a dozen types of fire-roasted meats, paraded on huge skewers from kitchen to diners' plates.

So it's sizzling lamb chops, chunks of filet mignon, chicken breast pieces wrapped in bacon, baby back ribs, *linguica* sausages and more. The Brazilian steakhouse experience pays tribute to the rugged gauchos who long ago slow-roasted meat over campfire flames.

In Milwaukee, customers begin by grazing at the *rodizio* (an exotic salad bar). Each diner gets a coaster and quickly learns to place the green side up, if they want hot food.

When the parade of meat begins, it doesn't stop until the coaster is flipped the other way. Pace yourself: Side dishes such as fried bananas, rice/beans and cheese bread also are a part of the deal. Vegetarians likely will find enough on the rodizio to satisfy their appetite.

For more about Wisconsin's first Brazilian steakhouse, which opened in 2006: **www.saborbrazil.net** **414-431-3106**

•

The daily specials, when we last checked, included Rum and Coca-Cola —and it was possible to have it delivered!

What sounds like a cocktail to you may be a flavor of the day at **Kopp's Frozen Custard**, which has locations in Glendale (5373 N. Port Washington Road), Brookfield (18880 W. Bluemound Road) and Greenfield (7631 W. Layton Avenue). Each has a "flavor line" as well as a phone number for other inquiries.

Custard is serious business here. Ten-pack pints, plus hot fudge and pecans, can be (and are) shipped nationwide in dry ice.

This is all the doing of the late Elsa Kopp, a native of Germany who started the business in 1950, after her husband's diagnosis of Parkinson's disease. She needed a way to support her family. Now son Karl Kopp is in charge, and the flavor of the day experimentation continues. Pink Ribbon contains white chocolate chips, a raspberry liqueur and raspberry fruit swirl. Grizzly Bear has chocolate-covered peanuts and a ribbon of butterscotch, in chocolate custard.

And the Imperial Torte, a rum-caramel flavor with French pastry pieces and chocolate? That one is named after Elsa and served once a year, on the Sunday closest to April 18, her birthday. **www.kopps.com**

Road Trip: Suds It Up in Milwaukee

Milwaukee is about more than beer, but brewing helps shape the city's character and enhances its prosperity.

1. Brews. Miller Brewing Co., 4251 W. State Street, began as a German brewer's dream in 1855. That's when Frederick Miller bought the Plank Road Brewery for $2,300.

Today, SABMiller produces 130 million barrels of beer annually, in 40 countries and as hundreds of brands. The Milwaukee plant is touted as the oldest major brewery in the U.S. One-hour, guided tours are free and include product samples. Tour times are updated daily. **www.millerbrewing.com 800-944-5483**

2. More brews. Sprecher Brewery, 701 W. Glendale Avenue, Glendale, exists because of the initiative taken in 1985 by an ex-Pabst brewing supervisor. The brewing occurs in a former elevator car factory.

Sprecher's Imperial Stout, Dopple Bock and Pipers Scotch Ale were among medal winners in 2007 international competition. The company sells a barbecue sauce with root beer, as well as root beer and other gourmet sodas by the bottle.

Tours occur year-round, but reservations are required. Tours end at the indoor beer garden, with a sipping of beers and sodas. **www.sprecherbrewery.com 414-964-2739**

3. Brews on the lake. Lakefront Brewery, 1872 N. Commerce Street, has earned a case full of awards and also counts the nonalcoholic Golden Maple Root Beer among its liquid assets.

The cream city brick building includes Lakefront Palm Garden, a big and no-nonsense banquet hall where you can find a polka band and fish fry on Fridays, which also is an ideal time to take a tour. It's easy to meander from warehouse to patio to Milwaukee's downtown RiverWalk.

The brewery uses organic malt and hops, which then become compost. Renewable energy is a priority, and the business has earned Travel Green Wisconsin ecotourism certification. **www.lakefrontbrewery.com 414-372-8800**

4. Live music is commonplace at **Milwaukee Ale House**, 233 N. Water Street, also on the shore of the Milwaukee River, but in the city's trendy Third Ward, a formerly musty warehouse district.

Unusual specialty pizzas, sandwiches and salads, seafood and steaks make up the menu. Stout Pot Roast may be "Mom's recipe," but it also simmers in the brew-pub's Sheepshead Stout. **www.ale-house.com 414-226-2337**

5. Rock Bottom beer. Rock Bottom Restaurant and Brewery, 740 N. Plankinton Avenue, is part of a Colorado-based chain that spreads into more than a dozen states. It specializes in "familiar American food" and the onsite brewing of good, but corporate, beer recipes.

Members of the Mug Club who are loyal patrons are rewarded with merchandise: beer glasses to T-shirts to barbeque sets. The Rock Bottom brewpubs are one part of Rock Bottom Restaurants Inc., whose other holdings include the Old Chicago pizza and pasta chain. **www.rockbottom.com 414-276-3030**

Brewery tours via boat stop at Lakefront, Milwaukee Ale House and Rock Bottom during good weather weekends. **414-283-9999**

6. Antiques and collectibles are numerous at the **Water Street Brewery**, 1101 N. Water Street, Milwaukee, and 3191 Golf Road, Delafield. Thousands of beer cans, coasters, tap knobs, tap handles and openers turn both locations into minimuseums.

Open since 1987, Water Street Brewery is especially proud of its Sunday brunch and Friday fish fry. Any of the handcrafted creations can be ordered to go, as in filling a growler (64 ounces), which is not the same as leaving with an open container. **www.waterstreet brewery.com 414-272-119, 262-646-7878**

7. Best place for a nightcap, then bed? County Clare, 1234 N. Astor Street, is a cheery Irish inn with a sister property near Athlone, Ireland. Expect bangers and mash on the pub menu, Irish ales by the pint, occasional live Irish music. Friendly and cozy, plush and authentic. **www.countyclare-inn.com 888-942-5273**

Milwaukee Ale House is on the brewery boat cruises along the Milwaukee River.

TELL ME ABOUT:
Supper Clubs

The quintessential Wisconsin supper club: the HobNob in Kenosha.

Could it be that the tendency to drink less alcohol, order smaller portions and seek more healthful foods may be endangering Wisconsin's reputation as a supper club state?

Add growing competition—from pricey restaurant chains, classy bistros in small towns, resort condo developments with full kitchens—and some supper club operators have responded by tacking "for sale" signs on their doors or websites.

We tend to think of a supper club as a place that doesn't open until around 4 p.m., where the owner often is the person to greet and seat customers.

We may have to wait an hour for a table, but we don't care because the atmosphere is friendly and the cocktails are cheap and honest, ample portions, with (easily) a full shot of liquor.

At the table, we expect to see a relish tray. It typically contains raw vegetables and one or more unpredictable choices—sweet and dill pickles, homemade cottage cheese, herring or a house specialty cheese dip.

Great steaks and fish fries lure us into supper clubs. So does hot, fresh bread, served with real butter. There may be an elaborate salad bar, or just iceberg lettuce with homemade dressings.

What happens after dinner? We might order a generous Brandy Alexander, back at that friendly bar, among neighbors and friends.

This is Midwest tradition, but things are slowly changing.

Only a decade ago, Wisconsin was about little more than meat and potatoes, says **Ed Lump**, executive director of the **Wisconsin Restaurant Association**. "Now people order a salad and no potatoes" and "have more sophisticated tastes because of their travels, and what they see on the Food Network."

Such trends as grazing on appetizers, and splitting a meal or entrée, require some types of restaurants to reinvent themselves if they are to survive. "The restaurant business, as a whole, is very good," Ed says, "but the individual restaurants are not always rising with the tide."

Being obese "is out of style," he notes, and moderation—at the bar, at the dining table—is becoming the norm. Adult customers tend to drink less, but might want to "drink better"—fine wines, microbrews, flavored martinis.

At mealtime, bigger quantities and many courses don't necessarily mean more customers.

"The appeal of these kinds of extras is not as great," Ed says. "If you don't want the food, then it's not a value to you," regardless of portion size or cost. So if more supper club customers say no to the first course of tomato juice or a soup, or order steak without a potato, it may be time to consider new menu options.

Although supper clubs "still have popular appeal," the conundrum is how to address changes in dining habits while satisfying the regulars. "Maintaining the status quo means slipping behind," he says.

"One of our roles is to educate our members about these trends, and there is some resistance to" making changes, says Ed, whose former Brat Und Brau restaurants peaked in popularity during the 1970s, an era when franchising was a new concept and upscale restaurant chains didn't exist.

"After quick service, it was all independents," he notes, but the wider swath of chain restaurants today—with budget to high-end menus—challenges all levels of locally owned competition.

Restaurants with healthful dining choices are easy to find through the Wisconsin Restaurant Association, which includes about 7,000 locations in its online dining guide. Besides searching by geographical area or type of cuisine, consumers can look for restaurants with healthful options.

Is skim or 1 percent milk available? Egg substitutes? Low salt and no MSG options? Low-carb choices? Vegetarian fare? Smoke-free dining? There are a dozen categories in this part of the search engine.

Wisconsin Restaurant Association
2801 Fish Hatchery Road, Madison
www.wirestaurant.org
800-589-3211

•

ALGOMA:
Rent This Kitchen

The retail outlet is small but stacked with appetizing surprises: Bloody Mary mix made with homegrown tomatoes. Apricot-zucchini and chopped-cherry jams. Plum-pear, rhubarb-pomegranate and pumpkin-apple butters. Gumbo. Gourmet cookies. Toffee. Maple-coated popcorn. Double chocolate biscotti. Asiago pepper rolls.

Dozens of businesses use the **Algoma Farm Market Kitchen** to prepare their products. This specialized business incubator, which opened in 2001, sets a precedent in Wisconsin, and perhaps the nation. This commercial kitchen has succeeded as similar ideas elsewhere have withered at the discussion or research stage.

Dozens of new products get their start in Algoma.

"This proves it can be done," says **Greg Lawless**, co-director of the Ag Innovation Center at University of Wisconsin Extension. He attributes the project's success to the leadership and grant-writing tenacity of **Mary Pat Carlson**, facility director since 2005.

Mary Pat got interested because she needed a kitchen to make jam and jelly with the fruit from her family's Sister Bay business, **Carlson's Island View Orchard**, established in 1846.

Three years of research prior to the Algoma facility's opening involved Cornell University. Ninety percent of funding for kitchen operation comes from private donations. Agri-tourism events—from cooking demonstrations to product samplings to food workshops—plus room rentals for weddings and corporate events increase public exposure and the revenue base. These features make the facility unusual nationwide.

Mary Pat is a lifelong teacher and student of economic development who says the Algoma project's multifaceted mission helps build momentum and exposure for the food processors. A next step is to add a second commercial kitchen.

Food preparers pay $12 to $20 per hour to rent the commercial kitchen, which can be accessed 24 hours a day. Their goal is to build sales and "graduate."

One successful graduate is **Nutorious**, makers of gourmet nut confections. "The kitchen has allowed us to effectively manage the precious cash that we have," says Nutorious co-owner **Carrie Liebhauser**. "If we had to spend the money for equipment and facilities that would have been necessary to produce our first package, we would have been doomed. Instead, we were able to pay as we go and use any excess funds for product promotion—something that has paid off very well for us."

At Nutorius, walnuts, pecans and almonds are given sweet or savory coatings; some are mixed with dried fruit. Product varieties include Door County Cherry Vanilla, Cranberry Orange, Chocolate Coconutty and Cha Cha Chipotle. The products were made at the Algoma kitchen for two and a half years, until the company moved to Green Bay.

Door County Signature Spices of Sturgeon Bay, which blends herbs and spices in Algoma, also was launched there. "The kitchen facilities are wonderful since we would be unable to start our business and maintain it," say proprietors **Betsy Rossberg** and **Brenda Schumacher**. They began using the kitchen in 2006 and now sell their spice blends at retail outlets, from Two Rivers to Sister Bay.

Although the Algoma Farm Market Kitchen targets entrepreneurs in four counties—Door, Brown, Kewaunee and Manitowoc—Mary Pat fields calls and assists small businesses from as far away as Madison, Milwaukee, Eagle River and Wausau.

People who rent the Algoma kitchen for business purposes are required to develop a business plan and carry at least $1 million in product liability insurance. Some products, by state law, also require completion of food handling classes.

"Our biggest issues are food safety and security," Mary Pat says. "After that comes business success."

JoAnne Penny of **Penny Lane Farm** in Baileys Harbor has used the Algoma kitchen since 2005 to make two sweet-sour dipping sauces: Southeast Asian Spicy and Cherry Ginger. Before that, she made her sauces at home, for only family and friends.

"The amount of time I am needing the kitchen is increasing as my product is getting more exposure," JoAnne says. She describes the technical assistance—regarding licenses, labeling, insurance—to be invaluable, and the marketing opportunities incredible.

Another plus: although some entrepreneurs who have used the kitchen have found out it isn't for them, they were able to do it with little financial loss.

The Algoma Farm Market Store is open to the public, but hours vary, so call before trying to visit. Store events include Saturday Samplings—product tastings and a cooking demonstration—but the schedule is sporadic. Group tours and samplings can be arranged, at cost and by appointment, for a minimum of ten people.

Algoma Farm Market Kitchen
520 Parkway Street, Algoma
www.farmmarketkitchen.com 920-487-9750
•

Art, whimsy and friendly faces greet you at The Flying Pig.

TIDBITS

Less than two miles south of the Algoma Farm Market Kitchen, near Lake Michigan, is the **Flying Pig Gallery and Greenspace**, N6975 Highway 42. It is a terrific and whimsical place to nibble and sip as well as shop.

Order a biscotti and latte with real maple syrup while strolling through the sculpture garden. Nurse a microbrew as folk musicians perform in the garden on sultry summer nights. This is a class act in a country setting. **www.theflyingpig. biz** **920-487-9902**

•

About 10 miles south of the Flying Pig, at N3176 Highway 42, is **Diggins Cafe and Fine Rocks**, a deliciously odd mix of stone-oven pizzas and gemstones that are big enough to use as lawn art. **Dave Belton** also sells jewelry, fossils and stone carvings. Add sandwiches, salads, soups and bottled Baumeister pop (made in Kewaunee since 1907).

The former tavern has a beautiful lake view, and Dave hauled his rock collection from the Chicago area in 2003, the fulfillment of his dream to "live and work in the same location."

Just look for a dazzling splash of colors, at the south end of Kewaunee and facing the lake. **www.digginsonline.ws** **920-388-4849**

Food, fossils and a view at Diggins Cafe

This steakhouse is a tribute to the legendary football coach.

APPLETON: Lovin' Lombardi

A remarkable tribute to one of the country's most beloved coaches thrives quietly in downtown Appleton.

Vince Lombardi's Steakhouse, inside of the **Radisson Paper Valley Hotel**, is a classy museum as well as a fine dining spot that has earned *Wine Spectator* awards. Covering walls and display cases are more than 400 artifacts from the life and career of the Green Bay Packer coach, who died in 1970.

The framed photographs, game plays, letters from U.S. presidents, player jerseys and coaching trophies have had a home here since 2000.

Why Appleton? No one else asked, says **Vince Lombardi Jr.**, who lives in Washington. We chatted before he and buddy **Paul Hornung** of Louisville, a running back during the Lombardi years, came to the Fox Valley to sign books, "eat a good dinner together" and catch a Packer game at Lambeau.

Paper Valley Hotel owner **Dennis Langley** took the initiative to approach Lombardi's family in 1998. Vince Jr.'s concern was that "if you don't do it right, it could detract from" his father's reputation instead of reaffirming it.

"I had been at the hotel and restaurant many times," Vince said, "so when they called and said they'd rename the restaurant" he knew what the space was like. It was then a French restaurant called Christie's.

As **Jay Schumerth**, the hotel's senior general manager, tells the story, Dennis soon was with Lombardi's children in Washington and Florida, going through box after box of treasures stored in attics and garages.

"Better there than in my basement," Vince eventually concluded, regarding the decision to bring parts of his father's estate to Appleton. The football halls of fame in Green Bay and Canton, Ohio, have less Lombardi memorabilia than that on display at the steakhouse in Appleton.

Game plays from coaching the New York Giants were discovered in a leather briefcase. A St. Cecilia (New Jersey) High School yearbook shows Lombardi in his first coaching jobs, for the school's football, basketball and baseball teams.

Sprinkled elsewhere is fan mail, from Gerald Ford, Richard Nixon, Ethel Kennedy and others. "It's as much a museum as it is a restaurant," Jay contends.

Photos capture Lombardi with his high school diploma and golfing with Jack Nicklaus, as well as with his team at significant games.

"We have this mythical image of Vince Lombardi," notes Jay. "Here, people can see that he was a dad, a grandfather—more than a football coach."

In addition to its main dining rooms, two private areas each seat up to ten people. Fall menu specials include Brazilian Lamb Chops, Twice Cooked Cranberry Pork Roulade, Pepper Crusted Ribeye with Mango Chutney, Tuscan Chicken, Grilled Halibut with Sweet Chile Ginger, and Crab Stuffed Filet of Sirloin.

The signature dessert: Chocolate Super Bowl, a handmade chocolate shell filled with strawberries and cream.

The restaurant, which has its own bar, is open only for dinner. The menu is à la carte, with entrées ranging from $16 to $50-plus.

Lombardi's Steakhouse
333 W. College Avenue, Appleton
www.vincelombardisteakhouse.com
920-380-9390
•

TIDBITS

Strawberry soup is a delicious seasonal treat at Mary's Family Restaurant in Appleton.

Where else can you get your fill of food and Green Bay Packer memorabilia? **Fuzzy's #63**, a casual bar and grill at 2511 W. Mason Street, Green Bay, is owned by **Fred "Fuzzy" Thurston**, the starting guard from Super Bowl I and II.

Order Fuzzy's Special, a hamburger and brat patty with cheese, then head to the room with the pool table and size up the Packer and other NFL memorabilia that is in display cases.

Fuzzy (now in his seventies) sometimes hangs out here during Packer games, and on the Fridays before a home game. **920-494-6633**

•

Wisconsin may well be the Hot Beef Sandwich Capital of the World, so it's perhaps unwise to suggest who makes the best. Let's just say that you won't regret ordering the hot beef sandwich or platter at **Mary's Family Restaurant**, in operation since 1958 at 2106 S. Oneida Street, Appleton.

This friendly fixture in the Fox Valley is a perennial award winner, for its soups, chicken, breakfast and chili. When we visited in summer, a cup of the chilled strawberry soup was a grand treat: It was a thick puree, not too sweet, with a fat dollop of whipped cream on top. Served seasonally.

www.foodspot.com/marysrestaurants.com 920-733-1546
A second Mary's location is at 2312 N. Richmond Street, Appleton.

Who is the king of both wine and cheese in Wisconsin? You could make a strong case for **Troy Landwehr** of **Kerrigan Brothers Winery**, N2269 Highway N, Appleton (near Little Chute).

Troy makes more than a dozen fruit-based wines—plum to pear, Dutch Apple to Cranberry White—and he carves cheese. The latter involves much more than turning a block into a wedge.

He's turned a 700-pound chunk of cheddar into a carving of Mount Rushmore, as a marketing tool for Cheez-It crackers. Other blocks have been chiseled to look like the prime minister of Ireland, comedian Tom Arnold, baseball player John Kruk and David Letterman's *Late Show* sidekick, Biff Henderson.

At the winery, staff cheerfully offer free tastings daily, and they have many ideas about how to make their products more versatile. Use the blackberry wine as a marinade or a rub on wild game, for example, or mix it with sour soda for a spritzer.

www.kerriganbrothers.com 920-788-1423

Troy Landwehr makes more than a dozen fruit-based wines.

ELLISON BAY:
In-Home Christenings

Janice Thomas helps the cooking-impaired make friends with their new appliances.

Janice Thomas will christen your new baby, but it will be done in the kitchen, not in a church.

The co-owner of **Savory Spoon Cooking School**, open seasonally and by private arrangement, also travels nationwide to help new homeowners feel more at ease with their appliances.

These kitchen christenings began in 1999, in an old adobe house in Tucson, Ariz. The kitchen was tiny, and an interior designer had recommended that Thomas help acclimate the homeowners to their revamped space.

Today Janice tends to work with high-end appliances, such as lines produced by Madison's Sub-Zero/Wolf. She typically arrives when construction or remodeling has finished, the movers have left and it's time for a housewarming.

There's just one problem: You don't know how to use the stove. Or maybe that's the first of several technical challenges.

"A $2 million house needs the right level of equipment to go with it, for resale value, if no other reason," Janice says.

What do you place in the kitchen's cold drawers? (Try ingredients that you need for a meal but are not quite ready to chop or shred.)

How about the warming drawer? (Heat plates, before adding food, or keep one component of a meal warm while waiting for another to get finished.)

Timing isn't everything, but it is important. This often is a part of the lesson plan when Janice is the teacher. She owned her own catering company for 14 years, studied at Le Cordon Bleu in Paris and has conducted classes at Savory Spoon since 2003.

Heat the oven grill 15 minutes before adding steaks, she advises. Turn on the oven fan 10 minutes before broiling. Result: The meat will sear nicely, and the air will remain clear enough to see it.

"Sealed burners, open burners and stoves can have all kinds of different grills on top," Janice notes. Each feature can come off as an added complication or intimidation factor for the novice cook. It is the teacher's job to demonstrate the convenience.

Her kitchen christenings often are camouflaged as a family gathering, girls' night out or couples' dinner party. The event is personalized and may begin with an Irish blessing, toast or family anecdote.

Making pizza might be appropriate if the homeowner wants to learn more about cooking with a convection oven, which enhances air and heat circulation. It also helps grab the attention of children.

An overall goal is to help people succeed with their first big social event at home, "without having the stress of whether or how the equipment works."

Private cooking classes at Savory Spoon, an 1877 schoolhouse, are more expensive than attending a class that is a part of Janice's seasonal schedule.

Savory Spoon's Culinary Marketplace, also in the schoolhouse, sells specialty foods that are made on the premises, kitchen tools and gadgets, products from other specialty food businesses.

On staff is a chocolatier, who produces truffles, turtles, toffee and more.

Savory Spoon Cooking School
12042 Highway 42, Ellison Bay
www.savoryspoon.com
920-854-6600

•

Tim Krolczyk says inside rounds are the way to go.

MINOCQUA:
BEEF ON PARADE

As the weather cools, out come the pots of chili, the Packer sweatshirts and the long-simmering beef roasts. It is this way in Minocqua, too, especially during the last weekend of September.

That is when local retailers pay homage to their customers, and they do it in an unusual way, by cooking almost one ton of beef, then parading it through the downtown.

More than one-half of the 85 roasts, which average 20 pounds each, brown and simmer on rotisseries, kettle grills and open fires along Main Street. Many of the cooks wear strange costumes as they babysit the meat and dream up ways to bribe the judges—like offering wine, to cleanse the palate.

The **Beef-A-Rama** in 2008 was the city's forty-fourth. The hoopla starts with music and dancing on Friday night. The Rump Roast Run takes place Saturday morning. Winners of the 5K and 10K events earn—you guessed it—rump roasts. About 500 people participate.

All the activity occurs in a relatively contained space, about four square blocks, which locals call "the island." The average tourist listens to bands and munches on free appetizers at local businesses as the smell of beef permeates the air.

The late **Harold Helterhoff** established this festival, and wife **Thelma** would bake thousands of foot-shaped sugar cookies to give away. They owned a moccasin shop, and each cookie had a dab of red frosting on the toes.

"They called it the Fish-A-Rama during the first year, but didn't actually cook any fish," says daughter **Shyla Helterhoff Wiesendanger**.

These days, there are rules, but not many. The roasts can't be cooked at home. They have to be ready for the parade at 2:45 p.m., after judging.

Some cook the meat over scented wood chips. Some roasts are injected with garlic, spices, wine.

"We all have our secret recipes," says banker **Vickie Shughart**, judged Best Chef with husband **Scott** in 2006. "We don't clown around" was their theme, but beneath the frivolity is serious competition.

There is no way you'll pry away their recipe. We have tried. Not even the Shughart children know it.

TJ's Butcher Block for ten years won the bid to provide the beef. "Inside rounds," owner **Tim Krolczyk** says of the cut. "They slice easily." He won the cook-off in 1997, 1998 and 2004.

"We all snoop at everybody else's beef" while it's cooking, he admits.

The Parade of Beef, led by a firetruck that transports the judges, takes all of 15 minutes. Tops. The cooking teams—with their roasts in wheelbarrows, displayed as mannequin heads, carried by hand, in wagons—march to Torpy Park, where volunteers quickly slice the goods and stuff thousands of sandwiches. Each sells for $3. People with pets get the scraps.

"It's a gigantic 'thank you' from the merchants for a wonderful summer," says **Dick Strucel**, operator of the **Aqua Aire Motel** and an event volunteer for at least 25 years.

The beef gets wolfed down, au jus or with sauces of horseradish or barbecue. What you get may be a surprise of seasonings, Jamaican jerk to Hawaiian pineapple, and there is no method for categorizing the bounty.

You eat what you get, and the locals say it's almost always pretty good.

Proceeds benefit local charities. Awards go to the best overall chef and winners in three sub-categories. Appearance and presentation (of both the cooking team and the product) count as much as taste.

There have been M*A*S*H characters transporting their cooked beef on a gurney, and a team in hospital garb that used an ER cart. Elvis impersonators, cows, witches, pirates, men in grass skirts and women in Superman outfits also are a part of this event's proud history.

Minocqua Beef-A-Rama
Minocqua-Arbor Vitae-Woodruff Area Chamber of Commerce
www.minocqua.org
800-44-NORTH

•

Expect fine dining—and trivia—at Bernard's Country Inn.

PORTAGE COUNTY:
Tale of Two Chefs

Their restaurants are ten miles apart, each with easy access from U.S. 51. Cost for dinner averages $20-25. The chefs have studied or worked with culinary icons. Food is their passion, and each provides a fine dining experience that may seem out of place in small-town Wisconsin.

There also are differences.

Bernard Kurzawa, a European master chef, began his training in East Berlin at age 14, influenced by the teachings of Auguste Escoffier, who popularized traditional French cooking methods. Bernard and wife **Irene** have operated **Bernard's Country Inn**, Stevens Point, since 1973, and he turns 70 in 2008.

Bernard's is a traditional fine dining experience, with one exception: Each table has a booklet of odd trivia, to entertain dining companions between courses. These are the things you can learn: Human thigh bones are stronger than concrete. A cat's ear has 32 muscles. The memory span of a goldfish is three seconds.

So cover thin bread sticks with a spread of creamy cheese, or liver pâté, and chuckle while waiting for soup or salad to appear.

The menu is full of Old World specialties: wiener, jaeger, schweine and zigeuner schnitzels; stroganoff and coq au vin; duck a l'orange and veal cordon bleu. It's about potato dumplings and spaetzle, cooked red cabbage and stewed apple sweet potatoes, traditional tortes and strudels—all made from scratch.

Bernard was chosen the **Wisconsin Restaurant Association**'s top restaurateur in 1994.

Ten miles south, **Christian Czerwonka**, a New York native, is a part of the entertainment at **Christian's Bistro**, which he and wife **Leah** opened in Plover in 2007. The restaurant's open design means customers can be seated at the kitchen counter, instead of a dining table, and watch the meal preparation.

Christian Czerwonka turns his work into theater at Christian's Bistro.

The chef spent 15 years working for Emeril Lagasse, first as a line cook. He eventually earned key roles in opening the celebrity chef's restaurants in Las Vegas and Atlanta. "Those experiences are what enabled us to do this," Christian says, referring to the bistro. "It is our chance to live life" instead of being swallowed up by work.

The restaurant serves lunch and dinner but is closed on Sunday and Monday. It serves breakfast only on Saturday.

Leah Czerwonka is a native of Wisconsin, which is why they are in Plover. "It is a good place to raise a family," she says; they have three daughters, preschooler to preteen.

Simple preparation of quality food is a priority, but the chef considers hospitality a key ingredient to success. "It's about the whole experience," he says. "We're throwing a party every day for our friends and family." Leah strikes up conversations with customers at each table.

The "open kitchen atmosphere" adds to the ambiance; "there's nothing to hide behind" and the cooking becomes an attraction.

The bistro menu is described as "homestyle/comfort cooking with a gourmet twist." Roasted duck, grilled flat iron steak and seared wahoo have been options.

Choices employ locally grown foods as well as favorite regional products from elsewhere in the U.S.—like heirloom grits that are ground to order, and garlicky, spicy-sweet Wickles Pickles.

The Czerwonkas also appreciate fresh seafood, but don't head there for a traditional fish fry. You'll find salmon and two or three other options on the menu, but they will be grilled, baked or sautéed—not deep fried.

•

More than 30 years of age separate Christian and Bernard, and they don't approach work in the same way, but they have one big thing in common: a commitment to quality.

Bernard's versions of sauerbraten and holiday stollen are his grandmother's recipes, and he still has her handwritten cookbook. He cooks red cabbage in goose fat, and accumulates about 20 pounds of it when preparing the Christmas geese.

Before coming to the Midwest, he worked at the Savoy in London, and on an oceanliner that routinely traveled between Europe and New York. "I always wanted to see what the cooking business was like in America," he says.

In 1973, "I didn't have a lot of cash and no bank would give me a loan" because he was not yet a U.S. citizen, so Bernard bought the Stevens Point restaurant on a land contract and thrived as local companies brought their events and executive meetings to him.

He's not in a rush to retire, but "if somebody came in with cash and wanted to buy" the restaurant, Bernard suggests that he'd sell it in a flash.

In recent years, "business isn't what it used to be," largely because local corporations today have in-house dining and catering staff. So Bernard's no longer is open for lunch.

"The local economy has rendered my business worthless," the chef laments, but he has yet to improve his bottom line by cutting corners in the kitchen. "Not as long as I'm running this restaurant," he vows.

Bernard's Country Inn
701 Second Street North, Stevens Point
www.bernardscountryinn.com
715-344-3365

•

Christian's Bistro
3066 Village Park Drive, Plover
www.christiansbistro.com
715-344-3100

Seymour citizens take their title, "Home of the Hamburger," seriously.

SEYMOUR: A Meaty History

A 15-year-old boy flattened a few meatballs near the Seymour horseracing track in 1885, and many lives have not been the same since then.

Charlie Nagreen from Hortonville gets credit for inventing the hamburger sandwich, made from "Hamburg steak," which he sold at the fairgrounds for more than 60 years. People in other states have tried to tug at his title, but Seymour fights back or simply ignores them.

A proclamation from **Governor Jim Doyle** concludes that Seymour is home of the hamburger. Oklahoma's governor issued something similar in 1995. Akron, Ohio, hosted the first National Hamburger Festival in 2005. Seymour's annual Burger Fest is entering its second decade.

While historians bicker, we're reaching for the ketchup and having a nice lunch. We love a good burger, and nobody celebrates the sandwich with more enthusiasm than Seymour.

"Who likes Seymour's hamburgers? We like Seymour's hamburgers." That is the start of "The Seymour Hamburger Song." For the second verse, simply substitute "cheeseburger" for "hamburger."

This is not the only jingle in the city's repertoire.

Harleys, horses, hula dancers, hot rods and harvesting equipment participate in the community's **Hamburger Parade** in early August. This and the morning **Bun Run** are precursors to the annual **Burger Festival**.

Kids slide down a ketchup-coated slide. A 60-pound burger is grilled outdoors, near the 12-foot Hamburger Charlie statue, then divvied up among spectators.

Even bigger is the city's other prominent piece of public art, a giant hamburger that is perched high above every living creature. The most outlandish antic was the grilling of an 8,000-pound burger a few years ago, for entry into the Guinness Book of World Records.

The annual burger-eating contest, a friendly competition, doesn't attract professional food eaters. That's probably because the top prize in 2007 was one free burger per week for a year, plus a Hamburger Charlie bobblehead.

The festival record is 5.25 burgers, eaten in ten minutes, and the 2007 winner came close—4.75. There is no contest entry fee, and one contestant admitted he was competing just to get a free lunch.

For other festival trivia and paraphernalia, head to the **Seymour Community Museum**, Depot Street, 920-833-2868.

Seymour Burger Fest
Lake Park, Seymour
www.seymourwi.com
920-833-6053
•

Mickey-Lu's stays open until 12:30 a.m. during summer.

TIDBITS

Good burgers and burger makers are not in short supply. Three examples:
Mickey-Lu's Bar-B-Q, on U.S. 41 (710 Marinette Avenue) in Marinette,
turns into a swirl of neon at night. The little box of a burger joint opened in
1942, and owner **Chuck Finnessy** still uses the original bun and meat recipes.

On the menu are eight sandwiches, nothing unpredictable, except for
maybe the fried egg. Prices were raised in 2007, to a whopping $1.70 for a
burger, $1.10 for an ice cream sundae.

A burger weighs less than one-quarter pound, but Chuck wouldn't size
it any other way. "We make them so they taste right," he says of his flame-
kissed charcoal grilling. "This is the size they need to be."

The business has outlasted seven bakeries and is loyal to local vendors:
Brandon Meats in Green Bay, **Stephenson Bakery** in Menominee, **Joe's
Cheese House** and **Hoppy Dairy**, both in Marinette.

"If I need something and it's late, I'm not going to get help from a guy
down in Milwaukee," says Chuck, who took over in 1988. He was 50 in 2007

and loves what he does.

"We have three or four generations of customers in some families," he says. "It's a very special place to a lot of people, and that makes it rewarding to me. I've had people bring in their grandchildren and tell them 'when I was your age, my grandmother brought me here.' That shared touchstone means something."

Countertop jukeboxes play three songs for a quarter, from "Louie Louie" to "Sugar Sugar" to "Wooly Bully." A framed 1955 menu shows 30 cents for a hamburger, 25 cents for a sundae. Decor seems untouched from the same era.

Mickey-Lu's stays open until 12:30 a.m. during summer but is closed on Mondays. Business begins at 9 a.m. and, yes, burgers are sold that early. And so is the Porterfield Special: ham, egg and cheese on toast. "You have to know about it to order it," Chuck says. It was named after the hometown of the waitress who created it. **715-735-7721**

•

The biggest scoop at **Mihm's**, 342 Chute Street, Menasha, is the charcoal-grilled steak sandwiches, made here since 1958 with ground sirloin from a local butcher. The cook automatically adds an ice cream scoop of onions, then pickles, unless you order the sandwich another way.

The business is small in size but big in reputation, at least around the Fox Valley. Look at the wall to read the menu. The extra-creamy malts also draw raves. Flavors include butterscotch.

www.mihmscharcoalgrill.com 920-722-0306

•

Football fans know **Kroll's West**, 1990 South Ridge Road, Green Bay, is the best place to catch a burger, brew and huge helping of Packer spirit.

The fourth-generation family business began at a Main Street boarding house, where **Harry** and **Caroline Kroll** sold meals for 35 cents. Charcoal-grilled burgers—served on a toasted bun, with butter—made their debut in 1936, and Kroll's moved across the street from Lambeau Field in 1974.

The Signature Wall of autographs shows that Kroll's fans have included John Madden and Al Gore. Kroll's South Loop opened at 1736 S. Michigan Avenue, Chicago, in 2005; great-granddaughters of the founders run the show.

Can't get enough? Kroll's ships its cooked burgers ("seared the Kroll's way") and soups to fans across the continental U.S., via UPS.

www.krolls-greenbay.com 866-464-7306

Sister Bay Bowl plays it straight, has been tops with customers since the 1950s.

SISTER BAY: Bowling for Chicken

Take a look at a **Sister Bay Bowl** picture from the 1950s, and then think about how the place has changed. Not much, right? That's why we love it, especially as the years stack up.

A third generation of the **Willems** family owns the business, which started out as a hotel and dance hall, but adding a six-lane bowling alley in 1958 proved to be a brilliant move. *Money* magazine has dubbed this one of the nation's top tourist destinations, and it's not because of the glitz or gourmet fare.

Da Bowl rates high because of its authenticity, the real people who nurse a brew while eyeing the gutter balls and strikes. Come mealtime, an accordion-like room divider opens, and there you have it: a no-nonsense supper club setting, with salad served by the big bowl and hot mini-loaves of white or rye bread at every table. Count pork chops and whitefish among the dinner entrées.

The bowl . . . it means bowling, and Bowl Combos ("your choice of two: perch, whitefish, shrimp, scallops, ribs or sirloin steak"). The steak sandwich, 7 ounces of sirloin served open-faced, goes for $13.95, but don't let that mislead you. The only entrée that exceeds $30 is the sirloin for two, 28 ounces at $30.95 (it was $5.50 in 1965, and the owners don't hide the old menu or make apologies). Almost every meal today is under $20 (including salad and potato).

Not in the mood for rabbit food? Substitute cottage cheese with peaches for salad. Just need bar food? Order chicken wings or potato skins, by the bowl.

Daily dinner specials include liver with bacon and onions, on Thursdays. A market price is assigned to perch, so let's bet that it's not likely to come from Europe or Asia. Burgers and brats, cheese curds and homemade soup are served for lunch, even when the tourists scoot during the dead of winter. Expect a couple of hours of down time between lunch and dinner, as staff shift menus, moods and gears.

That's enough for a few frames on the lanes, which you'll score yourself. No automation will spoil the mood.

Sister Bay Bowl
504 N. Bay Shore Drive, Sister Bay
www.sisterbaybowl.com
920-854-2841

•

TIDBITS

Mission Grille, a mere block from the **Sister Bay Bowl**, earns accolades for its wide wine list and ambitious epicurean endeavors. *Gourmet* magazine considers this restaurant among the top 12 in Wisconsin.

The building was formerly St. Rosalia's, the first Catholic Church in Door County. Today the altar is the bar—we will resist making jokes—and other architectural remnants result in a mix of style and serenity.

Some seating is in the former choir loft, or on the glass-enclosed veranda. The menu ranges from Black Angus steaks to wild Alaskan salmon, prepared in inventive ways. For dessert: Four-Berry Cobbler—as in cherries, blueberries, strawberries and raspberries—big enough to share.

www.missiongrille.com 920-854-9070

•

STURGEON BAY: Cheery Cherry Diner

Wrapped in a paper napkin at every place setting is a fork, knife and spoon that is long enough to deal with the half-dozen types of thick malts and shakes served here.

We are in **Perry's Cherry Diner**, where it seems appropriate to order cherry pie, and it is served warm. Owner **Perry Andropolis** says three or four cherry pies are made daily, but the bigger draw is the shakes, which up to 75 percent of his guests order.

Less visible, because of its short supply, is the diner's Apple Jazz pie—apple pie accompanied by cinnamon ice cream and caramel sauce.

Greek food is the diner's atypical specialty: gyros, quesadillas (using gyro meat, with "Ann's cucumber sauce" on the side) and spanakopita (the spinach-cheese pie is "in very limited supply").

Salads (Greek, traditional veggie) come in full size and "mini me" portions.

This business dates back to the 1930s, when it was called Larsen's Lunch, then renamed Victory Grill (when World War II ended). Perry's parents—Jack and Ann Andropolis—took over in 1972, but after 20 years of business, it was their son's turn to take the reins.

Though Greek food remains on the menu, Perry has made a mark in other ways. One example is the chopped chicken, cherry and walnut salad, served with French vanilla yogurt dressing.

"If we move in another direction, it will be to add more natural food items to the menu," he says. The atmosphere is high-gear retro, and Perry feels strongly about not serving alcohol.

We notice a For Sale sign outside, which a server says has been up for years. Perry says it's only been in place since spring 2007. "We're trying to find the right couple," he explains, vowing that "the place won't close, but we may have another operator" sometime in the future.

List price is $259,000, and that includes the catchy name.

Guests waited in line for tables (at least one point during the day) for around 60 consecutive days during the high season for tourists, the real estate ad says. The 38-seat diner serves as many as 500 people per day.

Perry's Cherry Diner
230 Michigan Street, Sturgeon Bay
www.perrycherrydiner.com
920-743-9910
•

SUAMICO: Fresh Herbs & Chives

Refined dining isn't fussy at Chives.

Refined and high-quality dining flourishes in a small town, just north of Green Bay, and the chef-owner understands the many facets of Packer spirit as well as anyone.

J. R. Schoenfeld, the team's executive chef from 1997 to 2003, today owns the lovely **Chives Restaurant**, in a former general store, built in 1890. He is a Rhode Island native whose wife, Cindy, is from the Shawano area.

This is not the place to chug beer and look for a big-screen TV.

Diners are automatically poured a glass of Pellegrino. It is easy to study fine wine and cheese choices: a glass-doored cooler with both faces the 70-seat dining room.

The menu mixes local and imported ingredients. The cheese sampler, when we visited, had Irish and Vermont selections, but none from Wisconsin. Schoenfeld says he does not use frozen ingredients; seafood arrives fresh from Hawaii.

Order a cup of vichyssoise and a salad of mixed greens, or fried Brie with berry chutney. The menu is not all fussy; it includes steaks and burgers, but inventive twists and a French flair are evident.

The chef shows his sense of humor on the dessert menu, which includes the Chives Ho-Ho, an Amaretto cake filled with whipped cream, covered with a layer of fudge and garnished with a raspberry puree.

Chives Restaurant
1749 Riverside Drive, Suamico
www.chivesdining.net
920-434-6441

TIDBITS

The **Chives Schoolhouse Wine & Food Specialty Shop**, operated in conjunction with Chives Restaurant, is a place to shop as well as attend cooking classes and wine and cheese tastings.

Cheeses are sold by the pound, and the "five-artisan cheese assortment," with crackers and condiments, costs $25 and changes weekly. Gift baskets of specialty foods can be customized.

Cooking class topics vary with the seasons, begin at noon on Saturdays and last two hours. Topics have included the technique of braising, one-pot meals for winter, and choosing and cooking fish.

Chivefest, on a Saturday in September, features samplings of food, wines and microbrews, with a backdrop of jazz performances. The pre-purchase of tickets is recommended.

•

Owners of Chives also operate **Pie from the Sky**, a pizza place, at 13201 Velp Avenue, Suamico. Watching employees hand-toss the crusts is part of the fun.

Originally a church built in 1857, the restaurant offers, among other pizzas, the Holy Moly (like a traditional deluxe) and Basilica (pesto, fresh garlic, feta, sun-dried tomatoes, olives and balsamic glaze). All are baked in a stone oven.

Sandwiches, salads and pastas also are served.
www.piefromthesky.com
920-662-1766

•

When not at Chives, chef-owner J.R. sometimes is at the helm as a Professional Golf Association chef, feeding pro athletes and fans at PGA tour stops.

What goes up, must come down as great pizza crust at Pie from the Sky.

NORTHEAST

Paul LeClair, holding smoked chubs, hopes Suzie Q will last five generations.

TWO RIVERS: In the Smoker

When *you* think about fishing season, it's likely a lazy summer day, hook in water, beer in boat—and as much interest in landscape as the possibility of a nibble.

So you may be surprised to hear **Paul LeClair** chat during winter about how busy this time of year is at **Susie Q Fish Market**. Brother **Mike** sets out seven days a week, sometimes 12 hours a day, to battle the waves, wind and moody weather of Lake Michigan, much the way great-grandfather Charlie LeClair did it back in the mid-1800s.

Today's daily catch of up to 1,000 pounds—whitefish, chubs, smelt—stocks area restaurants, grocery stores and the LeClair family's own small market. Some of the fish are sold freshly gutted and scaled; others go into a smokehouse.

Smoked fish is Susie Q's specialty. Chubs are caught from fall to late January. Then comes the smelt, whose harvest extends into spring. A third brother, **Dan**, takes charge of sales and marketing. Paul is in charge of the business of processing the fish.

"We put on a lot of smelt fries in Wisconsin," Paul says. "It's 30 to 40 clubs—American Legion posts, Lions clubs—a good way for them to raise money."

His daughter, **Jamie**, helps process the fresh fish that Mike catches. Paul's youngest, son Jack, born in March 2007, brings hope that a fifth generation of the family will continue the business. "It's getting tougher to make a living," Paul says. "We are a dying breed." Some of the challenge is about customer demand being higher than supply.

Susie Q Fish Market
1810 East Street, Two Rivers
920-793-5240
•

TIDBITS

"I have seen them from 1812 to 1815, swarming the rivers so thickly, that they were thrown out with a shovel, and even with the hand." That description of Great Lakes fishing during its boom in the 1800s is from Margaret Beattie Bogue's *Fishing the Great Lakes: An Environmental History, 1783-1933.*

In the early 1980s, Wisconsin had more than 200 licensed commercial fishermen. Now there are about 65 licenses for Lake Michigan and another ten for Lake Superior, says Bill Horns, Great Lakes fisheries specialist for the Department of Natural Resources.

The only way to get a commercial license in the state, he says, is through a transfer of a license from an existing fisherman. Limiting licenses strengthens and stabilizes the industry.

•

The **Susie Q Fish Market** is not far from the Historic Rogers Street Fishing Village, 2010 Rogers Street, a museum of historic buildings with exhibits about commercial fishing. It includes an 1886 lighthouse and a 1936 wooden fishing tug. Artifacts from shipwrecks and antique fishing fleet equipment help explain a 170-year history of work that has been called "America's most dangerous profession."

Open May to October, or by appointment. **www.rogersstreet.com 920-793-5905**

•

Two Rivers calls itself the Birthplace of the Ice Cream Sundae, since the first was served there in 1881, and locals gladly confront challengers to the title.

NORTHEAST

One example: To help Ithaca, N.Y., say "uncle," the city of Two Rivers placed a coupon for a free sundae in the opponent's newspaper. "By honoring this coupon," the ad read, "I acknowledge that Two Rivers is the REAL birthplace of the ice cream sundae."

The best place to buy a sundae in Two Rivers is at the old-fashioned ice cream parlor in the **Historic Washington House**, 1622 Jefferson Street. An unusual seasonal specialty is the Ruby Sundae: rhubarb sauce, hot caramel, butter pecan or vanilla ice cream. Topped with nuts and a cherry, of course.

The building, a former immigrant hotel, also is one part local history museum, and the lessons continue one block away, at the former St. Luke Convent, which is now the Two Rivers History Museum, 1810 Jefferson Street. **888-857-3529**

•

For fine dining in downtown Two Rivers, check out the snazzy **Element American Bistro**, 1513 Washington Street The name is a reference to being "in your element," comfortable with both the artsy setting and cuisine.

Designer **Kevin Voysey** has created an open-kitchen, two-level setting that is unusual because it's both spacious and intimate in atmosphere. Glass walls allow diners to see into the bike and fitness shop next door.

There is room for live music, jazz to folk. On the menu, which is adjusted seasonally, are mainstays (Angus burgers and perch sandwiches) plus inventive surprises (like the Apricot Chicken Salad Sandwich, Amaretto Shrimp Salad).

Self-taught chef **Jason Prigge** aims for sustainability and patronage of local food and beverage producers, whose names and locations are listed online. Fryer oil goes to a company that blends it into bio-diesel fuel for Manitowoc's city-owned vehicles, including buses. Compostable scraps from the kitchen go back to the gardens of local farmers. **www.elementamericanbistro.com 920-553-3568**

WASHINGTON ISLAND:
At Death's Door

Death's Door Spirits may lift your own.

Leah Caplan knows how to fill a liquor cabinet. First came Death's Door Vodka, a slick and smooth libation made from wheat grown on Washington Island, at the tip of Door County.

Then Death's Door Gin made its entrance, also produced with wheat from the same fields, plus juniper berries that are grown there. The liquor contains other botanicals from Wisconsin, and work has begun to find places to grow them on Washington Island.

Wisconsin's liquor choices have expanded because Leah, who operates the **Washington Hotel, Restaurant and Culinary School**, has long been an advocate of using locally grown or harvested ingredients in her cooking.

That means more than using the area's ever-present whitefish in her inventive menus, or growing a garden with fresh produce.

Leah persuaded local farmers to grow more wheat, so she'd have a local crop to grind into flour for her artisanal breads and bakery. When the farmers grew more than enough, the excess was shipped to **Capital Brewery** in Middleton and became Island Wheat Ale.

The creation of hard liquor from the wheat was a next-step project, since crop yields were good and Island Wheat Ale has gone over well. It's possible that a Death's Door Whiskey also will be produced, but Leah says that'll be it.

For the liquor cabinet, anyway. Her recipe experimentation, to include the liquor, has barely begun.

Brothers **Tom** and **Ken Koyen**, who harvest the crop that is used in the Island Wheat that Ken sells at his bar (**The Granary**), started off with 30 acres of wheat on the island. Five years later, farmers were growing 800 acres.

Other grains (oats, flax, barley) are rotated with the wheat, to ensure the health of the terrain. Not all products made from the wheat are edible: A line of lotions and soaps are on the market, too.

Death's Door Spirits
Washington Island
www.deathsdoorspirits.com
608-441-1083

•

Side Dish: **Death's Door Vodka & Miso Braised Ribs**

5 *yellow onions, sliced*
6 *cloves garlic, crushed*
1 *tablespoon fennel seeds*
5 1/2 *pounds pork country ribs*
1 *teaspoon sea salt*
1 *cup Death's Door Vodka*
2 *cups water*
1/2 *cup red miso*
2 *tablespoons buckwheat honey*

Preheat oven to 300 degrees. In a large skillet, over medium heat, heat olive oil. Add the onions, garlic, fennel and salt. Sauté until aromatic, no need to brown. Turn the heat up, add the Death's Door Vodka and boil until reduced by half. Add the water, miso (a condiment used in Japanese cooking) and honey. Place ribs in an oven-safe baking dish. Pour onions and liquid over them. Cover tightly with foil and braise in the oven 2-3 hours until very tender. Can be prepared a day ahead, refrigerated, fat skimmed and reheated at 350 degrees for one hour. Serve with mashed potatoes or rice and a nice cold martini. Serves 6-10.

—*Recipe by Leah Caplan*

NORTHEAST

226   **HUNGRY FOR WISCONSIN**

At Bread and Water, Valerie Fons (with daughter Micala)
operates a bakery and kayak excursion business.

TIDBITS

Valerie Fons considers Washington Island "a remarkable place" that attracts interesting people who have done well in various professions, from the arts to science.

Husband **Joseph Ervin** was a water quality research scientist at Michigan State before retirement. Fons is a United Methodist minister and a writer/kayaker who made news in the 1980s by paddling from the Arctic Ocean to South America's Cape Horn.

They opened **Bread and Water**, a bakery and kayak excursion business, in midsummer 2007 and rent the house where Valerie's grandparents lived. The family—which includes six adopted children, all with African American or Haitian roots—moved from Michigan.

Townsfolk demonstrate "a great deal of sharing everywhere—even at the town dump, where we've gotten some great finds. We exchange, share, pass back and forth," says Valerie. The islanders know each other by name, so "you don't get lost in a crowd. This is the context of a real, honest-to-goodness community—this is good for us."

Valerie hopes to bring more at-risk youth to Washington Island for a visit. That already has happened through Sierra Club and Sturgeon Bay non-profit projects, which Valerie calls LAUNCH (Lake Adventures Uniting Nature and Children with Hospitality).

The family sells soups, sandwiches, breads and bakery at Bread and Water, a business that also has a couple of rooms for rent. When you buy a loaf of bread, you get a poem to go with it. Island children come over on Wednesdays, for an after-school sewing circle. Low-income residents get a coupon for a free soup lunch when they retrieve food pantry rations.

Valerie likes the idea of "praying in my grandmother's pantry" and knowing that a dozen cedars, planted by her grandfather to thwart lakeshore winds, "shelter his great-grandchildren today."

"I want to show my children what it means to dream, and to take a risk," she adds, regarding the family's move to Washington Island. "I felt I was providing leadership as a mom by doing this."

Bread and Water is at 1349 Main Road, Washington Island.
920-847-2393

•

Foodies who exercise will want to consider "Harvest Fest Ride to the Island," a 260-mile and five-day bicycle ride from Middleton to Washington Island. The mid-September event is presented in cooperation with **Capital Brewery**.

The backroads route passes farmland and follows the Lake Michigan shoreline, with stops at family farms and other agricultural businesses. Meals will be big on locally grown ingredients. Overnight stays will be in cities along the way, such as Beaver Dam, Port Washington, Two Rivers, Sturgeon Bay and Washington Island, where the group will arrive in time to kick off the Wheat Harvest Festival.

The event is organized by **Midwest Scenic Bicycle Tours**, based in Dodgeville.

www.midwestscenic.com 800-675-2295

Van Der Geest Dairy can milk 100 cows at a time in their milking parlor.

WAUSAU: Sharing the Dairy

The family began farming with 17 cows in 1969 and today works about 4,000 acres to feed their herd of 3,000. Until recently, this was Wisconsin's largest dairy farm operation.

You'd think there would be enough going on at **Van Der Geest Dairy**, northwest of Wausau, without having a bunch of visitors underfoot, but outsiders are welcome to stop and learn about the business.

The farm's milking parlor and freestall shelter, constructed in 2000, were specifically designed to accommodate a crowd of people as well as Holsteins. A short set of stairs connects to a catwalk, for watching the near-constant convoy of cows, which are milked 100 at a time, three times a day.

It is a smooth and high-tech process that, amazingly, requires the hands of only five people to milk 500 cows per hour. Output is measured and recorded automatically by computer. Each cow wears a number and small box that the computer system recognizes. If it's time for hoof trimming or other individual attention, the cow is automatically and mechanically routed away from her peers as she exits the milking parlor.

"My husband's dream was to build a facility where people could see where milk comes from—and see that it's not just a jug from a store," says **Mary Kay Van Der Geest**, president of the operation. Husband Gary died without warning in November 2000, five months after the project's completion.

Son **Lee** assists his mother with executive business decisions, and this four-generation family enterprise demonstrates progressive environmental practices. Cattle bedding is an example. What looks like dried sawdust actually is dried, recycled and odorless manure. The manure liquid is extracted and ejected into soil as fertilizer, to ease runoff concerns. Dried manure also is used as furnace fuel in winter.

These techniques demonstrate the sophistication that this size of farm, in this era, demands of the people whose work results in food for us to eat.

Van Der Geest Dairy averages 50 employees, and they include people who specialize in farm mechanics, animal nutrition and business agriculture. A veterinarian visits daily. From March to December, about a dozen temporary workers join the crew, and they include harvesters who come from South Africa.

"It's getting harder to find labor," Mary Kay says. "We used to find the help in other farm families."

To support interest in agriculture as a career, the dairy annually awards $1,000 college scholarships to two graduating seniors. "Farm life teaches you about responsibility and chores at a young age," Mary Kay notes. "These are concepts that I think we're losing" as lifestyle conveniences multiply.

The farm is open to visitors from 9 a.m. to 5 p.m. Monday through Saturday. Tours are self-guided, but groups larger than 12 may call to arrange for a tour guide. Donations of $2 per person ($4, with tour guide) are collected. Not all parts of the dairy operation are accessible to the public, but a video explains the areas where visitors can't go.

Van Der Geest Dairy
5555 County A, Wausau
www.vandergeestdairy.com
715-675-6043

•

TIDBITS

It is especially easy to get a taste of farm life and products in June because many counties host at least one June Dairy Month meal or celebration. It's an excellent time to take a country drive. The payoff is educational and a fresh, healthful meal of good value.

On-farm events include tours and agricultural displays. The meal typically includes ice cream sundaes as well as pancakes or scrambled eggs and sausage. The cost averages $6 per adult, less for children.

For more: **www.wisdairy.com**

WAUTOMA: CALL OF THE WILD

Head into Waushara County, and the population of deer starts to outnumber people. Small and pretty lakes with walleye and white bass dot the landscape. Wild pheasants and turkeys thrive.

It is close to paradise for **Jeremy Thoren**, executive chef at the **Buck Rub Restaurant** at Pine Ridge of Wautoma, a rural complex that includes a 12-room boutique lodge and banquet facilities (for up to 325 people) that are adjacent to 1,000 acres of woods, water and wildlife.

"I moved here because I wanted to get away and not raise my family in the city," Jeremy says. The chef's specialty is preparation of wild game, which is what makes this restaurant unusual. Customers have come from both coasts and routinely make their way to him from Chicago.

Jeremy Thoren makes wild game entrées his culinary specialty.

Elk and buffalo cuts are from **Navarino Valley Elk Ranch** in Shiocton. **MacFarlane Pheasants** in Janesville and **Golden Dreams Ostrich Farm** in Almond also sell to Jeremy, but sometimes the chef shops much farther away—like quail from Manchester Farms in South Carolina, boar from farms in Texas.

"Most places don't have what we have to offer," he says, and that is an understatement. He also tries to "use as much Wisconsin produce as I can" and plucks fresh herbs from his own garden in summer.

Recent dinner entrées, which are under $25, included Ostrich Loin Steak, Antelope Parmesan and Wild Boar Ribs. Sautéed Breast of Pheasant, topped with papaya and tart cherry relish, is a signature dish, offered all year.

For breakfast: Elk Benedict—poached eggs, elk summer sausage and hollandaise on an English muffin.

More traditional options also are on the restaurant menus. The marquee dessert

NORTHEAST

is Chocolate Trilogy, layers of a crushed Oreo crust, milk chocolate and an espresso/dark chocolate mix.

"Wild" doesn't mean "shot in the back yard," of course. "No restaurant in this country can do that," Jeremy notes. All meats and fowl are farm raised—although Hunters Exchange Television crew shot a deer on the property, then had the chef pre-pare stuffed venison tenderloin as their cameras rolled. That episode has morphed into a five- to eight-minute regular gig about cooking with game, shown nationwide through satellite TV (see **www.he-tv.com**).

"It's a lot of fun for me," Jeremy says, and he feels fortunate to be able to pursue two passions—cooking and hunting—in Waushara County.

Large windows in the dining room and bar look out onto gardens, woods and a pond in summer. Snowmobile trails skirt nearby, but cross-country skiing and hiking are not allowed on the grounds at this time.

Accommodations include balconies or patios. In the sun-filled lobby is a cozy stone fireplace. Elsewhere is a hot tub atrium and game room.

Baird Creek Outfitters, also on the premises, offers archery and sporting clay practice, plus hunting and fishing expedition assistance.

Buck Rub Restaurant
Pine Ridge of Wautoma
N3387 Highway 73, Wautoma
www.pineridgeofwautoma.com
920-787-5519

•

ELSEWHERE IN THE NORTHEAST

Many people assume that sauerkraut is a German food, but it actually was created in China, then brought to Europe by Genghis Khan. All it requires is salt, cabbage and patience.

Wisconsin's once had 15 sauerkraut companies. Only one plant remains, but it's the largest producer of the shredded and fermented cabbage in the world. This **Great Lakes Kraut** plant adds its distinctive aroma to Bear Creek, near Appleton and Green Bay. The company's brand names include Krrrrisp Kraut, the official sauerkraut at Wisconsin's major sports venues.

The company is based in Shortsville, New York, and has a third plant is in Shiocton. The trio produces 125,000 tons of kraut per year. **www.krrrrispkraut.com**

•

Belgian trippe, a mild sausage made with cabbage and pork, is a rarity in Wisconsin but a specialty at **Marchant's Foods**, 9674 Highway 57, Brussels.

This small but proud Belgian community of 1,100 is part of the nation's largest known Belgian American settlement. Nearby is Namur, a historic district that was declared a National Historic Landmark in 1990. In some circles, French is spoken with a Walloon accent. Most of the settlement's buildings were destroyed during the Peshtigo Fire of 1871.

Namur, "in multiple private ownership, is threatened by adjacent tourism development," the National Park Service has observed.

A new four-lane highway, completed in 2008, bypasses Brussels and Marchant's. Still to be determined is the impact that the rerouting will have on business, which opened in 1947.

Marchant's also makes and sells Belgian pies, which have a sweet yeast dough and fruit filling. **920-825-1244**

•

The name Chanticleer comes from the rooster in Chaucer's *Canterbury Tales*. Roosters of all sorts—figurines, wall hangings, carvings—adorn this Eagle River resort's restaurant.

The Chanticleer Inn, a summer-only resort until 1965, has been in business since 1922. Now it is open year-round, and winterized condo units and motel rooms have replaced the cottages.

The property at 1458 E. Dollar Lake Road borders Eagle River and the resort's Dollar Lake, which means some diners boat over for dinner or an outdoor Beer Garden grilled lunch. The water views are generous and meal

You can make the chili as hot as you want at Chili John's in Green Bay.

options wide-ranging, from burgers to lobster.

www.chanticleerinn.com
800-752-9193

•

Everybody seems to be a chili expert in Wisconsin, but who can match the level of accolades and endearment earned by **Chili John's**, 519 S. Military Avenue, Green Bay?

Bean or no beans. Spaghetti (not elbow macaroni) is another option. Most important: mild, medium, hot or extra hot? We're talking sweat level as in spice, not temperature. You can get the same saucy meat mixture plopped on top of a dawg. Order it "to go," and a scoop of oyster crackers is shoveled into the takeout bag. The chili, by the pound, also can be shipped around the country. Last time we checked, a 2-pound sampler pack went for $75.50.

The chili recipe comes from a Lithuanian immigrant, and it hasn't changed. Fans include NFL broadcaster John Madden. The operation has been around since 1913. A Chili John's Cafe exists at the Lambeau Field Atrium during Packer training camp, the NFL season and special events.

www.chilijohns.com 920-494-0187

•

An 1899 railroad depot, where the Packers used to depart for road games, today houses **Titletown Brewing Company**, 200 Dousman Street, Green Bay. Handcrafted beers include "Johnny Blood" Red (after 1930s halfback McNally) and (Tony) Canadeo Gold.

The brewpub is hard to miss because of the 22-foot concrete football player statue in front of it. Look familiar? The statue long stood in front of the Packers Hall of Fame, until Lambeau Field Atrium completion in 2003.

www.titletownbrewing.com 920-437-2337

•

When the destination is true backwoods, like Sylvania National Wilderness Area, the place to head for dinner is **Bent's Camp**, 6882 Helen Creek Road (off County B, ten miles west of Land O' Lakes) for homemade pizza and walleye dinners.

The property has been a fishing/hunting lodge since 1896; the bar has the original birchbark walls and ceiling.

Walleye arrive pan fried, potato crusted, broiled, blackened or almondine. The North-woods Salad contains lettuce, tomatoes, cranber-ries, walnuts and bleu cheese. Meals are served on metal plates, reminiscent of bygone eras.

Upstairs at the restaurant is a small but appealing gift shop, with handcrafted jewelry and locally made foods, as well as more typical souvenirs. Housekeeping cabins are for rent. The property overlooks Mamie Lake, on the Cisco chain of lakes.

Northwoods denizen at Bent's Camp

www.bents-camp.com 715-547-3487

•

One of the more trendy meeting spots in Land O' Lakes is **Bucksnort Coffee House**, 4262 Highway B. The business doubles as a home furnishings and gift shop, selling stained glass and duck decoys, pottery and tableware, mirrors and handmade clothing for children.

www.northwoodsliving.com 715-547-6998

•

The chicken dumpling soup at **Skipper's Family Restaurant**, 812 E. First Street, Merrill, is so tasty that you might want to order a quart to take home. That's what we did, and when realizing a dozen miles from town that we for-got to take it with us, there was no hesitancy about turning around.

Owner **Rick Scott**, from Chicago, says the recipe dates back to the 1930s and the original skipper of this laid-back restaurant. Rick sells it by the quart for under $10, by the cup (one dumpling) and by the bowl (two dumplings).

We spent less than $5 for a cup and half-sandwich—chicken salad, which has a pleasant hint of sweetness. "Top secret," says Rick. "Nobody will

Slow food and delicious lunch—with no shortcuts—is served at Way Back When.

get it out of us."

Gourmet touches include homemade crepes on weekends, a portobella mushroom omelet, "root beer ribs" and baked chicken on Thursdays. **715-536-9914**

•

Although the highway sign made it clear, as in "road open for **Wilson's Cafe**," we had our doubts while navigating the gravel ruts and barricades. Not much was going on in Pound (population 350) and in Marinette County, but then we spotted an unassuming building.

Sure enough, it was the cafe, and the room on the other side of the door was big, busy, brightly lit and wood paneled. Customers lingered with friends, a newspaper, a book.

Owners **Mark** and **Paula Dembroski** want people to feel at home here and as if they're getting a deal. One way to do the latter is with freshly made cake doughnuts.

Order a plain one, and it's 15 cents. Add a dime for a coating of sugar, another nickel for a creamy vanilla or chocolate frosting. It's a longtime tradition here.

The cafe is at 4065 Highway 141. **920-897-3100**

•

Lunch at the **Back When Cafe**, 606 Third Street, Wausau, showcases chef-owner **Jolene Lucci's** reverence for Slow Food principles, like the luncheon crepes filled with a creamy sauce of chicken and mushrooms (plus broccoli, if you ask).

"No canned sauces or cheap ingredients such as powdered spices or imitation herbs," she promises.

The setting, antique-shop-meets-industrial-design, is a century-old building with two dining rooms. One is full of natural light and contemporary decor;

Whitelaw wieners are just one part of the inventory at Berge's.

the other mixes more intimate lighting with historical prints and hardwood floors.

The business thrives on the former Third Street Pedestrian Mall, which was reopened to vehicular traffic in 2007. The area had been closed off for 25 years.

www.backwhencafe.com 715-848-5668

•

Some great butcher shops operate under the radar, and **Berge's Whitelaw Sausage Company**, in Manitowoc County, is one of them. Its products don't get entered into state or national competitions, but locals rave.

When **Ralph Berge**, daughter **Sally Peck** and son **Ralph Jr**. took over the business in 2006, they inherited more than 100 meat recipes. The butcher shop has served this community of 730 for at least 80 years.

Most popular product? The Whitelaw Wiener, known locally as "the funeral wiener" because everybody seems to serve them for lunch after a burial.

Sally says it doesn't hurt to have St. Michael's Catholic Church right across the street from the butcher shop.

A secret combo of spices and other ingredients "change the texture and moisture" of the Whitelaw Wiener, which is precooked and tastes fine cold or hot.

NORTHEAST

Buy wieners made with Hoss's recipe (he works there), and the results are distinctively different but still perfectly acceptable.

Gourmet burgers, veggie to beef/pork patties, are newer products that go over well, Sally says. The place is turning into a full-service deli ("you have to appeal to the busy person"), and a small cafe should be open by summer 2008.

What does Sally like best about her work? "You get to be in on everybody's family function," like the Super Bowl party that requires 150 links.

The shop is at 107 W. Menasha Avenue, Whitelaw.

www.whitelawsausage.net 920-732-3222

•

The mailing address is Whitelaw, "which is the largest small town nearby," but the location is Branch (unincorporated, population unknown).

That's what you get with a community name like Branch. The biggest thing going for it, outside of the volunteer fire department's summer picnic, is **Nibby's**, a down-home restaurant where meals are served family style.

It's homelike cooking in friendly confines, and the signature dessert is the Kneecap. Small in size and light in weight doughnuts are rolled in powdered sugar and topped with whipped cream. Mmmmmm.

Karri Wiegert, who started working at Nibby's one year after its opening in 1992, says they'll go through at least 300 Kneecaps per week. Where did that name come from? "Good question," is her response.

We do know that Nibby's is the nickname of **David Doolan**, owner of the restaurant. He is the son of the folks who used to run Doolan's Supper Club in Francis Creek, but that is another story.

For more about Nibby's, 3921 Branch River Road: **www.nibbys.com 920-682-0998**. It's easy to find; just take the Highway 10 exit west, off of I-43 in Manitowoc County.

Door County cherries star in all kinds of products, from jam to wine at Bea's.

Road Trip: Door County Cherries, in All Courses

Door County is wild about cherries, especially the tart Montmorency. About 4.5 million pounds are harvested from mid-July to mid-August, enough for a fourth place finish nationwide. The pretty blooms peak about 60 days before the berries are ready for picking.

For more about the rhythm of cherry production: **www.wisconsincherries.org**

Pick your own, or enjoy the endeavors of others. It's not hard to find **Sprecher Ravin' Red** soda, a blend of cherry and cranberry juices, plus ginseng and honey.

But there's more:

1. Ice cream dreams. Schopf Hilltop Dairy, 5169 Highway I, near Carlsville, makes Door County Cherry ice cream and up to 30 other flavors. Tour the farm, walk the corn maze (in summer or fall), then order a scoop in the ice cream parlor. A country store keeps parents busy while kids check out the playground.

www.dairyview.com 920-743-0212

2. Brews for choosing. Shipwrecked Brewery, 7791 Egg Harbor Road, Egg Harbor, serves Door County Cherry Wheat on tap. Other choices: Bayside Blonde to Pumpkin Patch (a fall offering). On the food menu: smoked chicken topped with a cherry wine sauce.

www.shipwreckedmicrobrew.com 920-868-2767

Orchard Country Winery makes more than 30 wines, many incorporating Door County cherries.

3. Bing-cherry wine and more. Orchard Country Winery and Market's 30-plus wines incorporate several types of cherries at 9197 Highway 42, Fish Creek. Two examples: Cherry Chardonnay, a nice tug between dryness and Montmorency fruitiness, and Nathan John, a semi-dry made with Bing cherries (and named after the orchard owner's grandson).

www.orchardcountry.com
920-868-3479

4. Cherry pie is everywhere, or so it seems, and the great local bakers tend to keep their recipes secret. One excellent choice is the **White Gull Inn**, 4225 Main Street, Fish Creek, whose casual summer fish boils end with cherry pie à la mode.

www.whitegullinn.com
888-364-9542

5. For a fine dining setting, head to the **Inn at Kristofer's**, 734 N. Bay Shore Drive, Sister Bay, where Sautéed Quail in Door County Cherry Sauce is a signature entrée for chef Terri Milligan. Sip a flute of Door County Kir, cherry juice with Champagne, while enjoying the rich sunset and marina view. Savor Door County Cherry Panna Cotta, an Italian-style custard, for dessert.

www.innatkristofers.com 920-854-9419

6. Stay at the **Eagle Harbor Inn**, 9914 Water Street, Ephraim, and chef Kathy Brady likely will work cherries into her snacks or breakfast menu. She also bakes and sells hundreds of from-scratch cherry pies each summer and, nope, won't share her recipe.

Cherry cider, cherry-filled pastries and cherry strudel muffins also are not unusual here. Neither is french toast stuffed with cherries and cream cheese, typically served on Saturdays.

www.eagleharborinn.com 920-854-2121

7. For a wide assortment of homestead-produced foods, pickled beets to cherry jam, stop at **Bea's Ho-Made Products**, 763 Highway 42, Gills Rock, a four-generation family business.

It all began one summer when **Linda Landin** sold her parents' cherries from a roadside picnic table. The next year, she added surplus beans and cucumbers from the family's garden, plus her grandmother's chopped cherry jam. **Bea Landin** was Linda's mother, and today Bea's consists of a commercial kitchen, bakery and retail store that sells 100-plus types of local products.

www.beashomadeproducts.com 920-854-7299

Panna cotta with cherries, Inn at Kristofer's, Sister Bay

RESOURCES

Home Grown Wisconsin

A cooperative of organic farmers who raise vegetables, fruit and herbs for restaurants, some of which are nationally known. A Community Sustainable Agriculture component provides produce shares to Chicago area families.
www.homegrownwisconsin.com
608-347-3054

Savor Wisconsin

A joint effort of the state Department of Agriculture, Trade and Consumer Protection (DATCP), University of Wisconsin-Extension and Wisconsin Apple Growers Association to enhance the state's agriculture industry and economy. Organizers of Something Special From Wisconsin, a branding program that identifies member producers, restaurants, food co-ops and specialty retail stores.
www.savorwisconsin.com
info@savorwisconsin.com

Slow Food Wisconsin

The local component of a global effort to experience, celebrate and preserve food traditions. Supporters of artisan food and beverage producers.
www.slowfoodwisconsin.com
608-849-8199

Wisconsin Apple Growers Association

The state's commercial orchards, which exist in 46 of the 72 counties, produce about 56 million pounds of apples annually. The biggest production areas are Crawford, Door, Bayfield and Milwaukee counties.
www.waga.org   920-478-4277

Wisconsin Beef Council

The state's 28,000 beef and dairy producers earn about $878 million per year from livestock and livestock product sales. Wisconsin has about 1.25 million dairy cows.
www.beeftips.com   608-833-7177

Wisconsin Berry Growers Association

Members are devoted to the production and promotion of strawberries, raspberries and blueberries.
www.wiberries.org   info@wiberries.org

Wisconsin Cherry Growers

Members produce red tart cherries as orchard growers, processors and roadside market operators.
www.wisconsincherries.org
mstasiak@wisc.edu

Wisconsin Milk Marketing Board

Funded since 1983 by the state's dairy producers, to increase the demand for raw milk, primarily by marketing and promoting Wisconsin cheese. Wisconsin produces 2.1 billion pounds of milk per month. About 14,000 dairy herds are licensed in the state.
www.wisdairy.com   608-836-8820

Wisconsin Pork Producers Association

Members work to ensure the future success of the pork industry. The state's 2,300 pork producers market about 948,000 pigs per year. The top five production counties are Grant, Sauk, Dodge, Dane and Lafayette.
www.wppa.org   608-723-7551

Wisconsin Potato & Vegetable Growers Association

Formed in 1948 to unify the state's potato growers, of which about 150 are association members. Wisconsin's potato producers harvest about 65,000 acres of potatoes yearly.
www.wisconsinpotatoes.com
715-623-7683

Wisconsin Restaurant Association

The Madison-based trade association represents businesses in food service.
www.wirestaurant.org
800-589-3211

Wisconsin State Cranberry Growers Association

About 250 growers in 20 counties produce Wisconsin's top fruit crop. About 300 million pounds of cranberries are harvested annually, more than any other state's production—more than one-half of the amount of cranberries that Americans consume.
www.wiscran.org
715-423-2070

Wisconsin Winery Association

About three dozen businesses, most family-run operations, unite to promote wines produced in Wisconsin.
www.wiswine.com   608-443-2465

Wisconsin's Farm Fresh Atlases

Free regional food guides that identify farms, farmers' markets, restaurants, stores and other businesses that sell local food and make sustainable practices a priority. Five guides (Eastern, Western, Southeastern, Southern and Central) are published and distributed annually.
www.farmfreshatlas.org
cecarusi@wisc.edu

Cherry pie à la mode—a perennial favorite at Perry's Cherry Diner, Sturgeon Bay (page 219).

INDEX

TEXT CREDITS

PHOTO CREDITS

La Baguette, an authentic French bakery, opens in 2008 in Madison's Cambridge Court shopping center on Mineral Point Road. The Vigys ran a bakery by the same name in Minocqua for several years.

You can fly in, or walk in to Picadilly Lilly Diner, Lone Rock
(near the Tri-County Regional Airport, Sauk County).